The Heart Word

How I Lost It All and Found Myself

Lauren Chava Rose

#19080343

Author Photo: Ashleigh Vlieger, Sonora Photography

For Coco

Chocolate ice cream with chocolate sauce is all I ever needed.

For Claire

I hope my story travels through your bones

Until you see

That my liberation is your liberation.

Some of the names that appear in this book are aliases, and some are not. If I told you which names have been changed, it would defeat the purpose.

TABLE OF CONTENTS

A NOTE FROM THE AUTHOR

The story that you are about to read is told from my perspective and my memories.

I know, from being a therapist, that no two recollections of an event will ever be the same.

I'm not sure when we became so obsessed with the concept of a single truth.

But I don't subscribe to that ideology.

Instead, I stand in the knowledge that this book is my truth.

And I am the only one who can tell my story.

The same is true for you.

The Heart Word

I see you
Up late at night
Tossing and turning
Pacing and yearning
For a different life.

I see you
Callously emerging
In the light of day
As you laugh away all your wild.

There's only one problem
And you know what it is.

Once the heart speaks
There is no going back.

--

I lived your life
For so many years.

Until one day
I woke up
And I stayed.

And though my voice quivered
And my hands were caked in sweat
Tossing and turning
I stayed.

And though my mind fought it
And my fear almost won
Pacing and yearning
I stayed.

It's no wonder

That courage is the heart word.
It will drive you to the edge and back again.
It will ask you to rattle your own cage until it breaks.

That's what it takes to live.

OFF TO THE RACES

Every summer, when I was young, we would leave the suburbs of Chicago to spend a few weeks in New England with my maternal grandmother. These trips always began the same way. We would arrive at Logan Airport, rent a car, and drive to the small town outside of Salem, Massachusetts, where my mother was raised. I could always tell when we were getting close to my grandmother's house because after a certain point, I would begin to smell the salty ocean air. For a Midwestern girl, this was such a treat. I loved how complex the ocean smelled. Sometimes, it was fishy. Other times, it smelled more like seaweed. But no matter what, it was alive.

As soon as we arrived at my grandmother's house, we would order the exact same meal each year, like clockwork. As a child, I loved both the ritual and its consistency. There were so many aspects of my family that felt chaotic and unsafe. But, on these trips, I thrived. As I look back on it now, it's a little surprising that this is such an important memory. I suppose that's because my adult life has been defined by so much upheaval and so many losses. Perhaps it does make sense that I would cling to a memory of a time when my life felt predictable.

Once we arrived at my grandmother's house, we would all sit around her bright yellow kitchen table as we ordered fried clams, clam chowder, and the assorted sides. And if we really wanted a treat, we would go to this amazing restaurant on the ocean and eat fresh lobster. It was the best lobster I have ever tasted in my life.

Everyone in my family loved lobster. It was one of the only things that seemed to bring all of us together. I craved any moment where I felt like I belonged with my family. Most of the time, I felt lost. I believed there must have been a mistake. It seemed like the universe had plopped me down with a group of people who didn't understand me at all, and frankly, didn't really like me that much. But when we were all eating lobster, everything made sense.

* * *

Back in Chicago, my nuclear family (which consisted of my parents, my brother, and I) created a very specific tradition around eating lobster. We didn't have it very often outside of New England, so when we did, it was most definitely a treat. Perhaps we were also trying to make up for the fact that we were eating seafood in the Midwest (which many people in our extended family felt was outrageous). Or maybe we knew that it was one of the few ways that we could connect to each other. Honestly, I have no idea where this tradition came from, or who suggested it, but it was ours. And I have never shared this with anyone.

On lobster night in Chicago, my father would get home from the local seafood market with a Styrofoam box that appeared to be moving. There were air holes at the top of it. I remember the first time I realized that he had come home with lobsters that were still alive. I felt a pang in my gut. *Did I really want to go through with this?* If I wanted to eat my dinner, clearly, I would need to watch it die first.

I will warn you; our family ritual is probably inhumane. Scratch that, it's *definitely* inhumane. To begin, we would take the lobsters out of the box and place them in a row at the back of the kitchen. There were four lobsters: one for my mother, my father, my brother, and me. We would watch the lobsters as they began to move steadily and slowly across the floor. That's because we were racing them.

The four of us stood back and cheered for our respective lobsters. Sometimes, we even named them. Most of the time, the lobsters barely moved forward. It was as if they were throwing their claws up in protest. Maybe they knew how ridiculous this event was, even if we did not. Nonetheless, the lobster that got the farthest was declared the winner. And guess what the winner received? That lobster went into the pot of boiling water first.

14

Eventually, all four lobsters were sent to their demise. For years, I would leave the room during this portion of the evening. I couldn't watch it happen. But one night, I decided to stay. I forced myself to watch the lobsters sink into the pot of boiling water as they were still alive. That was bad enough, but I was completely consumed by what happened next. One of the lobsters attempted to escape. I stood over the pot, wide-eyed and in disbelief, as the rogue lobster began to claw its way up to the top. *It looked like this lobster might actually get out.* I stared at my father, wondering if he was going to do something. But my father didn't look very concerned. Then I watched in horror as the other three lobsters pulled the rogue back into the pot, plunging the lobster to its death.

I asked my father why lobsters did this. Why they killed one of their own. He told me that the three lobsters who pulled down the rogue lobster were ultimately doing it a favor. It was the humane thing to do because they were all going to die anyway. I accepted this explanation. Until now.

We held lobster races for many years. It's possible that my family still does this, though I wouldn't know. Honestly, I always thought it was a little strange, but it was tradition. It was ours. It wasn't until I began writing this book that I was struck by something particularly eerie. The strongest lobster, the one who got the farthest, was sent to die first. And if that wasn't bad enough, my family seemed to accept the fact that any lobster who tried to escape from the pot was ultimately killed by its own kind. Apparently, these were the things that happened to lobsters who asserted themselves. They were gravely punished.

That mentality – *if I'm going down, so are you* – might well have been our family motto. And I would come to learn that it didn't originate with my parents. The *lobsters in the pot* mentality went back multiple generations. It took me years to realize that I had been socialized to believe that all of this was humane; that it was the natural order of things. I have only recently been able to see it for what it is.

Perhaps I can only see it now because I am the rogue lobster. But, unlike the myriad of lobsters who came before me, I got out.

WHEN THE END IS THE BEGINNING

May 2018

I woke up on Mother's Day and immediately burst into tears. I clutched my floral bedspread against my chest. *I can't do this anymore.* I dried my eyes as I rolled over in my bed. My long, horizontal blinds danced in the artificial wind created by my air conditioner. They formed shadows that moved across my bedspread like weeping willow branches. Somehow, I felt comforted by that. Apparently I wasn't the only one weeping today.

I continued to cry into my deep purple sheets. *Great, I guess I'll be washing these later.* I was only a few minutes into this day, and already I had no idea how I was going to get through it. No one in my life struggled this much on Mother's Day. Not like me. I felt isolated and alone. I continued to watch the shadows dance back and forth on my bedspread as my vision began to blur. Light, then dark, light, then dark. It all felt the same to me.

At least I loved my apartment. That might not seem like something that could quell an aching heart on Mother's Day, but it did. I lived on the top floor of a large, brick walkup on the northside of Chicago. I lovingly referred to my home as The Treehouse. There were strong, beautiful trees outside every window. I felt as if the trees were there to hold me up. They supported me, especially on the hard days. This apartment was the first place where I felt safe. It was the first place I ever really loved. Even then, it felt too good to be true.

I grabbed my phone from the nightstand and unplugged my charger. I began to scroll through Instagram as I violated the first self-imposed rule of Mother's Day. *No. Social. Media.* Frankly, I knew better, but it was like a drug. I scrolled past photo after photo of friends and acquaintances smiling with their mothers, thanking them for being such incredible role models and confidantes. They clearly looked up to these women. *Wow.* My brow furled. I kept scrolling. My curiosity became jealousy, which morphed into resentment, then rage, and ultimately landed on pain. Suddenly, I went off the rails.

I cried into my sheets again as I threw my phone against the wall. Mother's Day always began this way. I would wake up incredibly upset. Then I would toss back and forth as I resisted the urge to go on social media, ultimately giving in to the temptation. *Honestly, who has that much willpower?* After a few moments of self-inflicted punishment, I would inevitably lose my shit. I repeated these cycles year after year until I ended up right back where I started: ugly crying into my sheets and wishing that the day ahead of me would somehow vanish into thin air. All before my morning tea.

But this time, it was different. I hadn't spoken to my parents on the phone in over a year. It had been even longer since I had seen them in person, and they only lived twenty minutes away. My relationships with both of my parents had been in the process of steadily eroding for the past decade, and in January, I had reached my final breaking point. I arrived at the devastating decision to estrange myself. Over the months that followed, I wrote letters to each of my parents, informing them that I was leaving our family. I set a firm, no-contact boundary. We were not to speak in any form once I mailed these letters. It was over. I was walking away for good.

That winter, I planned my escape from the family like Andy Dufresne in *The Shawshank Redemption*. At night, I chipped away at the prison wall as I mapped out every detail. I met with a financial planner and got my personal finances in order. My parents were wealthy, and I had to be prepared to leave that legacy behind. Once I decided that I could, I continued with my plan. I retrieved copies of my birth certificate and other essential documents from city hall. I ran through a laundry list of keepsake items that my parents might still have in their possession. It turned out that I had taken everything I wanted from my childhood home when my parents moved out of it a few years earlier. Truthfully, I didn't want much. I took my old figure skates and a string of VHS tapes containing my skating competitions and dance performances. That was it.

Slowly, methodically, my plan came together. But, just like Andy Dufresne, I had to keep covering up my work every time a guard walked by. From time to time, my mother would text me. I had been low contact with both my parents for over a year. There were no real boundaries to this situation; low contact simply meant that we didn't speak for extended periods of time until someone caved. Both sides of these cycles were almost always initiated by me. I would go months without speaking to my parents, always in the aftermath of a huge betrayal. Eventually, the heartache would set in. I would begin to miss them. So I would reach out, hopeful that we could move forward. Sometimes we managed to patch things up temporarily, but there was always another rupture. This cycle went on for years. Until one day, I was done.

From January to May, I felt like I was living a double life. I managed to plan my escape without anyone in the family knowing about it. By the time Mother's Day rolled around, the planning was complete. Actually, I had been ready since March. I just couldn't find the right time to blow our lives up. I stared at my calendar as I tried to choose a day to end it.

Well, my birthday is in March, so that's out. And Mother's Day is obviously out, and then it's their wedding anniversary followed by Dad's birthday, and then Coco's yahrzeit,[1] which brings me to sometime in July. So maybe after the 4th of July? Well, no ... my parents love summer... everyone is always at the lake house. So maybe next fall? It would need to be after the high holidays. But then it's Thanksgiving. And then Hannukah. Shit.

All of a sudden, I couldn't wait anymore. I had thrown one too many Mother's Day pity parties, ending with that morning. I didn't have any more tears left to shed. I was not going to spend another second living my life like this. I was thirty-six years old. I had wasted so much of my life desperately yearning for everything to be different. I had spent the past five years begging my parents to repair their relationships with me. I had gone to therapy with my mother and her therapist. Twice. At this point, I knew the truth. Nothing was ever going to change. My life was not going to get better unless I went rogue and took control of it myself.

I paced back and forth in my living room, still in my pajamas stained with tears and sweat. I texted Amy, one of my closest friends. I told her that I was done and that it was happening today. She didn't seem surprised. I asked if she was available to accompany me to FedEx later that morning so I could mail my estrangement letters. Twenty minutes later, I walked out of my apartment with a flash drive, my parents' keys, and a plan.

HALLMARK CERTAINLY DIDN'T MAKE A CARD FOR US

I climbed into my car and drove the short distance to Amy's place. Luckily, she wasn't celebrating Mother's Day with her family until later that evening. She had plenty of time to help me leave mine. My entire body began to fill with electric energy as I gripped the steering wheel. I felt all my senses activate. The colors around me were brighter. The sounds were more pronounced. I was alive for the first time. Either that, or it was a pure adrenaline rush.

I pulled in front of Amy's apartment and texted her that I had arrived. A few minutes later, she emerged from her building and waved at me as she walked down the sidewalk to my car. I opened the door as she slid onto the passenger seat. She immediately leaned over and gave me a hug. I was shaking. Amy smiled as she grabbed my hand. She told me that I was doing the right thing. I laughed as I stated the obvious: "But it's Mother's Day. Are you fucking kidding me? How could I have chosen this day? This is the worst possible day to estrange myself."

As we drove to FedEx, we talked about how eerily poetic it was that I was estranging myself on Mother's Day. For most of my life, I was told to celebrate my mother. I was forced to celebrate my mother. It didn't even matter if I wanted to celebrate my mother. Frankly, I desperately *wanted* to want to celebrate her. Year after year, I had gone through the motions of giving my mother obligatory cards and flowers. But each time I wrote her the kind of card she needed to receive, I felt like I had to cut off my arm to do it. I couldn't quite name that icky feeling I felt each time I signed another card. Now I can. It's self-betrayal.

My mother and I had a very complicated relationship. Hallmark certainly didn't make a card for us. My mother was not my role model nor my confidant. Instead, I had been terrified of her emotional unpredictability when I was a child. As I grew older, we fought constantly. Our relationship had two speeds: all-out war and neutral. There was no warmth. There was no comfort. I could never let my guard down. I feared that as soon as I did, I would be annihilated. The truth is, I was consistently haunted by our relationship. There was nothing else like it in my life. I desperately wanted to love my mother, but it was never safe to love her. That's what my Hallmark card would say.

We pulled into the parking lot of our local FedEx, which was stationed at the edge of a small strip mall. Amy and I walked through the large double doors and were hit with a burst of air conditioning that didn't quite match the weather outside. It was May in Chicago. Sometimes, that meant sweater weather. Other times, it was hot and humid. Today lingered somewhere in between.

I made my way to the computer station and inserted my flash drive. My hands shook as I scrolled through my documents until I found the two files I needed to print. Amy asked me if I wanted to sit down. I continued to hover over the computer, barely listening. I double-clicked on a Microsoft Word document that said *Mom* and pressed print. Amy walked over to the printer to wait for it. I immediately closed that document and opened the one that said *Dad*, mechanically trying to complete this task without thinking too deeply about what any of it meant. I ended my computer session and met Amy over at the printer.

I retrieved the first letter, stuffed it into an envelope, and scribbled *Mom* on the front of it. I waited for the other one. It was much longer. I began to take each page out of the printer as I reflexively read the words I had written to my father. Amy immediately stopped me. She reminded me that I had spent months working on this letter and that reading it right now was not a good idea. I knew she was right. I also knew why I hesitated. My relationship with my father was complicated in a whole different way. Leaving him was tremendously painful. My mother and I had never been close, but I had been close to my father. The fact that our relationship had eroded past the point of repair was absolutely devastating for me. This would never be the outcome I wanted for any of us. But somehow, we had gotten here. We had gotten to the place where I was prepared to walk away from my own family forever.

I shoved my father's letter into an envelope and hastily wrote his name on it. Then, I placed the keys to my parents' lake house in the third and final envelope. I loved that house. It was breathtakingly beautiful, with floor-to-ceiling windows that faced a private, serene lake. My parents went there almost every weekend in the summer and often in the winter. It was undoubtedly their happy place. I had even taken Amy there. The energy of our family was different in that house. There was less fighting; fewer moments where I felt the need to escape. Still, there were some. And that was enough to reinforce my decision. It was time to build a different kind of life. A life with less continuous heartbreak and more peace.

Amy and I walked over to the counter and waited for a FedEx attendant to approach us. There were only a handful of people in the store. *Not a surprise.* I rang the bell, and an attendant quickly approached us. I greeted him with a forced smile as my whole body began to shake uncontrollably. I bent down and dropped my head, still gripping the side of the counter. Amy rubbed the small of my back and told me to breathe.

I regained my composure and handed the three envelopes to the attendant. He glanced at the one that said *Mom* and asked if I would like to expedite shipping so that it would arrive in her hands later today. Amy and I both screamed, "NO!!!"

The attendant quickly redirected himself. He tried to disguise his utter confusion, but I knew it was still there. This was clearly the beginning of a lot of these moments in my life. People would continue to ask about my family and how they were doing. There would be many, many assumptions made about where I spent the holidays. I began to prepare myself for a life of sifting through countless microaggressions.

I watched the attendant place my envelopes into a large FedEx envelope. I forced a polite smile as I gave him the address of my parents' condo. I asked for three-day shipping. That way, the package would arrive sometime next week. Clearly the week of Mother's Day, but not *on* Mother's Day. That was an important distinction. As I stood at the FedEx counter, I realized that I hadn't been able to pick a day to estrange myself because I had been focusing on when my parents would be ready. From that perspective, I would be waiting forever. That morning, something had changed. I flipped the script. I focused on when I was ready. And clearly, I was ready now.

I handed my credit card to the attendant. I watched him seal the envelope and casually toss it onto a pile of outgoing mail. He returned my card and told me that I was "all set." I looked at Amy and realized that neither of us knew what to do next.

We walked out the door and breathed in the fresh air. Amy asked if I had eaten anything that morning. Of course, I hadn't. We walked over to the coffee shop at the end of the strip mall. As we stood in line, everything hit me. I had thought about this moment for months. I had processed it in therapy. I had even tried to preemptively prepare myself for a barrage of emotions. But I was shocked at what I actually felt in that moment. It was the one thing I hadn't anticipated.

Amy looked at me as she asked me what was going through my mind. She seemed prepared to hold everything from extreme grief to complete elation.

I smiled. And then I said: "I'm free."

THE BLACK SQUARE

Spring 2007

I was twenty-five years old when I decided to return to the one place I never wanted to live again: my hometown. I had promptly left Chicago at the age of eighteen, and though I had been home sporadically for holidays and summer breaks, I had done my best to get as far away from my home as possible. I had spent seven years gallivanting all over the place. Life had taken me from Michigan to Cape Town to Washington, DC. But the harder I'd tried to run away, the harder I'd seemed to run headfirst into the most wounded parts of myself. The parts who had seen too much.

My trauma followed me all over the globe. Sweaty nightmares haunted me in Cape Town. Triggers and flashbacks permeated my college life. These moments began to add up so significantly that it was hard not to take notice, though I absolutely tried. I wanted to believe that I could outrun all the bad things that had happened to me. That proved to be impossible.

I didn't want to look under the hood of the car when it seemed to be running just fine. At least, that's what I kept telling myself. I once had a friend whose sideview mirror was haphazardly sideswiped by someone too cowardly to leave a note. Instead of getting the car fixed, my friend wrapped silver duct tape all around the mirror and fastened it back onto the side of her struggling Volkswagen Jetta. Since her car was also silver, we joked that the duct tape fit right in. At first, I found this situation hilarious. But every time I was in her car, I became distracted by it. Sometimes I would stare at the mirror, expecting it to fall right off. Other times I would wonder if she was ever going to get it fixed, or if she planned to keep it that way indefinitely. It felt like an omnipresent problem. What began as a Band-Aid quickly became all-consuming. That's exactly how I felt about exploring the things that happened to me when I was a child. I thought I had found a solution to my problem by living everywhere except Chicago. But it wasn't that simple. I left home at eighteen and duct taped my life back together. But that's not a real solution. And now, all those years of tape were beginning to unravel.

A piece of tape almost came off one night in college. I was sitting on a dorm bed with my best friend (and crush). We were drunk. His roommate was at a house party. My friend looked at me and said, "Tell me something I don't know about you."

I stared into his eyes, and for a moment I became intoxicated by the combination of cheap beer and my unrequited feelings for him. I said, "I want to tell you about the worst thing that's ever happened to me."

His eyes grew wide. He blurted out, "No. Not like this. I think we should both go to bed. You can tell me in the morning if you still want to."

I walked back to my dorm room in a haze. It was a true walk of shame, without any of the perks. I felt horrified and rejected. But I also felt relieved. In the end, I never told him. That moment promptly went back into the vault with loads of duct tape to hold it shut.

I spent the next seven years repeating all kinds of destructive relational patterns while I struggled to keep the vault taped shut. Until one day it became abundantly clear that there was only one path forward. I knew I needed to go back to the place where it all happened. Back to the one place I swore I would never live again. My soul was calling; yearning for me to do the work. It started as a whisper, and I ignored it. But the whisper grew louder during the three years that I spent in Washington, DC, after college. I desperately wanted to stay in DC and pretend that I was fine. My life made sense there. I had a great boyfriend, a job I loved, and amazing friends. Everything was good on paper. But I knew that's all it was. One night, in the fall of 2006, I woke up crying uncontrollably. I had been jolted awake by yet another nightmare. I stumbled into the dimly lit bathroom in my small studio apartment and stared at myself in the mirror. And then, I heard a voice emerge from deep inside of me. I think it was my heart. She whispered: *It's not working, Lauren. Running away is not the same thing as freedom.*

* * *

In the spring of 2007, I applied to a graduate school program for social work at the University of Chicago. I decided that if I got in, I would take it as a sign and return to my hometown. I was promptly accepted into the program, with an attached email from the admissions director asking why I hadn't applied for a merit scholarship. I wrote her back and blurted out that I was just happy to be accepted and that was more than enough. Her response consisted of two sentences, "Lauren, I personally read your admissions application and I'm telling you to apply for a merit scholarship. I'll look out for it." Even after that extraordinarily strong nudge, I almost didn't apply for the scholarship. But, I figured, what the hell. A few weeks later, I received a letter from the university telling me that I had been awarded a merit scholarship that paid for half of my tuition. That's how badly the universe wanted me back in Chicago.

That summer, I packed up my life in Washington, DC. I broke up with my boyfriend, and I said goodbye to all my friends. Even amid all the losses, I felt alive for the first time in years. I was going to be a part of a social work program that lit my soul on fire. I wanted to be a therapist so badly, and this was such an incredible opportunity. It really softened the blow of how hard it would be to return home.

Spring 2008

No one told me that getting a social work education would require a deep dive into the vault I had duct-taped shut. In retrospect, I'm glad I didn't know this ahead of time because it would have prevented me from going. Having come out the other side, I can understand why so many social work programs are organized this way. After all, there's no way that anyone can confidently hold someone else's trauma without being acutely aware of their own material. As someone who has practiced as a psychotherapist for thirteen years, I believe this kind of entry into the field is completely necessary. However, graduate school proved to be one of the most harrowing and eye-opening experiences of my life.

I was sitting in a class called Family Systems, Approaches to Practice when I opened the vault for the first time. Our professor made a comment at the beginning of the quarter that stayed with me. She said, "Many of you will hate me for assigning this work. That's because the assignments will require that you analyze your own family. In depth. And if you are afraid to do that, you don't deserve to sit with anyone else's family."

I shuddered as I agreed with her. In many ways, this class was my biggest fear realized. But it would also present me with the perfect opportunity to peel back years of duct tape and get that damn car fixed.

The turning point came when we were asked to produce a genogram of our own families. A genogram is basically a family tree, but therapist style. We want to know who is in the family, but we also want to know about the relationships between everyone in that family. So a genogram looks like a family tree, but with colorfully coded symbols and lines that describe different relational dynamics such as: *close, apathetic, distant, admiration, physical abuse, conflict,* and *controlling.* Those are just a few examples.

I dreaded this activity way before I started it. I replayed the years I had spent running away from myself and running away from home as if they were a movie reel. I saw myself exploding on well-meaning friends and partners. I saw myself bursting into tears apologetically and on repeat. I watched in horror as I attempted to use my trauma as an excuse for bad behavior. I knew this was the moment when I had to begin facing it all. I had shoved down a major secret for most of my life and now it was tearing me apart. There was no way to avoid it anymore. I decided to make this genogram my Hail Mary moment. And that's a lot coming from a Jew.

A good genogram (and the one we had to do for this assignment) maps out three generations in a family with the focal person (the client) in the center. For the purposes of the assignment, I was the client. So I drew a circle for myself (the code for cisgender female) and wrote my name in the center. Then I mapped out three generations on the genogram. That was the easy part. Now it was time for me to share my opinions of these relationships. My stomach hit the floor.

I started with the easiest one. I drew lines that looked like railroad tracks connecting me to my paternal grandmother, who I had affectionately renamed Coco. This was the code for *very close.* Then I looked at my parents. I drew two parallel dotted lines between my mother and me. This was the code for *conflict.* Next I looked at my father. I hesitated for a moment. Then I drew one dotted line to connect us. This was the code for *distant.* We had been close when I was a little girl, but things were different now. My heart began to ache thinking about it.

I moved on to my brother, Peter. I drew a red, dotted line connecting us. This was the code for *indifferent/apathetic.* Frankly, that code didn't quite match how I felt about Peter, but it was the closest one I could find. We had gone through phases where we were close in a way that almost resembled a friendship. But now, I could barely sense his presence in my life.

As I made my way through the rest of the chart, I realized that most of the lines I had drawn were in the *ambivalent, not very close,* and *distant* categories. My grandmother was the only one in the *very close* category.

I was almost done with the genogram. There was only one Black Square (the code for a cisgender male) who remained. He was off in the distance, almost at the edge of my peripheral vision, on my mother's side of the genogram. I stared at the Black Square as the breath left my body. All of a sudden, the duct tape began to unravel:

Everyone was congregating in the foyer of my parents' home. The home I was raised in. It was Rosh Hashanah, which was just a few months ago. My parents were standing a few feet away from me as the Black Square and his family entered our house. I was wearing a red, short-sleeved, collared shirt with a long black skirt. I was dressed more appropriately for work than for a holiday. I placed my left hand on the banister that led upstairs, ready to run at any moment. The Black Square immediately greeted me and began asking me questions. It was the first time we had seen each other in years. He wanted to know why I moved back to Chicago. I told him I was here to go to social work school. That I was becoming a therapist. I watched as his eyes began to glaze over. I stopped speaking. Then he said, "Sorry, I stopped listening to you because I was too busy picturing you naked."

My gut filled with rage. I couldn't keep this in anymore. Without thinking, I swung the vault wide open and drew two parallel jagged lines etched in a deep red. The lines seemed to slice through the entire chart. It was all I could see.

This was the code for *sexual abuse*.

A WHITE TANK TOP WITH HOT PINK STARS

Shortly after I completed the genogram, I spent Passover with my family. The Black Square was there because we were celebrating the holiday at his house. I almost didn't go. Drawing that genogram and writing the attached paper changed everything. But I wanted to spend the holiday with my family. It was the first year that I was home for Passover since high school. I decided to try and make the most of it.

We often spent Passover at the Black Square's house when I was growing up. Of all the Jewish holidays, this was by far the worst one for me. First, the seder was always long, and he managed to make it longer with his speeches and his performative piety. It also felt like the story of Passover was directly mocking my life. During Passover, we recount a time when the Jews fled persecution in ancient Egypt. I had to sit in his house, year after year, and relive a story where a bunch of Jews escaped exile when I remained deep in exile. Sometimes the Black Square would call on me to read the section where the Jews are still being persecuted. I could feel him getting off on his own power trip.

That evening, it took me over an hour to get dressed. I kept changing my clothes because everything I tried on seemed to reveal too much of my body. I finally settled on a long-sleeved pink shirt, a floor-length grey skirt, and ballet flats. I laughed when I looked at myself in the mirror. I was dressed like an Orthodox Jew, which I most certainly was not. It was a warm April night, and if I wasn't so concerned with hiding my body, I would have undoubtedly worn something different. I emerged from my apartment and immediately began to sweat. I didn't care. This was the right outfit.

Halfway through the seder, we broke for dinner. I had reached my brink. The Black Square was staring at me from across the table. His eyes were fixed on my chest. Despite my best attempts to hide my body, it felt like he had x-ray vision. I could feel his glare penetrating my skin. I looked down at my hands. They were sweating. I finally looked at the Black Square, hoping that if I met his gaze, he would look away. Instead, he licked his lips in a sexualized manner and continued to stare at me. I felt a shiver run down my neck. In an instant, the Black Square began walking toward me. I froze. He stood behind my chair and began to give me a back rub. I quickly moved his hand away from the small of my neck. *He put it back.* And then he slid his right hand down the front of my shoulder, catching my bra strap under his forefinger. I pushed my chair back and almost clipped his foot. He moved on.

As soon as the Black Square walked away, I texted my friend from under the table. It was Saturday night, and I knew that she was going to a house party in the city later in the evening. I told her that I wanted to meet her there. She was surprised, but excited. I said I needed to go home and change first. We laughed about what I was wearing.

Passover ended, and I quickly gathered my things. I told everyone that I had plans. I sped back to my apartment and threw off my clothes, as if the events of the evening were all their fault. Intellectually, I knew that my outfit was not to blame. But it's amazing how many times I had fooled myself into thinking that I could control the outcome of the Black Square's bad behavior. It wasn't until I had been a therapist for many years that I realized just how many survivors blame themselves in this exact manner. *If only I hadn't worn that. If only I hadn't been drinking.* Now I know the truth. What he did to me will always be his fault. It will never, ever be mine.

* * *

I changed into a white tank top with hot pink stars, tight jeans, and black stiletto heels. A true departure from my earlier outfit. This time, I wanted to feel sexy. Since I had just been forced to be sexual, I might as well turn the night around by owning it. As if it ever ends up that way.

I got into a cab and quickly applied my lipstick. I had escaped the exile of Passover and I was finally headed to the party. However, I had an ulterior motive. There was a guy I had met a few times through this friend group, and he had taken an interest in me. I knew he was already at this party. I wasn't sure if I liked him, but I decided that it would feel really empowering for me to be around someone whom I could have the freedom to reject.

I entered the party after 10:00 p.m., and everyone was already drunk. I needed to make up for lost time. I strutted through the hallways of an apartment in Wicker Park that belonged to someone I didn't know, until I found everyone hanging out in the kitchen playing beer pong. I threw my hands in the air and announced my arrival as if I was a celebrity: "Hello everyone, I have arrived. Get excited!"

My friend squealed with joy and barreled me over with a hug. I turned my head, hoping that the guy who liked me had seen my entrance that reeked of artificial popularity. *He had.* I watched as he made his way over to me. We talked for a few minutes as he caught me up on the events of the party so far. The conversation was boring, but I feigned interest. He got me a beer and asked how my night had been. I took two shots before I grabbed my beer from him. I laughed as I said, "I need to get so drunk that I forget this night ever happened."

His eyes widened with curiosity as he said, "Oh, it sounds like you have a crazy story! Let's hear it!"

I decided to resume the part I was playing as a celebrity by announcing to everyone in the kitchen that I had a crazy, dramatic story to share. Everyone stopped what they were doing and looked at me. Suddenly, I had their undivided attention.

"Alright everyone, you want to hear some crazy shit? I had to spend yet another Passover dodging unwanted sexual advances at the dinner table. There's someone in my family who has always weirded me out, and he really lived up to his track record this year. Tonight, he licked his lips from across the table in front of everyone and then he gave me a creepy backrub. What a fucker. I really think my parents saw him do it. It's whatever though. It's been going on for so long. That's my family for you. Seriously, it's fine! It's all good. Everyone has at least one relative in the family who has oversexualized them from birth. Am I right?"

I couldn't stop laughing. I was laughing hysterically. At some point, I looked around the room, and I realized that no one else was laughing. *Actually, no one was breathing.* The life had been drained out of the room. The beer pong game was over. My friend was in the corner crying.

The guy with the crush looked at me in horror. He asked me if I was being serious. He looked incredibly genuine as he displayed his shock and concern.

That set me off: "Oh, come on. Seriously, give me a break. This is nothing. You're so sheltered. Why do you like me anyway? You are a good ole Midwestern boy looking for some basic chick with a basic life who can be your girlfriend. You can't handle me. Spare yourself the trouble, and just move on."

He didn't even know how to respond, so he said nothing. I didn't either. *Ugh, there goes more duct tape off the vault.* I knew I had successfully pushed him away. I had overexposed myself. The truth is, I did like him. I had managed to convince myself otherwise because he was a good person. He was caring. He was stable. He was everything I wasn't used to and believed I didn't deserve.

After I destroyed the mood in the kitchen, I moved into the living room and proceeded to drink more alcohol than I ever have in my entire life. As it got increasingly later in the evening, most of the *good ones* started to head home, including the guy I had insulted and then alienated. But I wanted to stay. I needed to stay. I wasn't done.

I met a guy at that party, sometime after midnight. He was clearly one of the *bad ones*, so naturally, that was perfect. That was what I deserved. We started kissing in a corner of the living room and ultimately made our way onto the couch. As I kissed him, I heard a small voice deep within myself say, *What are you doing, Lauren? You don't want this.* I ignored that part. I told myself that I was in charge. I was on top of him, and I was calling the shots. Unlike the events of the Passover seder earlier that evening.

It didn't take long before the Bad One was pressuring me to go into his bedroom, which was just down the hall. Apparently, this was *his* house party. I refused. I said I needed to get home. And that's when he grabbed my wrist. *Hard.* He pulled me back down to the couch. I rolled out from under him, grabbed my purse, and ran. I sprinted out the door of his apartment and almost directly into oncoming traffic. I was drunk and disoriented. I was in a part of town that felt foreign to me. I ran further down the street and tried to hail a cab. No one was coming. I turned around and saw the Bad One running after me. He was catching up.

I faced forward and threw my hands in the air, waving them all over the place and screaming at every cab that drove by. I looked like someone who was stranded on a desert island and was trying to flag down a helicopter. Without warning, a yellow cab swerved across two lanes of traffic to get me. I slid into the cab and slammed the door, just as the Bad One caught up and tried to grab the handle. I yelled to the cab driver, "GO." We sped away violently.

Then I burst into tears.

NOW DISH IT

The week after the party, I had dinner with my grandmother. Coco and I were incredibly close, and we had been for my entire life. She was my father's mother, and she'd moved to Chicago from New York City after my parents were married and before I was born. She was a permanent staple and protective factor in my life. I will always feel so grateful to have grown up in her presence. There's no way I would be here without her.

Coco and I didn't have a typical granddaughter/grandmother relationship. That's because there was nothing typical about her. Coco was a character in her own right. She would dress in fancy velour tracksuits, complete with a floor-length black mink coat and large rose-tinted sunglasses with gold rims. Most days, she adorned herself in delicate, gold statement necklaces with understated stud earrings. And when it rained, she covered her couture in a traditional beige Burberry trench coat with a matching headscarf. She insisted on having her hair done and her nails manicured to perfection at all times. She dressed better than almost all my friends. She definitely dressed better than me.

I didn't know any other grandmothers like Coco. She would wear the same fancy outfit to the Jewish holidays and to the grocery store. But she didn't dress in fabulous clothing to impress other people; she derived a sense of joy from the clothes themselves. And Coco made sure to pass that gospel on to me, any chance she got. One time, she even looked at me and said, "Honey, in a world with Chanel, what is there to be upset about?"

Coco and I used to sit in the corner at every family gathering and gossip about everyone as if they weren't staring us in the face. She had a habit of using the phrase "cuckoo for Cocoa Puffs" when she wanted to make fun of someone. She stole that line from a commercial that ran incessantly in the eighties and nineties for the General Mills cereal. I wasn't sure that Coco was using that phrase correctly, but it made me laugh every time.

Like me, Coco was an outsider. She was bold and

41

outspoken. She wasn't afraid to share her unpopular opinions with everyone in the family. And those were not traits that went over very well. She and I felt a kinship that was so clear to everyone else that I'm sure it bordered on annoying at times. During moments when I was being particularly feisty, she would laugh and say, "That's something I would say! How come you aren't my daughter? We are the same person. That's a riot."

It was true. Coco made me feel like I belonged in our family – despite her fabulous fashion sense, which I managed not to inherit. We were undoubtedly two peas in a pod. We were the two black sheep. At least I had company. Great company.

One of the biggest perks of returning to Chicago was that I got to spend more time with Coco. We developed a ritual where I would drive down to her swanky apartment in the middle of the Gold Coast on Friday nights, and we would walk arm in arm to the adorable French bistro down the street for dinner. All the waiters in this restaurant knew us. As soon as we walked in, they would immediately usher us to a small, dimly lit table in the back corner of the restaurant, away from everyone. This was our spot. We would sit there for hours, talking about everything.

In addition to clothes and jewelry, Coco had another love: ice cream. As she got older, she became a firm believer in eating anything that made her happy. This ranged from a good cheeseburger (which she ate with a knife and fork on a china plate) to her favorite desert: chocolate ice cream with chocolate sauce. *Not hot fudge.* Chocolate sauce. She was very particular about this. The first time we went to that French bistro together, she tried to order her special desert by saying, "I will have a bowl of chocolate ice cream with chocolate sauce."

The waiter looked confused. He said, "Would you like us to make you a sundae, ma'am?"

Coco scoffed as she threw her hands in the air. "No! I want a bowl with one scoop of chocolate ice cream and some chocolate sauce. Like I said."

The waiter nodded as he anxiously scribbled down her instructions. I didn't *see* his notepad, but I imagine it looked like this: JUST A BOWL OF ICE CREAM WITH CHOCOLATE SAUCE. The waiter looked at me as I said, "I'll have what she's having." Coco and I burst into a fit of laughter.

After that, every time we went to the French bistro, the waiter always brought us two bowls of chocolate ice cream with chocolate sauce as soon as our meals had been cleared.

* * *

The week after Passover, I sat at the French bistro across from Coco as we waited for our bowls of ice cream. We had been engaging in small talk for the past hour, which mostly consisted of me telling her about my graduate school program and the new friends I had made.

As soon as our ice cream arrived, Coco looked at me and said, "Ok, Lauren, enough with the niceties. Our ice cream is here. Now dish it. And don't give me the grandmother version. Tell me what's really going on."

This was customarily the way we spent our time together. Dinner was for all the things that were going well, but once the ice cream arrived, it was time for me to tell Coco the rest of the story. It was time to *dish it.* And I did. She knew everything. She knew about everyone I dated. She knew about all the fights I had with friends. She knew about the Black Square.

I looked down at my bowl of ice cream, and I told Coco all about that night at the house party. She looked at me as she shook her head. "I knew something bad was going to happen that night when you left, Lauren. I was worried about you. He was especially bad at Passover."

I stared into Coco's rose-colored glasses. "I can't continue down this road, Coco. It's time for me to tell my parents about how long this has been going on. I need it to stop. Look at what happened at that party. I really want to become a therapist. I finally care about my life now. I have too much to lose, and if I continue down the path I am on, I am afraid that I won't make it."

What happened next was shocking. Coco and I proceeded to get into the only fight we ever had in the entire time that she was alive. Coco was a straight shooter. She always shared the truth about how she felt about a given situation. This was a character trait that consistently bonded us. We were very similar in that way. The only problem was, in this situation, we were on strictly opposite sides.

Coco looked at me sternly. "Lauren, I don't think you should tell your parents. What are you going to do if they don't back you up? I know you. I know how important it is for you to respect the people around you. I am afraid that you might lose a lot of respect for your parents over this. I don't know how you will be able to have a relationship with them if that happens. You could lose everything."

I dipped my spoon into my melting ice cream. I swirled the chocolate sauce around the edge of the bowl as I tried to process what Coco had just said. Then I spoke:

"Why do you think they won't back me up? There's no way that my dad is going to hear about all this sexual abuse and do nothing. There's no way he is going to allow me to be in the same room as this asshole if I come forward. I know him. He won't let this happen to me ever again."

Coco looked at me. The glare in her eyes burned a hole in my throat. Then she said, "Lauren, I know my son. Trust me, I do. And I hate saying this to you, but you need to hear it. It's unlikely that your mother is going to back you up. You already know this. She won't stand up to anyone on her side of the family. And if she tries to push this under the rug, then so will your father. He won't take a stand if it will alienate your mother in any way, even over something like this. Not even for you."

I began to cry. Then I defended my father. "I just don't think you're right about this. I'm his only daughter and he loves me. There's no way that Dad will allow this to continue.

There's just no way. I don't have a lot of faith in Mom, you're right about that. But Dad is different. He will defend me. I know it. And anyway, I've already made my decision. I'm going to tell them. I have to. I can't live like this anymore. I can't have another house party experience like that ever again. I was almost raped at that party."

Coco reached across the table and grabbed my hand. Her blue veins glistened in the candlelight. "This is heartbreaking for me to say, Lauren. But when it comes to your mother, your father has a huge blind spot. I've seen it. He will do whatever she wants him to do in this situation. And she is not going to support you."

Neither of us ate our ice cream that night. We both watched as the chocolate ice cream and the chocolate sauce melted into one another until they became one. The restaurant was closing, so it was time for us to leave. There was a heaviness in the air. So much had been said, and yet, so much was left unsaid. I hooked arms with Coco as we walked back to her apartment in silence. We never argued about anything. Ever. There was an uncomfortable tension that I didn't know how to fix. We got to the lobby of Coco's building and said goodbye.

As I walked away, Coco called out, "Lauren, wait. I just want you to know that whatever you decide, I will be here for you."

CALENDAR OF CARE

June 2018

The weeks that followed my estrangement were exceedingly complicated. I felt free, and I was deeply plagued with grief. My heart ached for my parents, and I was simultaneously terrified of running into them. One time, I was walking around my local Trader Joe's when I thought I saw my mother. I dove under a fruit bin. My reaction was akin to hiding from an active shooter. I had no idea how to move through these feelings. There was no blueprint for being in liberation, mourning, and fear all at the same time. There was nowhere to turn.

But it was even more than that. While it always felt complicated to rely on my family, at least I had one. And my parents had been there for me during some critical times. In January of 2013, I was in a terrible car accident on my way to work. I totaled my car in the middle of the highway during a particularly brutal Chicago winter. While I was changing lanes, the front wheel of my car caught on a patch of ice, and I spun across three lanes of traffic until I smashed headfirst into the highway divider. I managed to avoid hitting another car. And somehow, I emerged from the wreckage without a single scratch on my body. But emotionally, I was a mess. The first person I called was my father. He left work immediately and drove straight to the scene of the accident. When he arrived, I was still shaking. I couldn't think. I couldn't breathe. He took over in all the right ways. He drove me home. He picked up my favorite chicken noodle soup. He helped me call the insurance company. He sat with me in the living room as I burst into tears.

Now, that safety net was gone. I sat alone in my treehouse apartment and curled myself tightly into a ball. *What if I get into another accident? Who would I call?* I began to cry. I swaddled myself in a blue and yellow blanket knit by my maternal grandmother. Lately, I had been yearning for the energy of my ancestors. At least, some of them. Coco had passed away in June of 2016, leaving me without a buffer. As soon as she died, I knew that my estrangement would be imminent. I rocked myself back and forth like a baby, remembering all I had lost. I cried from a place I didn't even know existed. The truth hit me like a ton of bricks: I had become an orphan.

I was thirty-six years old, but I felt like an infant. I began to understand why preschools rely on routines and structure to get through the day. Children feel safe when they know what happens next. That must be why preschool rooms often have colorful, interactive calendars with large block letters that say SNACK TIME, NAP TIME, and RECESS. In graduate school, I did my first-year internship in a series of preschools, screening children for autism. The students loved pulling me by the hand as they skipped over to the large, laminated schedule. I would bend down and watch as they proudly pointed to the next activity. And when a child would correctly identify what came next, I would exclaim, "Good job!" It was fun to see these children smile ear to ear during these moments. I always thought that was adorable. Now I understood why this kind of structure is imperative. I had no idea what activity was next in the larger calendar of my life. I had no idea what came after estrangement. And the terror was real.

I felt like the floor had been ripped out from under me. I had no routine and no conception of time or space. I ate trail mix for dinner. I cried myself to sleep. I woke up in the middle of the night wailing for help, but no one was around. I lost track of entire weekends as I zoned out to *The Real Housewives* and barely remembered to shower. I couldn't believe how quickly I reverted to infancy. I was scared and lonely. I needed help, but I was too afraid to ask for it. I had a long history of getting through things alone. At a young age, I figured out that I couldn't rely on my mother, so I relied heavily on myself. But this was becoming too much. This was overpowering. I needed my friends.

Still swaddled in my grandmother's blanket, I called my

friend Heather. I told Heather that I was lost. I barely had the right words to describe the aching loneliness in my heart. She asked me what I had been doing in my spare time. I barely answered her. Instead, I just continued to cry.

* * *

Heather and I met during graduate school, and we became fast friends. She had a light about her that was infectious. Her natural blonde hair and blue eyes matched the brightness of her spirit. Every time I was around Heather, I felt seen. I was not accustomed to that feeling.

Over the years, Heather and I built a friendship that felt more like a sisterhood. Neither one of us had a blood sister, so we both craved that kinship. We would get together and talk for hours, until our tea turned cold. We spent our Sundays driving to random neighborhoods in Chicago and getting lost on long, winding walks until it became dark outside. This was the kind of friendship I had always wanted.

By the time I estranged myself, Heather had become my best friend. We had been there for so many pivotal moments in each other's lives. I watched Heather get married, have a child, and separate from her husband. I watched Heather buy her own house, fix it up, and raise a toddler completely on her own. She made all these things look so much easier than they were. In my eyes, Heather was secretly a superhero. That was the only possible explanation. I had no idea how she managed to do all of this while also thriving as a therapist. Heather never let the events of her life break her spirit. That's still my favorite part about her.

* * *

When I told Heather how badly I was struggling, she had an idea. Heather suggested that she contact all my close friends and put together a calendar where each person could sign up to spend time with me every weekend for the next month. *Oh my God, my very own preschool routine!* That's the beauty of Heather. I could barely form a sentence. I felt like I had launched myself into the abyss of orphanhood with no security system in place. But Heather has always been deeply intuitive. She knew exactly what to do. So Heather devised a plan to help me see that I had let go of a false sense of security, and I had all these people waiting to catch me on the other side. I knew she was right, but I needed to see it for myself. So I referred to our little experiment as my calendar of care.

Later that day, I sent Heather my empty Google calendar for the next month as well as the email addresses of all my other close friends. I am the kind of person who spends time with each friend individually. I have never been part of a group. My closest friends grew accustomed to seeing each other at my annual birthday party, and not much else. But my estrangement brought everyone together in a whole new way, and that was a little bit exciting. It also felt a little scary. I could relate to that scene in *Seinfeld* where George Costanza freaks out because two people in his life are about to meet. He doesn't like Relationship George merging with Friendship George. Just like George Costanza, I had so many versions of Friendship Lauren, and each one was slightly different. I wondered how all of this would go.

A few days later, Heather emailed my calendar back to me, but this time, it was full. My friends had signed up to take care of me during every single weekend over the next month. They had even planned a girls' night out at the end of the month. I was floored. I also felt like the luckiest person in the world. All the Friendship Laurens would just have to get over it. This was good.

I survived the month of June by following the routine and structure outlined in my calendar of care. Since I had no decision-making capacity, I came to rely on my friends in a whole new way. Every Friday, I glanced at my Google calendar, which glimmered with colorful plans. Like a kid in preschool, I got excited as I pointed to each new activity. It was so comforting to be cared for in this way. It was so comforting to be taken in. All of this was new to me.

My friends were also in charge of planning our time together since I made it clear that I was relinquishing control over everything. This was a shocking departure from my adult self, but it turned out to be a welcome one. I let my friends take me to brunch and to dinner. All I had to do was show up. Sometimes, we went to yoga or walked through a park. I needed them so much more than I realized.

In the middle of June, it was Heather's turn. She picked me up outside my apartment, and I walked over to her white Subaru hatchback. Her daughter, Willa, waved gleefully from her car seat. We drove down to Hyde Park and walked around our old stomping grounds. It was so much fun to take Willa around campus as we told her stories from our graduate school days. Willa loved hearing about the fact that I knew Heather before she did. She thought it was hilarious that her mother had a life before motherhood.

I loved telling Willa the story of the first time I met her. When I would stay late at Heather's house, Willa would run into the living room and ask me to put her to bed by reading a book and then telling her this story. I would cradle Willa in my arms as if she was a newborn. Now that she was almost four, her long body hung off the chair. I would look into Willa's eyes and tell her that as soon as I saw her, I knew that she was going to be a very special girl.

Over the years, I developed a unique bond with Willa. Sometimes, Willa felt like Heather's clone. She was the sweetest child I had ever met. She had her mother's blonde hair and bright blue eyes that seemed to shimmer with the same lightness. She loved being outdoors, just like Heather. She also loved a good craft project, just like Heather. But Willa was bold, outspoken, and inquisitive. She formed quick opinions and wasn't afraid to share them. And in these moments, she reminded me more of myself.

I have a photo from the day the three of us spent in Hyde Park. We found this rock and decided to take turns jumping off it. I snapped photos as Heather jumped off the rock first. I laughed as she imitated those cheesy wedding photos where people are posing in the air. Then, it was my turn. I stepped onto that rock, and I launched myself upward. I could hear Willa yelling, "WOW, Auntie Lauren! You jumped so high!"

I had no idea what all the buzz was about until Heather showed me the photo. I *had* jumped incredibly high. I joked that my new name should be Air Lauren. I borrowed that pun from Michael Jordan's Nike commercials that ran all the way through the glory days when the Chicago Bulls dominated basketball in the 1990s. His nickname was Air Jordan, because he soared through the air higher than any other player at the time. I wasn't a basketball fan per se, but I grew up in Chicago when the Bulls were on fire, and Michael Jordan was the standout player. He seemed especially ethereal. I hoped that by nicknaming myself Air Lauren, some of that magic might rub off on me.

Willa asked me how I had managed to jump so high. And then I told her that I had grown up as a competitive figure skater. She looked at me with wide eyes and said, "Cooooool." It was cool. I loved talking about my life as a skater. I had skated from the age of five all the way through my junior year of high school. I competed all over the Midwest, and I won a prominent regional competition when I was fourteen years old. Winning that competition was one of the best days of my life. I had trained so fiercely and worked so diligently for that moment. And it paid off. I skated the best program of my career. As I stood at the top of that podium, my teal competition dress shimmered in the spotlight. I bent down as the head judge placed a gold medal around my neck and handed me a glass sculpture that said Regional Champion. I remember thinking to myself, *I am going to make it.*

As I told Willa these stories, I realized that figure skating had saved my life. It gave me something positive to focus on while I grew up in a family riddled with chaos. Figure skating had provided me with structure, routine, and purpose. Skating also gave me a community that felt safe. And as soon as I launched myself off that rock, my body remembered it all. My body wanted me to remember that I really am Air Lauren, and that meant that I could survive anything.

* * *

As June drew to a close, I began to feel more like myself. My friends truly brought me back to life. They swooped in and took care of me when I needed them the most. I was eternally grateful. It turned out that I wasn't alone. I had a fierce network of friends who truly loved me. I even had my very own calendar of care.

At the end of June, my friends and I gathered at a trendy sushi restaurant in Wicker Park for our girls' night out. It was the perfect summer evening in Chicago. We sat on the patio and ordered fruity martinis. I looked around the table and smiled. I wore my best jeans, a frilly shirt, block heels, and fresh lipstick. It felt so good to dress up again. Coco would have been proud. I listened as my friends told each other hilarious stories about their most recent dating escapades. Everyone was getting along swimmingly.

Hearing their stories made me realize that I had completely neglected my own love life. For the past three years, I had been so immersed in the disillusionment of my family that I had no capacity to focus on anything else. It was so nice to listen to my friends discuss their regular problems. This is what we were supposed to be doing with our spare time. We were in our thirties, and we wanted to have fun. I no longer felt the need to take up space crying into my martini as I recounted the events of one horrible Jewish holiday after another. Instead, I sat back in my chair and laughed along with my friends.

After dinner, we walked over to a new hipster bar that had just opened down the street. Once inside, I immediately began mocking the Caribbean décor. *Um, this is Chicago.* Nonetheless, I couldn't dispute the fact that it was cool. After all, I had a love-hate relationship with everything hipster. There were shuffleboard tables and piles of board games. We decided to park ourselves around a table that contained Giant Jenga. One of my friends went to buy us a round of drinks, while the rest of us began to stack the large Jenga pieces. We laughed and danced to the background music. At one point, I pulled out my phone and downloaded a dating app. My friends cheered. I was so glad we were all together.

It was the perfect evening.

THE OTHER F-WORD

July 2018

As June spilled into July, I began to feel a newfound sense of purpose. I was hopeful about my future for the first time. I even let myself dream. Where did I want to live when I grew up? What kind of partner would be right for me? It had been years since I had the bandwidth to explore these things. Instead, my dreams had constantly been derailed by reality. Over the years, I worried that my relentless family drama would scare away a potential partner. I could tell that my friends had become exhausted by the vortex of chaos that had engulfed me for the past decade, even though they would never admit it. But everything was different now. I got out. I was finally in charge of my own destiny.

The only people left in my life were my friends. That was such a relief. Not only had they come to my rescue for the entire month of June, but we also had fun. I certainly wasn't expecting that to happen. In fact, I couldn't remember the last time I really had fun. At girls' night, we brainstormed ways that I could bring more joy and levity into my life. I had no idea what to do with that conversation. I sat at the table like a confused child as I exclaimed that fun was the other F-word. We all laughed.

* * *

One weekday morning, in mid-July, I sat on my patio and tried to follow the advice of my friends. It was time to experience joy again. I didn't have to be at work until the early afternoon, so I decided to take advantage of an easy summer morning. July in Chicago is highly coveted. We don't receive nearly enough sunlight during the rest of the year. It felt so good to bask in the glow of the sun and all its warmth.

I extended my legs straight in front of me until they brushed up against the railing of my patio. I drank my loose-leaf chai and took in a breath of fresh air. My covered patio always managed to reveal just the right amount of sunlight. I popped in my headphones, and I began to listen to a Bon Iver album on my phone. A smile crept across my face.

I put on my sunglasses as I watched my favorite tree move delicately in the wind. I stared at the light green leaves as they swept against my wooden staircase. I loved The Treehouse apartment. It had been my home for almost three years. That may not sound like a long time, but it was for me.

A TEAM OF MEN IN PROTECTIVE GEAR

July/August 2018

At the end of July, strange things began happening in my apartment. One afternoon, I took a work call in my second bedroom, which doubled as a home office. While I was on the phone, I noticed a black dot moving within my peripheral vision. I tilted my head and glanced up at the ceiling. *Ants.* Well, that's annoying.

I walked back into the living room as I scanned for more ants. I noticed a few more scurrying across the ground beneath my glass coffee table. *Shit.* I retrieved a spray bottle from the kitchen and ran back into the living room to kill them. First, the ones under the table, and then the ones in the second bedroom. I sat down on the couch and attempted to regain my composure. I was never a fan of ants, but I wasn't especially bothered by them either. I thought, *You live amongst nature, Lauren. Sometimes nature comes inside.* Nothing to worry about.

I turned on the television and flipped to Bravo, hoping to distract myself. A few hours later, I heard the same scurrying noise coming from my windowsill. I paused the television and walked over the window. It was dusk, and the sun was beginning to set. I gasped. Suddenly, hundreds of ants began coating the windowsill. They were accumulating right before my eyes. There were so many ants that all I could see was black. They had not been there a few hours earlier. *Nothing had been there.* I know this for a fact because I had just watered the plants that sat along the window. Not a single ant. Now, there was an army. An army of ants climbing on top of one another, scrambling to get in.

I stood at the windowsill, frozen in time. I looked down and saw hundreds of oval, iridescent eggs. My mouth agape, I watched in horror as baby ants began to break out of their fresh eggs. *They were coming to life by the second.* It was like watching a nature video. The ants began to multiply faster than I could count. Within minutes, there wasn't enough room on the windowsill for all of them. I watched the ants pile on top of each other, as they squeezed their way through a small crack in the window and into my apartment. It was officially time to panic.

* * *

I searched the web, desperately yearning for an explanation. I had never seen anything like this before. I had gone camping. I had spent time in nature. I had even dealt with ant problems in former apartments. *Nothing like this*. Google was useless. The internet couldn't provide any answers except for: infestations happen, and we don't always know why. I shook my head. That wasn't good enough. I stared at the line I had just typed into my search bar: *hundreds of ants just came out of nowhere*.

I turned the television back on. A new episode of *The Real Housewives* had just started. Perfect. I began to make dinner. As my pasta boiled, I walked back over to the windowsill and continued to stare at the horrifying situation that was unfolding in real time. The ants were still multiplying right outside my window. Some of them were coming inside, but not as many as I would have thought. Instead, they were hatching and immediately stepping on top of one another until they formed a large black line against the glass. The line kept getting taller and taller. I had never seen ants behave like this.

I pulled a dining room chair into the living room so that I could eat my pasta and watch television without needing to be anywhere near that window. I tried to pay attention to the show, but my gaze kept gravitating toward the windowsill. *Something isn't right.* I turned to Google once again. I searched for pictures of infestations. I didn't see anything that came close to what was happening in my home.

I tried to continue my nighttime routine. I changed into my pajamas and brushed my teeth. But I kept walking back over to the window. The ants had stopped reproducing, but they were still there. They weren't trying to get into my apartment; they were just perched on top of one another. I didn't understand.

Then again, I certainly wasn't an ant expert. I climbed into bed and turned off the lights.

I didn't sleep at all. I lay in bed, paralyzed in fear. I didn't want to know what was happening in the other room. I tossed and turned until daylight began to creep through the blinds of my bedroom. I still had a few hours before my alarm would sound, and I would need to figure out how to get ready for work as though nothing was deeply wrong. I closed my eyes and took a deep breath, attempting to center myself. Slowly, I got out of bed and crept over to the windowsill. I squinted. *I didn't want to look.* My eyes began to dart around the living room. *No ants.* I opened my eyes the rest of the way and peered over the windowsill. All the ants and their eggs were gone. *What the fuck!?*

I had never done drugs in my life. I had never taken a puff of a cigarette. But now, I felt like I was living in a hallucinogenic haze. How could this have happened? *Where did all the ants go?* There was no way that a full-blown infestation could somehow disappear into thin air. After going back and forth about it, I decided to call my landlord. In the three years that I had lived in The Treehouse apartment, I had called maintenance twice. Once because my dishwasher broke, and the other for a routine furnace repair. That's it. Apart from the occasional garden spider, I had rarely encountered bugs inside of this apartment. And nothing like this had ever happened to me. That's for sure.

My landlord was incredibly responsive. He showed up later that day, armed with a face shield and a huge canister of toxic chemicals. Even though neither one of us could locate the plague of ants I had described from the night before, my landlord sprayed the entire perimeter of my apartment anyway. He walked onto my patio and sprayed there too. He even hired someone to go onto the roof to see if there was an ant colony that had spontaneously taken up residence there. But no one found anything. A few days later, I still hadn't seen any more ants. Perhaps the whole thing had been a fluke. I did my best to move on.

That weekend, I went out to dinner with my friend, Silvia. We ate amazing Persian food and got gelato afterwards. We sat in the middle of my favorite neighborhood park on a warm, summer evening as we ate our dessert. I looked at her and smiled. I told Silvia about our girls' night out, since she hadn't been able to make it. She laughed when I told her that I finally downloaded a dating app. I listened intently as Silvia described a problem she was having at work. Everything seemed fine. *Finally, back to normal life.* Then, I glanced down at my feet and caught a glimpse of a large, black ant zigzagging across the ground. I froze.

* * *

The next day, the plague of ants reappeared in my apartment. Once again, ants lined the windowsill in my living room, their eggs encased in that white gel that's now burned into my memory. They climbed on top of each other just as they had done the first time; multiplying in minutes. I ran out the back door and onto my patio. *More ants.* They were scurrying up and down the wooden banister. I was confused. I thought ants usually walked in single-file lines. These ants looked like a dark force had taken hold of them. They were zigzagging all over the banister and running into each other in the process. They looked intoxicated. *More strange ant behavior.* I heard a weird noise and looked up at the sky. I saw one huge ant with wings, circling my patio. It was the largest ant I had ever seen in my life. It was three times the size of the ants scrambling drunkenly up and down the banister. *What is THAT?*

I pulled out my phone in a frenzy as my palms began to sweat. My fingers shook as I tried to unlock my phone. I opened my web browser and began to search for answers. Google told me that once you see a flying ant, you are in deep shit. Flying ants are responsible for the reproduction of an entire colony. Where there is one flying ant, there are bound to be hundreds of babies that follow.

I closed my web browser and called my landlord. This time, in a panic. He came right over. We stood at my windowsill, and he saw everything. I examined his face, studying his confused look as he watched the ants climb on top of each other. He remarked that it was strange that the ants weren't really trying to get inside. *Ok, I'm not losing my mind.* We walked out the back door and onto the patio. My landlord looked perplexed as he watched the drunk ants scramble all over the banister. He confessed that he had no idea what to do. He had owned this building for years and yet, he had never seen anything like this before.

My landlord stated that this situation was way above his paygrade, so he called a professional exterminator. A team of men in protective gear arrived the next morning, armed with more large canisters of pesticide. They banished me from my unit so they could get to work creating the most toxic environment imaginable. Feeling defeated, I walked down the stairs and watched them from the street.

The exterminators went onto the roof and discovered a large ant colony in the making. That colony certainly hadn't been there the week before. They eradicated everything. They climbed ladders and sprayed the outside of my entire windowsill. Ants fell from the sky like small black droplets. It was apocalyptic. The exterminators barged into my unit and fumigated the place until my beautiful treehouse apartment was covered in a cloud of smoke. I looked up at my apartment from the street. Dense fog filled the inside of every window until all I could see from the street was a white haze. I had lost my only safe haven. Tears began to stream down my face.

Once they were done, the exterminators made their way down the stairs to come talk to me. I tried to move my legs, but it felt like I was stuck in cement. The exterminators approached me, dodging eye contact. They told me that they had removed every ounce of this infestation, but it was a peculiar one. They had never heard of an infestation vanishing and then reappearing a week later. They also confirmed that the ants' behavior was *uncharacteristic.* Nonetheless, they reassured me that sometimes, ants do strange things. No two infestations are ever the same. The exterminators said they had eradicated the problem and that it would be safe for me to go back into my apartment within a few hours. *Safe? What does that even mean.*

Once the exterminators left, I didn't know what to do with this situation. On the one hand, I was grateful that the exterminators had confirmed that I was experiencing something out of the ordinary. That also made it worse. What now? Would the plague suddenly return? Since these ants were behaving so strangely, it felt like just about anything was possible. How was I going to sleep through the night? My apartment had quickly morphed into a place that was terrorizing me.

* * *

That week was filled with paranoia during the day and insomnia at night. I kept waking up in the middle of the night and sleepwalking my way over to the windowsill, expecting to see another plague. But there was nothing. Not a single ant. They hadn't returned, but I was consumed by the fear that they would.

On Friday afternoon, I called Heather. I finally told her what was going on. Up until this point, I had kept this problem between me, my landlord, and the team of men in protective gear. I was afraid that my friends would think I had gone clinically insane. Heather was immediately empathetic, yet she couldn't believe the words that were coming out of my mouth. I asked if I could stay at her place for the night, even though there was *technically* nothing wrong anymore. She told me to come right over.

One night turned into two as I spent the entire weekend with Heather and Willa. Heather convinced me to stay in their guest room as she packed the weekend with fun and games designed to distract me from the horrors of the past week. It worked. On Sunday evening, we went to a block party on Heather's street where we all played together in a bouncy house. Willa clung to me, laughing as she jumped up and down. In an instant, I began to feel nauseous and claustrophobic. It was getting late, and I didn't know what was waiting for me at home.

I broke out of the bouncy house and began to hyperventilate. Heather grabbed Willa as they slid out of the large, inflatable red door behind me. Heather rubbed the small of my back as I tried to regain my composure. I told her that I needed to go back to my apartment. *What if my entire place is filled with ants again?* I had to be there to manage the situation before a swarm of angry, drunk ants took hold of my home. Heather urged me to stay with her instead. She told me that I didn't need to go home, and I could borrow some clothes to go to work tomorrow. She told me I could stay with her for as long as I needed. She did have a spare bedroom in the basement, after all. I thanked Heather for her open invitation as I promptly declined it. We began walking down the street so that I could get my things.

* * *

The ants did not return, so I had no choice but to try to continue with my life. Though that proved to be impossible. I struggled to sleep through the night. Any time I heard a sound, I shot out of bed. I tossed and turned, haunted by memories of ants breaking out of their slimy, iridescent eggs. I woke up at dawn and walked cautiously over to my windowsill. *Nothing.* I patrolled the halls of my apartment, unable to calm myself down. I waited for daylight to arrive so that I could get ready to go to work. My home quickly became yet another place I yearned to escape from.

I did my best to continue my summer morning routine. I woke up early and sat on my patio drinking loose-leaf chai and listening to music. But it wasn't the same. There was no joy. There was no levity. Instead, my mind wandered. Every time

I thought I saw a black dot move across the banister, my eyes grew wide. When the wind brushed up against my delicate arm hair, I jumped out of my seat. I couldn't seem to settle down, no matter how hard I tried.

In early August, Heather convinced me to spend a night downtown at a hotel. The ants had still not returned, but my nerves were completely shot. We both knew enough about trauma to know what was really going on here. I was haunted by what had happened to me. I hadn't slept in weeks. My body and mind were in desperate need of at least one night without a PTSD flashback. I decided to take Heather's advice. So I pulled out my laptop and searched for fancy hotels in downtown Chicago.

I found an incredible deal that allowed me to stay at the Drake Hotel on a Sunday evening without breaking the bank. It was perfect. In the morning, I could take a ten-minute bus ride from the hotel to get to my office. I packed an overnight bag, and I got into a Lyft. I was excited to treat myself to a relaxing evening in a hotel room that I wouldn't have to inspect every fifteen minutes.

The Drake is one of the oldest and most charming hotels in Chicago. It has tall ceilings and beautiful royal blue carpet. It has a grand entrance with crystal chandeliers that look like they belong in Buckingham Palace. I walked into the lobby, and I immediately felt like a movie star. I also felt like I didn't deserve it because I was playing pretend. I was only here because I was trying to outrun the horrible reality of my life. Visions of ants lining my windowsill infiltrated my mind as I approached the front desk to check myself in.

I rode the gold-plated elevator up to my fancy room and threw my overnight bag on a plush king-sized bed with crisp white sheets. I examined the perimeter of the room for a second before I realized what I was doing. I grabbed my purse and quickly left the room.

As I began to walk around the neighborhood, I regained my bearings. I was only a few blocks from my grandmother's old apartment in the Gold Coast. My heart began to ache. My feet seemed to have a life of their own as I gravitated toward Coco's apartment building. On the way, I passed the French bistro we used to frequent. It was hard to miss. The storefront was painted deep red, and it had large, slender windows complete with adorable flower boxes. The bistro resembled every quaint café in Paris. I stood outside and my heart sank. We had been here so many times. We had shared so many laughs over chocolate ice cream with chocolate sauce. It was also the scene of our one and only fight.

I forced myself to continue walking down the street until I got to Coco's apartment building. I sat down on the concrete steps and began to cry. I missed her with every bone in my body. All of a sudden, I felt alone. *Really alone.* The orphan feeling was back. I cried as I realized that it had been less than two months since I left my family. I barely had a chance to process my estrangement before the ants violently booted me from the one home I had left.

I texted Heather and told her that I wasn't doing so well. I told her that I was sitting on the steps of Coco's apartment crying. I told her that I was lonely. She said she was afraid that might happen. She apologized for not being able to spend the night downtown with me. I hadn't even considered that as an option, so it was almost worse to have it yanked away.

I peeled myself off Coco's steps and began to walk down the street. Tears streamed down my face. My grief felt like an endless pit of darkness. The triggers were everywhere. As I walked away from Coco's building, I felt like I lost her all over again. Coco had been my one true ally in the family. Without her, I felt cast adrift.

It was still early in the evening, and I had no idea what to do with myself. I wandered around the Gold Coast for a while and ultimately decided to indulge in a glass of wine. I rarely drank alcohol on Sunday evenings, and I especially didn't drink alone. But I needed something to take the edge off.

I found a cute American bistro and sat down on the patio

with a glass of chardonnay. I snapped a video of myself posing with my wine and posted it to social media. I looked like I was having the best time. I stared at this video, perplexed, as the likes piled up. I felt like a phony. None of this was real.

I walked back to the Drake, already a little tipsy from my single glass of overpriced wine. I went up to my room and took a long, hot shower. The bathroom was beautiful. White granite lined the floor and the walls. I let the hot water beat down on my back until my skin turned red.

I emerged from the shower and realized it was getting late. I ordered room service for dinner as I watched *The Real Housewives*, just like I would have done at my apartment. I went through all the motions of self-care, but none of it worked. I couldn't bypass any of these feelings. I felt displaced and ungrounded. I missed my grandmother with every ounce of my being. I had no family. I had no safety net in the event of a crisis. I couldn't call my father and cry on his couch anymore. And now, I couldn't bear to be in my own home.

COMING APART AT THE SEAMS

Mid-August 2018

After my night at the Drake, I must have glazed over the next three weeks. That time in my life is a blur. *And that's trauma.* The mind has a built-in shield that prevents us from remembering the aftermath of truly horrific events. Sometimes it's possible to recover these memories. Other times the brain will send a shockwave through the body when we get too close to them. It feels like touching a hot stove. When this happens, it's best to back up. That's because there are some events that are so devastating, so deeply disturbing, that we may not be able to fully comprehend them without going a little mad. I've always thought of that as one of our greatest survival mechanisms as human beings. Our brains come with this buffer because some events are simply indigestible. A plague of ants that accumulated in front of my eyes and then disappeared into thin air will always live in that category. I suppose I can accept that.

What I do remember about the aftermath of the ant plague is that I threw myself into my work, desperate to forget about everything that had taken place. Thankfully, I loved my job. I had been a clinical social worker for the past nine years. Five years prior, I opened my very own private practice. I had a caseload of clients that I absolutely adored. I saw them in my very own office suite in the Chicago Loop. I had secured my office two years ago, and it was quite the career milestone when it happened. I felt eternally grateful to all the clients who had chosen to work with me over the years. After all, I was only in business because of them.

My office felt like a serene living room. I supplied complimentary tea and coffee for my clients. I brought my favorite novels from home and placed them in the waiting room along with a series of coloring books designed for adults. Live plants lined the window of the main office, which boasted an incredible city view from the thirteenth floor. I had a suite in one of the oldest high-rise buildings in downtown Chicago. It was a historical site with a lot of character. It felt like my home away from home. My clients would often comment on how safe they felt there. I felt the same way.

But ever since the ants, my career held a sharp contrast to the rest of my life. Work was a sanctuary; home was a nightmare. I didn't know what to do with that schism. Every night, I went home and did my best to exist in my apartment, but it felt like a violent crime had taken place there. I struggled to feel safe in my home. I clung to my old routines, but nothing felt the same. I was going through the motions. I cooked pasta as *The Real Housewives* blared in the background. I glared at the windowsill in my living room, bracing myself for another plague of ants. And when it was time for bed, I tossed and turned until the first light of dawn broke through my blinds. I yearned for the moment when my alarm would sound so that I could be temporarily liberated from the invisible prison of life with PTSD.

* * *

I continued to go to work and sit in front of my clients with my legs crossed, and my arms clasped delicately in my lap. I looked at them with compassion as they shared intimate details about their lives. Secretly, I marveled at the fact that my clients had no idea that my life was falling apart. They didn't know I had left my family. They certainly didn't know about the mysterious plague of ants. *Nothing.*

At times, I wanted to tell them. Or rather, I wanted to tell them *some* aspects of my story. I had a lot of clients who could have benefited from knowing about my estrangement. But the field of mental health required me to assume the impossible task of becoming a blank slate. The field wanted me to be Regular Lauren, no matter what horrors I was facing in my own life. I understood this philosophy and generally agreed with it. But, in retrospect, I'm not sure it helped my clients to believe that I had everything figured out. Especially during moments when that couldn't have been farther from the truth.

Trying to hold on to Regular Lauren as a plague of ants overtook my apartment was a whole new level of unattainability. There was no way I could pretend to be a blank slate while my life began to disintegrate in front of my eyes. On the one hand, I felt like a fraud. I was playing the part of a stoic therapist while I was on the brink of total collapse. On the other hand, I was eternally grateful that I got to pretend that everything was fine. Perhaps I was really the one who needed to hold on to Regular Lauren. I stared at my clients, yearning to see myself through their eyes: Lauren is stable, Lauren is kind, Lauren is a regular person with a regular life.

In the evenings, I began to unravel. I walked through the door of my apartment hoping to hold on to Regular Lauren, but that identity was quickly ripped out from under me. I fought against this deterioration, clinging to the way things used to be. I did my best to continue my regular routine of changing out of my office clothes and into sweatpants. But only after I had patrolled the perimeter of my entire apartment. The ants never came back, yet I was irrevocably haunted by them. I frequently woke up in the middle of the night in a cold sweat. I launched myself out of every chair if I felt something touch my arm. I glared at the ceiling of my patio as I braced myself for the return of the flying ants. These moments became ritualized. I didn't know how else to function.

In the mornings, I continued to get dressed for work just like old times. I listened to music as I walked the short distance to the train just as I had done *before*. Sometimes, I would stare out the window of the blue line train and marvel at the tall skyscrapers as they lined the Chicago River. Other times, I would look out the window and catch my own reflection in the glass. I would quickly turn away, unable to face myself. *This wasn't working.* There was a limit to how long I could embody two vastly different realities, and it had the shelf-life of a dairy product. I could feel that due date quickly approaching. I was coming apart at the seams.

ONE FOOT IN FRONT OF THE OTHER

The end of August drew near, and summer in Chicago was in full force. I looked down from my third-floor patio as the neighborhood children played together in an inflatable pool. They looked so innocent, so blissful. I wondered how my life had taken such a dramatic turn for the worse. I couldn't begin to fathom what had happened in my apartment, but at least it seemed to be over now. Still, it was almost harder to experience so much intensity while the sun shined so brightly. Nonetheless, I did my best to take advantage of these easy summer days. I was ready to turn things around.

On a particularly beautiful Sunday afternoon, my friend Mila and I decided to go to the beach. I had known Mila since we were in middle school. She had been one of my closest friends. We went through periods in our life where we were extremely close and other times when we didn't speak as much. But each wave that brought us back together seemed to be purposeful. When Mila moved back to Chicago, we easily rekindled our friendship. She had recently gone through a divorce, and I had been in the process of divorcing my entire family. We were clearly back in each other's lives for a reason.

Mila and I decided to go to a secluded beach in the Rogers Park neighborhood of Chicago. One of the best parts about Chicago is that there are small, private beaches that line most of the coast. Those were always my favorite places to go to in the summer. I was never a fan of the overcrowded beaches that were much larger. I wanted to go to a beach where I could hear the waves crashing up against the shore. Mila was the same way.

Mila and I spent the day together, drinking iced coffee and reminiscing about the many years we had known each other. We soaked up the sun on our brightly colored beach towels and periodically ran into the water to cool off. We snapped a photo of our neatly pedicured toes and posted it to Instagram. Mila gathered a few stones and arranged them in a delicate circle as I read a book. It was perfect.

We also talked about my recent estrangement. Mila

admitted that she wasn't surprised by anything that had gone down in my family. Initially, I had no idea how the news of my estrangement would feel to someone who had grown up with me – someone who had known my parents. I imagined that most of the people who grew up around my family had been fooled into believing that I came from an ordinary household. But Mila was different. Mila had always been incredibly perceptive and deeply intuitive. So when she told me that she wasn't surprised about any of it, I felt so much relief.

* * *

I got home from the beach around dinnertime and took a shower. As I reached for my bath towel, I felt so grateful for the wonderful day I had with Mila and the power of being so close to the water. I threw on a pair of shorts and a tank top and ordered a salad from one of my favorite restaurants. As I waited for my dinner to arrive, I settled into my couch in the living room to watch a little television. Days like these made it slightly easier to be at home. It had been almost a month since the plague of ants swarmed my apartment. Perhaps that had been a fluke after all.

A few hours later, I started to get sleepy, so I decided to call it a night. I walked into my bedroom, still reminiscing about how lovely the day had been. I sat on the corner of my bed as my feet dangled off the edge. I looked down and caught a glimpse of the dark wooden floor. *Something was moving.* I froze. Small, white worm-like creatures were beginning to emerge from underneath my bed at a rapid pace. I hugged my legs against my chest in an upright fetal position as I stared down at the ground. *No.* Slowly, I uncurled my body and tilted my head so I could peek under the bed skirt. I saw more of those things than I could count. *NO, NO, NO.*

I reached down and picked up one of the creatures with my bare hands. I didn't even know what it was. I held it between my thumb and index finger as it twirled its head around in a 360-degree circle. I almost hurled. It was mealy white with a dark brown dot at the top. It was half a centimeter long. I threw it back down onto the floor. I grabbed my phone from the nightstand, and I went back to Google for answers. It didn't take long to identify these creatures. *Moth larvae.*

I grabbed my phone as I launched myself off the bed. I ran out of the room, vigorously slamming the door on my way out. I darted into the kitchen and grabbed as many terrycloth towels as I could hold. I began to line the crevice underneath my bedroom door with towels so that whatever was happening in my bedroom would stay there. I threw my body down on the couch and I stared at the ceiling. I couldn't breathe. I couldn't focus. I couldn't believe this was happening. *Again.*

* * *

A few hours later, my phone alarm buzzed. It was an anticlimactic start to Monday morning. *Did I even sleep at all?* I sat up on the couch as my head began to throb. I had never slept on my own couch overnight, and I was groggy from a combination of fear and insomnia. I avoided setting foot in my bedroom until it was essential for me to get dressed. I opened the door, hoping that by some miracle, everything would be gone. But, to my dismay, moth larvae still populated the room. They were just as I had left them. White larvae were scattered all over the floor like tiny pebbles. I thought about the fact that the ants had magically disappeared, and I became slightly hopeful. I closed my eyes and said aloud, "Go away, go away, go away." But when I opened my eyes, the horror movie was still playing. I shook my head, embarrassed that I had tried such a ridiculous intervention. *Come on, Lauren. You aren't a magician.*

I was about to be late for work, so I had no choice but to leave my home in a chaotic state. I threw clothes on and shut my bedroom door, resealing the room with towels. I brushed my teeth in a hurry and splashed water on my face. I began to cry. *NO.* I shut myself off from my emotions. I was back in survival mode even though I had barely left it. I needed to put one foot in front of the other so I could get myself to the office on time.

I walked to the train in silence. I didn't even bother listening to music. My mind raced as I approached the station. *How could this be happening again? Why did I suddenly have moths? Are the ants going to come back too?* I quickly decided that there was no point in asking any of these unanswerable questions. I didn't know much, but I knew that something was deeply, deeply wrong.

I stared out the window of the Blue Line, allowing my vision to blur as the train transported me to my office. Tears began to well up in my eyes. *No.* I stopped myself again, allowing my brain to become a combination of blur and mush. There was no way I was ready to comprehend this. Plus, I was afraid of what would happen to me if I paused, even for one second, to take it in. *Just put one foot in front of the other.*

At work, I continued to play the part of Regular Lauren. I sat with my legs crossed and listened intently to my clients talk about their lives. But after each one left, I walked around my office, pacing back and forth. My veins began pumping adrenaline. I searched the internet for answers; I scanned dozens of photos of moth larvae as if I was a biologist. Every time I heard a client enter my waiting room, I shut the computer and attempted to transition back to the role of Regular Lauren. The line between the two selves was beginning to shrink, just as I had feared. I didn't know how much longer I could keep up the charade.

* * *

That evening, I walked through the door to my apartment and threw my bag down on the floor. I prepared to enter my bedroom. I closed my eyes as I turned the doorknob, praying again that everything would be gone. I opened the door and glanced down at the ground. *SHIT.* Moth larvae still covered the floor. There didn't seem to be more of them, but there certainly weren't any less.

Now it was time to get serious. During one of my breaks at work, I had learned that the best way to eradicate moth larvae was to use a vacuum cleaner. Still in my work clothes, I ran over to the storage closet and grabbed my vacuum. I tore off my shoes and slipped on some cheap flip flops; the kind I wore in communal showers. I began to vacuum vigorously, as I averted my eyes from the horror of watching dozens of moth larvae fill up the bag. The vacuum didn't kill the larvae, so they were still inching their way around the inside of the bag. I stopped for a minute and bent down to look at the ones I had captured. The moth larvae slid around the inside of the bag, temporarily pausing to lift their brown heads off the ground in the same 360-degree circular motion I had seen the night before. I almost hurled again.

I looked at the time and realized it was almost midnight. I had been at this for hours. It felt like I hadn't even made a dent in this situation. Larvae continued to emerge from under my bed as if there were an infinite amount of them. I was exhausted. I hadn't eaten dinner; I had barely taken breaks to go to the bathroom. And now, I had to figure out how to go to bed.

I changed into my pajamas and shut the door of my bedroom. *There's no way I am sleeping in there.* I brushed my teeth and retired to my couch in the living room once again. I set my phone alarm and tried to get some sleep.

* * *

My alarm buzzed and I shot off the couch like a cannon. I sighed as I stood up and stretched my arms over my head. My whole body ached. I walked into the kitchen to retrieve a glass of water as I stared angrily at my bedroom door. I needed to walk back in there to get dressed, but it was the last thing I wanted to do. I tried to shut off my brain as I began to remove the towels from the space under the door. I turned the doorknob slowly. *SHIT.* There were fresh larvae everywhere. *How is that even possible?* I had spent hours eradicating them the night before and it looked as though I hadn't accomplished a thing.

I thought it was strange that I had only seen larvae without seeing a single adult moth. It reminded me of the way the ants came to life before my eyes. *What was happening? Was this another example of strange bug behavior?* Nonetheless, the adult moths had to be here somewhere, and I needed to know where they were hiding. I crept over to my bed, dodging larvae on the floor like I was playing hopscotch. I hit the side of my mattress and ducked as a handful of moths flew out from under my box spring. *Oh fuck.* There they were.

I glanced at the clock and realized that I was about to be late for work. I left the vacuum inside my bedroom, changed my clothes, and re-sealed the door to my bedroom with towels. I grabbed my messenger bag and headed out the door. I stuffed a piece of gum in my mouth as I ruffled my hair. I was a mess.

* * *

Somehow, I made it through the workweek, driven by a combination of adrenaline and denial. But the moths continued to accumulate at an unstoppable rate. Every night, I came home from my office, changed my clothes, and vacuumed dozens of larvae. Then I hit the mattress vigorously until adult moths flew out from the sides of the bed. I sprayed the airborne moths with Lysol until they fell dead on the floor. Finally, I vacuumed up the adults along with all their children. The whole process took hours.

Once I had successfully cleared out my room each night, I detached the vacuum bag and took it outside, where I poured the contents of the vacuum (containing dead adults and living larvae) into a garbage bag. I ran down three flights of stairs to the dumpster, where I disposed of this mess. This was my nighttime routine for an entire week. After all that work, moth larvae reappeared each morning as if I had done nothing the night before. I was caught in an endless cycle. Spray, vacuum, repeat.

I spent five sleepless nights on my couch. When my alarm sounded, I folded up my throw blanket and brushed my teeth. I drank a glass of water, glaring at my bedroom door as though we were in a fight. Surprisingly, the moth problem stayed confined to my bedroom, just as the ants had stayed confined to the living room windowsill. There was no time to question this strange behavior. I just had to get through it.

As I walked to work, I forced myself to transform into my alter-ego: Regular Lauren. I sat in my office as if nothing were going on at home. I began to wonder how I was able to keep up this façade. It seemed eerie, and a little problematic, that I had no issue pretending everything was fine. Even though it was becoming exhausting to live a double life, merging the two selves was not an option. I was desperately afraid of what would happen if I let myself begin to fall apart.

Later that day, at the office, I glanced down at my pants and noticed that a tiny hole had formed in the center of the right leg. *That's odd.* I continued to listen to my client tell a story about her in-laws when I felt a chill run down my spine. *Oh fuck. The moths.*

* * *

On the train ride home from my office that evening, I pulled out my phone and opened Google. Between the photos of the moth larvae and the hole in my pants, I determined that I had clothes moths. I had no prior experience with moths of any kind, except seeing them congregate around streetlights. As I read about clothes moths, my heart sank into my stomach. These moths destroyed clothing and bedding. *Shit, shit.* I hadn't had a chance to take a closer look at my closet, beyond stealing work clothes each morning. And clearly, I had overlooked the fact that they had already enjoyed a few meals. I had been so consumed with eradicating the plethora of moths from my bed that I hadn't even considered they might also be munching away at my clothes.

I reluctantly walked in the front door of my apartment. I crept over to the bedroom door and opened it. Larvae lined the floor of my bedroom as if I hadn't been trying to eradicate them all week. At this point, I was used to it. I jumped over patches of larvae as I made my way to the bedroom closet. I braced myself as I opened the white double doors and began combing through my clothes. Moths flew out of all my sweaters. *Fuck.* There were small holes in almost all my pants and shirts. I moved over to my dresser and lifted a pair of green legwarmers that Amy had knit for my birthday. I held them up to the window as light peered through dozens of holes like Swiss cheese. These had become my favorite legwarmers and now they were decimated. In that moment, I realized that the moths were about to destroy everything in my bedroom.

I grabbed garbage bags from the kitchen and threw all my damaged clothing into them. I tried not to think. I just did it. I removed the clothes I was wearing and threw them in the garbage bag as well. By the time I was done, I had one bra, one t-shirt and one pair of pants to my name. Everything else was gone.

A HAUNTING SENSE OF DÉJÀ VU

I shook my head in disbelief. I had nothing to wear to work the next day. There was no way I could wear a t-shirt that said *Feminist as Fuck* and a pair of leggings to the office. This had to be a cruel joke. All of a sudden, I remembered that I had recently ordered a summer dress. I checked the tracking information and realized that it had just been delivered. I ran down the stairs and grabbed a thin, white sealed bag from the landing area by the mailboxes. *Thank God.* I held the package up to my chest, clinging to it for dear life.

I tried the dress on and looked at myself in my bathroom mirror. It was a sleeveless, light grey, pencil dress that hit right above the knee. It was adorable. It was also skintight. When I spotted the dress online, I decided it would be perfect for a second date or dinner on a patio with a friend. Apparently, I would also be wearing it to the office. I rolled my eyes. I had no idea what my clients would think of this outfit. This was not the kind of dress they had ever seen me wear. I prayed that no one noticed or worse, said anything. I was afraid that a single comment would shatter me into a thousand pieces.

* * *

The next morning, I sat in my office chair with my legs tightly crossed as I attempted to pull the hem of my dress down lower than it would go. It was almost impossible to focus on what anyone was saying. This was not the kind of therapist I wanted to be. Part of me felt like I should have canceled my day. The other part of me knew I was here because *I needed to be here.* Or rather, I needed an escape from the hellhole that my apartment had become. I clung on to Regular Lauren for dear life. I needed her more than ever.

I made it halfway through my workday before I had my first break. I threw my dark green messenger bag over my shoulder and locked up my office. I walked down the street and made a beeline for Target. I was on a mission.

I quickly slid through the large revolving doors and ran upstairs to the women's clothing department, stopping briefly to catch my breath. I grabbed the first cardigan I saw and threw it on haphazardly over my dress. Next, I slung a pair of pants and a few tops over my arm, as I breezed through the department like I was on *Supermarket Sweep.* I breathed a sigh of relief. *It's going to be ok. I can totally come back from this.* But my hopefulness was quickly thwarted by reality. I had nowhere to store these clothes. I couldn't bring new clothing into an apartment swarming with clothes moths. I stopped dead in my tracks. I wasn't going to be able to life-hack my way out of this. Defeated and fighting back tears, I put everything back except the cardigan and walked toward the cash register.

* * *

By Friday afternoon, I was exhausted. The week had gone by in such a blur that I forgot to notify my landlord about the moths. I picked up the phone and called him, this time to tell my landlord that now my apartment was infested with clothes moths. He didn't even come over. He sent the same team of professional exterminators to my place. They arrived within the hour. The exterminators found moth larvae lurking underneath the floorboards. They told me that adult moths permeated every inch of my mattress and bedspring. They told me that it was only a matter of time before this infestation spread to my other furniture in the rest of the apartment. That's when they told me that this problem would be almost impossible to fix.

Nevertheless, the exterminators did what they could to alleviate the current situation until we could all figure out a more sustainable plan. Once again, I was banished to the sidewalk as they sprayed my entire apartment with toxic fumes. I stared up at The Treehouse with a haunting sense of déjà vu. I couldn't believe I was back here again. This time, with an entirely different infestation that was exponentially worse than the previous one.

The exterminators shouted down to me when the fumigation process was complete. I walked through the front door of my apartment and gasped. A thin, white powder covered every inch of my beautiful mahogany floor. Bug traps hung from the ceilings, all around the apartment. They looked like creepy party decorations. My home had become completely unrecognizable. Again. I cried to the exterminators as I begged them for an explanation. How could this have happened in *one day?* And why did the larvae continue to reappear each morning after I had gotten rid of them the night before? There had to be an explanation.

The two grown men avoided making eye contact with me. But they told me the truth. They told me that they had seen a lot in the thirty years they both had been doing this, but my situation was new. The exterminators confirmed that the moths were behaving *in an uncharacteristic manner,* just as the ants had. And then, they told me that they had never seen two extreme infestations, seemingly unrelated, appear out of thin air within three weeks of each other.

I walked the exterminators out of my apartment and closed the door. I glanced at the living room window and noticed that the sun was starting to set. I began to cry. My tears became louder and more pronounced. I paced back and forth, speaking to myself aloud: "What am I going to do now?" I began wheezing. Then hyperventilating. *NO, NO, NO.* I halted myself from going any further down the rabbit hole. This was too awful, too terrifying to comprehend. I forced my brain to deploy its emergency brake. *Hot stove! Hot stove!*

I stuffed my emotions down so that I could keep moving. Plus, the exterminators cautioned me that I needed to dispose of my bed immediately so that the infestation didn't spread to the rest of my furniture. Time was of the essence. I dried my eyes and launched myself into action.

I picked up the phone and called Mila. She lived in a nearby apartment that she shared with her family. I told her what was going on, and she offered to come over to my place with her older brother to help me dispose of my mattress and box spring. Mila and her brother arrived within fifteen minutes of my phone call and busted into my apartment like two superheroes. We gathered all our strength as we catapulted my full-sized mattress into the air and rolled it through the kitchen and out the back door of my apartment until it was resting safely on my balcony. Mila's brother was fiercely strong. He was far stronger than he looked. He reassured us that he could handle taking my mattress all the way down three flights of stairs by himself. I looked at Mila in disbelief, but she told me to let him do it.

We watched from the balcony as Mila's brother cracked jokes and rolled my mattress down three flights of stairs, leaving it propped up against the industrial-sized dumpsters that lined the alley. I gasped as moths flew out of my contaminated bedding and into the air. From a distance, they looked like sparks of light shooting off a flame. Once Mila's brother had removed my mattress, he came back and got the box spring. Mila was right, her brother made this look so easy and not nearly as disgusting as it was. His lighthearted attitude tempered my grief. And just like that, my bed was gone.

After Mila left, I called Heather. I told her that the exterminators had provided me with a grim diagnosis. They told me it could take months to eradicate this infestation and it would be challenging to do that while a tenant was living in the apartment. Heather immediately urged me to break my lease. She persuaded me to get out before this infestation escalated any further. I began to cry. All the emotion I had stuffed down came pouring out. I slid down the back wall of my second bedroom until I was on the floor. My tears hit the ground, splattering the white bug powder with each drop. *How could this be happening to me?*

Heather stayed on the phone, patiently, as I let myself break. At first, I fought her. I told Heather that she didn't understand the situation. And anyway, it's not like these infestations were lethal. Plenty of people go through things like this, and they don't just move out of their homes. She sat on the phone and sighed patiently. I continued to make my case. *Maybe I could sleep on the couch until I buy a new bed? Maybe I could switch bedrooms?* Heather didn't say a word. She let me cry. She let me fight against the reality that I had just lost my home. She sat there on the phone until I had exhausted myself. I wanted to keep fighting to remain in The Treehouse, but soon, I no longer had the energy. It was time to call a spade a spade. I had effectively been driven out of my apartment by back-to-back infestations. Finally, I agreed to leave.

There was just one problem. I had nowhere to go. Tears began to stream down my face all over again. I had just left my family. This was the exact scenario I had feared during the month of June. *What happens in an emergency? I can't ask my friends. That's too much.* My hands started to shake. I had no emergency contact. No plan. It was hard enough to step into the reality that I was an orphan. Now, I was an orphan with no home. I cried as Heather continued to sit silently on the other line.

I immediately launched myself into problem-solving mode. I talked about the fact that I could check myself into a hotel for a night and then immediately begin looking for a new place to live. Heather didn't like that idea. She argued that I needed time to come back from this. That's when Heather offered me a place to stay. She told me to move in with her and Willa while I figured out my next steps. I was overcome with emotion. I couldn't believe she had just offered to take me in like a stray cat. She told me it was no problem. That I could live with her indefinitely. I paused for a moment as I thought to myself, *my own family wouldn't have done that.*

I had no energy to tell Heather that her offer was far too kind or that I didn't want to be an inconvenience. So I just accepted it instead. Since I only had a few items of clothing to my name, I packed a bag in a matter of minutes. I looked around my apartment one last time, hardly able to register the magnitude of this turn of events. My bed was gone. Most of my clothes were gone. And now, I had lost my home.

LIVIN' MY BEST LIFE

End of August 2018

Thirty minutes later, I walked through the door of Heather's house in Evanston with an overnight bag slung over my shoulder. Willa ran into the foyer to greet me as she threw her little arms around my legs. "Auntie Lauren, are you here for a sleepover?" I looked at Heather. We hadn't exactly had a chance to tell Willa what was going on.

Heather looked down at Willa as she said, "Auntie Lauren is going to be staying with us for a while. She had to move out of her apartment so now she's here." Willa's big blue eyes grew wide as she let out a loud squeal. Apparently, my large-scale crisis was the best news ever. At least there was one person who thought so. I laughed.

* * *

The next day, I decided to go shopping. It was Saturday morning, and Heather had taken Willa to spend time with her father across town. I knew I had to buy some clothes, but the process of shopping for everything felt so surreal. A few of my friends tried to convince me to take advantage of the opportunity to re-invent myself and my wardrobe. But this wasn't fun. I wasn't being featured on *Queer Eye*. Instead, I felt like someone who had lost their home in a fire and needed to replace everything out of sheer necessity.

I decided to go back to Target. After all, I had chosen to shop there on a good day. Plus, I also needed toiletries to stay at Heather's place indefinitely. I walked into the nearest Target, promptly avoiding the clothing section. I grabbed a toothbrush and toothpaste as I began to circle the women's department like a shark. I became very overwhelmed as I stared at racks of dresses, pants, and tops. I had no idea where to start. I needed everything. This had never happened to me before. I was the kind of person who still wore clothes from college. I began grabbing shorts and tank tops and throwing them all into a shopping basket. I wasn't even asking myself if I liked any of it. It was methodical. Robotic. No fun at all.

All of a sudden, I began to panic. I backed up from a rack of dresses and texted Heather. She told me to slow down. She reminded me that I didn't need to replace my entire wardrobe right away and that instead, I should just try to pick out one or two items. Once again, Heather had managed to make sense of the mush my life had become. I remembered the way she created a preschool calendar after my estrangement when I was lying on the floor swaddling myself. Her ability to translate swirling emotions into direct action was a gift.

I returned the contents of my entire basket to their hangers. It turned out that I didn't like any of it. I stepped back, and I took a deep breath. And then, I looked around, waiting to be inspired.

Apparently, I was standing in the junior's section, which was a whole other situation. I saw a mannequin wearing a dark grey racerback tank top that was made of very lightweight material, so lightweight in fact that I could see the mannequin's white boobs (without areolas) peeking through the shirt. The shirt said, *Livin' my best life* in bold black letters. I couldn't contain myself. I stared at this shirt as I immediately screamed, "FUCK YOU, T-SHIRT!" A teenager nearby turned around, and I pretended to be on my phone. *Shit.* This had to be an all-time low.

As I stared at this shirt, my rage began to morph into something else. Something unexpected. Before I knew it, I was laughing hysterically. My eyes grew crazed and wide. I was laughing so hard there were tears in my eyes. Without a second thought, I knew I had to have this shirt. It was so absurd that it was perfect. I peeled the tank top off the mannequin, leaving her topless in the middle of the store. I didn't even bother to try it on. Instead, I promptly walked over to the cash register and bought it.

I returned to Heather's house as she came running into the living room. I pulled the tank top out of my shopping bag as I exclaimed, "This was the only thing I bought today." We both laughed. I changed into my new shirt, and we sat in the backyard. This was the first shirt I had chosen to represent my new life. Everything was falling apart. At least my sense of humor remained intact.

EVERYTHING MUST GO

Labor Day Weekend 2018

I had been staying with Heather for a week when I officially broke my lease. My landlord had been incredibly understanding when I told him that it was impossible for me to continue living there. He knew it was true. He allowed me to end my lease free of charge, under one condition: I had to be completely moved out by Labor Day.

I sent out an email to all the friends who had rescued me for the entire month of June. I asked anyone who was around to come to my apartment over Labor Day weekend and help me haul everything out of there for good.

The week I had spent at Heather's house had already given me a lot of perspective. I desperately wanted a fresh start. Plus, the exterminators told me there was no way to guarantee that the moth infestation wouldn't follow me to a new apartment – and I was not about to risk that. I decided to sell or donate just about everything that was left.

Luckily, I had a savings account that would allow me to replace the contents of everything the moths had destroyed. My maternal grandmother had taught herself how to play the stock market after her husband died, and she had done quite well. So well, in fact, that she started stock accounts for all her grandchildren. I'm sure she never imagined that I would be using her money like *this*, but I suppose you can't plan everything.

* * *

I woke up on the Sunday of Labor Day weekend and drove back to my treehouse apartment. I hadn't been back there since it all happened. Adorned in my *Livin' my best life* tank top, I braced myself to return to the mayhem I had left behind. I placed the key in the front door and took a breath. I opened the door slowly. Everything was just as I had left it. White powder coated the dark wood floors. Bug traps hung from the ceiling in every room. To my surprise, there wasn't a single moth in any of the traps. I walked into the bedroom as I held my breath. My eyes darted around the room. Nothing. No larvae. No moths. *What the fuck?* They had vanished, just like the ants.

I barely had a chance to process this strange occurrence before my friends began to arrive. Everyone smiled awkwardly as they ducked under bug traps. I felt so ashamed. It was so hard for me to ask for help, hence the reason I spent a full week vacuuming moths without anyone knowing about it. But this situation had gotten so bad that there was absolutely no way for me to get through it on my own. I suppose it was a blessing in disguise.

Amy volunteered to take photos and place ads for my furniture on Facebook Marketplace. Silvia began packing up my kitchen. Everyone launched into action, getting rid of the more generic items in my apartment. I walked over to my bookcase and dealt with the sentimental items. I picked up a photo of my family where we all looked happy and threw it in the trash. I couldn't bear to look at this photo anymore. I felt like I had gone through a massive divorce.

I managed to sell two chairs that had been in my second bedroom and were undoubtedly moth-free. I donated the rest of my furniture and all my kitchen supplies. My friends kept asking if I was sure that I wanted to get rid of *all of it*. I reassured them that everything must go. I still had no idea why this was happening, but I took it as a sign that I needed to start over completely. The only thing I was sure I wanted to take with me into my new life was my new tank top. And until I was sure about everything else, I would take my time finding a new home and replacing its contents, piece by piece.

When we were done, I walked my friends to the front door and said goodbye. I hugged each one, thanking them for everything. Silvia left with boxes of kitchenware to donate to Goodwill. I helped Amy haul my television down to her car because she needed a new one, and there was no way I wanted to keep anything from this phase of my life. As they each drove away, tears of gratitude welled up in my eyes. I couldn't believe they had done all this for me.

I turned around and stared up at my apartment. Visions of toxic gas from both infestations came flashing back to me. I shuddered at the memory of an exterminator spraying my ant-infested windowsill as black dots fell from the sky. I still didn't understand why any of this was happening. My head began to throb. I walked up the stairs and back into my apartment. It was nearly empty. The only items left were my living room furniture and my desk. I stood in my living room and waited for a truck from The Brown Elephant to arrive. I had decided to donate all my remaining (moth-free) items to a thrift store that was run by one of my favorite local LGBT social service centers.

A team of two movers arrived and began loading all my living room furniture into their truck. Once they were finished, I signed a form and offered them a glass of water, which I immediately rescinded once I realized that I had no glasses anymore. The men smiled and thanked me for my generous donation. I walked them out.

My eyes glazed over as I looked around the living room. Everything was gone. I took my keys out of my purse and began to remove the apartment keys from my keychain. I placed the keys on the kitchen island and walked out the back door.

There were no more tears left to cry. I was exhausted, defeated, and traumatized beyond belief. I no longer recognized my life. There was nothing left to do but move on. Maybe it was the universe, fate, or something else. All I knew was that it was time to leave all of this behind.

HEAVEN ON SHERIDAN

After I left my apartment for the final time, I got into my car and drove back to Heather's house in silence. Twenty minutes later, I walked through the front door and told Heather it was over. She hugged me and asked how I felt. My body went limp in her arms. She continued to hold me as neither of us said a word. A single tear began to form in the corner of my eye. It was all I could muster.

Within seconds, Willa came skipping into the living room. She sandwiched herself in between Heather and me. Willa looked at us and smiled as her big blue eyes lit up everything. She stared at me and said, "Auntie Lauren, will you come play with me?" Heather and I dropped our embrace, and I grabbed Willa's hand, allowing myself to be led into the magical world she was about create.

I walked into the basement as Willa ran over to her play area. She was going through a phase where she loved dressing up in princess costumes. I found this completely hilarious because Heather was such a devout feminist. Despite Heather's best attempts to derail Willa from her fascination with fairytales, the kid was irrevocably hooked on them.

I watched Willa adorn herself in a sparkly tiara to match her light blue Cinderella-inspired gown. She floated around the room mimicking the Disney princess with incredible precision. It was eerie and adorable at the same time. As Willa delicately lifted her little arms into the air, I was suddenly overcome with a desire to be whisked off into the sunset along with her.

Heather lived in a quaint house just north of Chicago. After she divorced Willa's father, Heather wanted a fresh start. She bought this house completely on her own, which was thoroughly impressive for a single parent on a social worker's salary. It was a two-story, three-bedroom house in a peaceful suburb. The house had two bedrooms on the main floor and a third bedroom in the finished basement. That was where I was staying. It felt like my own little apartment. Willa's princess clothes were scattered across the basement, adding just the right amount of irony to my situation.

When Heather moved into this house, she threw herself into a series of home improvement projects fit for a television series. I couldn't understand how it was possible to get *that* excited about a trip to Home Depot, but I envied it at the same time. I had never owned a home. I had moved so many times in my adult life that I could barely count all the apartments I had lived in. And now, I was staying in a house that someone had lovingly transformed into a home.

I did my best to soak that in.

Mid-September 2018

Before my life descended into a horror film, I had decided to take two full weeks of vacation time from my private practice. I had never been away from my clients this long. Now, I was in the middle of my *vacation.* And while this certainly wasn't the respite I had intended; I was supremely grateful that I didn't have to become Regular Lauren right now. My last day of work had been the day the exterminators told me that my home was uninhabitable. It was the day I moved in with Heather.

The week after Labor Day, I sat across from Heather at her pale wooden kitchen table. She had just come home from work. I had spent the day crying. I had no idea what to do with myself. All this idle time was beginning to work against me. I stared down at the floor, which was filled with laminated teal and white stencils that Heather had painted herself. Heather looked at me and smiled.

I told Heather that I needed to figure out how to move forward. I told her it was time for me to find my own place to live. Heather asked me if I was ready to take that step so soon. She reassured me that I could live with her and Willa indefinitely. I knew they loved having me around and the feeling was mutual. The three of us had grown so accustomed to each other. We went to Trader Joe's together and spent our evenings reading to Willa in her bedroom. I felt like I belonged in this house. After everything I had been through, that feeling was incredibly healing.

Emotionally, there was no way I was ready to move into a new apartment. Even though I had no proof, I was terrified that the plagues were following me. I still didn't understand how any of this had taken place. There were far more questions than answers. But at some point, I would need to face it all. And besides, I wanted my own space. As much as I loved living with Heather, it was also a constant reminder that I had lost my home. So I decided to push through my fear.

Heather asked me where I might want to live, and what kind of home I would want. I began to talk about how much I loved the lakefront. I had lived in Chicago for ten years, and I had never been able to see the lake from my home. Now that I had a real chance to start over, I wanted to be as close to the water as possible. I decided to make that my goal. I opened Zillow and began searching for apartments along Sheridan Road in the Edgewater neighborhood of the city. As a bonus, I would be much closer to Heather's house than I had ever been before.

I immediately found a listing for a stunning one-bedroom unit located in a large, black high-rise building. It was massive. The building had fifty-five floors and a doorman. I had never lived anywhere like it before. I began to get excited. I thrust my phone in Heather's face as I watched her eyes grow wide with amazement. I contacted the landlord and heard back within the hour. *How is this place still available?* I was shocked. I arranged a showing for the following afternoon.

* * *

The next day, I arrived at the high-rise building while wearing my grey pencil dress, my Target cardigan, and a pair of brand-new Birkenstocks. The revolving doors revealed a stunning lobby with marble floors and window walls. I smiled at the doorman and walked over to introduce myself. *A doorman?* I had never lived anywhere like this before. Given everything I had just endured, the thought of living in a huge building and having complete anonymity seemed incredibly appealing. I took a deep breath as I sat down on a tan leather bench, right across from a row of peace lilies. They even had one of my favorite plants here. It had to be a sign.

The landlord entered the building and waved to me. I shook her hand, and we stepped into the elevator. While we rode up to the unit, she told me that she owned this apartment with her husband, and they had lived there for a few years before moving to the suburbs to accommodate their growing family. I would be renting their condo. I had a good feeling about this landlord and about her unit.

As soon as I walked into the apartment, I knew it was my home. I opened the front door and breezed past everything until I was right at the edge of the living room window. The unit had floor-to-ceiling windows that faced the lake from the thirty-ninth floor. I had never seen a view like this one in my entire life. I stood at the window, and I was immediately at ease. The apartment boasted an unobstructed view of the entire Chicago lakefront. I looked down and saw the outlines of small figures riding their bikes along the lake path. And when I stared straight ahead, I watched the delicate, rolling waves of Lake Michigan stretch all the way to the end of the Earth. *How am I even here?* I was completely mesmerized, awe-struck, and eternally grateful. I turned around to look at the landlord, with my mouth agape. She laughed as she said, "Right? This view is the best part of living here. You will love it."

The landlord offered me the apartment on the spot. It had been vacant for a few weeks, and they were looking for the right tenant to move in immediately. I was thrilled; everything felt so right. And since I had very few belongings, I could be ready quickly. As we continued to walk around the unit, it felt increasingly more like my new home. It was also in great condition because the owner and her husband had completely remodeled it while they were living there. They had replaced the original flooring with beautiful, light wooden planks. They had gut rehabbed the kitchen and painted it deep red. And the bathroom was lined with blue and green tiles, which matched the unbelievable lake views. I loved everything about it.

I told the landlord that I was very interested, and this place felt like home. She jumped up to get the paperwork and my heart sank. In an instant, my hands became clammy. The breath left my body. I froze. A string of panicky thoughts raced through my mind. *What about the plagues? What if it's not over? I can't go through this anymore.*

The landlord walked over to me holding the lease as

I exclaimed, "Wait! I'm not ready." She seemed slightly disappointed. I glanced down at the light, wooden floor. I felt that I owed her an explanation for my knee-jerk reaction. However, it was hard to explain my situation without launching into the full-scale horror show my life had become. I decided to try disclosing at a four out of ten. I told the landlord that I was staying with a friend due to *unforeseen circumstances.* She looked confused. *Ugh, I guess I'll raise that to an eight.* I blurted out that I had just experienced back-to-back large-scale infestations that had robbed me of most of my belongings. She gasped. *Oh no. I guess that was a fifteen.*

I tried to backpaddle my way out of the overshare, doing more damage with every sentence that poured out of my mouth. I told the landlord that I had gotten rid of every moth-infested item so there was no need to worry that I would bring my bad luck into a new apartment. The landlord seemed to be only momentarily relieved. She told me to take the evening to think it over.

* * *

That evening, I walked into Heather's home, eager to tell her about my experience at the new apartment. I began referring to this home as Heaven on Sheridan. During the showing, I had taken an absurd number of photos, hoping to prove to myself that this place existed and was somehow in my price range.

Heather and I sat across from each other in matching living room chairs as I handed over my phone. She scrolled through the photos of the apartment as she said, "Lauren, are you serious? You have got to take it." I laughed as I reassured her that I knew it was perfect.

But I was extremely reluctant to pull the trigger. I told Heather that I was deeply afraid I hadn't seen the end of the plagues. So afraid that I almost regretted saying it aloud as if I could end up jinxing my fate. Heather talked about the fact that I had just been through something totally unexplainable, but that I had to *trust* that it was over. I desperately wanted to trust that it was over. But so much had taken place that seemed to blow the lid of all logic. My former landlord had never seen anything like it before. The professional team of exterminators had been stupefied. None of that was reassuring.

But I wanted to believe, I needed to believe that I could have my happy ending. Even if it was elusive or far-fetched. Even if it felt like a Cinderella story. But if there was ever going to be a way for me to ride off into the sunset, Heaven on Sheridan was it. I woke up early the next morning, and I called the owner of the lakefront unit.

I told her I was ready to sign my lease.

I DON'T WANT TO HEAR THAT

I drove over to Heaven on Sheridan and met my new landlord in the lobby. We smiled at each other as we rode the elevator up to the unit, where the paperwork would be waiting for us. I expressed my deep gratitude for having the chance to live in such a beautiful place. I thanked her for giving me a chance to start over after everything I had experienced in my previous home. My new landlord said she had a good feeling about me right from the start, and she knew this place would help me heal. I felt a sense of peace for the first time in months. That's when I realized that it had been far too long since my heart was filled with hope.

Unfortunately, my reprieve was cut short. As we walked through the front door, we gasped in unison. We were staring at a huge, gaping hole that consumed one of the large pillars in the living room. It looked like someone had taken an axe to the wall and demolished it for no apparent reason. The hole was the length of my entire body. The entire pillar was exposed, revealing a ring of light pink insulation that engulfed a large silver pipe. Pieces of the wall were scattered all over the floor. I slid my foot over the debris, forming an infinity symbol out of the dust. It felt like this nightmare might go on forever.

My landlord turned away from me and began making calls. I heard her on the phone with the maintenance department in the building. Apparently, a series of five units had flooded last night, right after I had seen the apartment. Maintenance had broken into all the affected units until they realized that the source of the flood was coming from this unit. So they smashed through the wall and closed the leak. They told my landlord that this situation would take weeks to repair, but that they had ultimately solved the problem. Maintenance said it was still possible for me to sign my lease and move in while this was going on.

My landlord got off the phone and looked at me apologetically. She began to ramble on about how *nothing like this has ever happened here.* My stomach hit the floor. *Oh no. I don't want to hear that.* I knew this wasn't over. My worst fears had been realized. The plagues *were* following me. I had just survived two infestations, and now there was a flood.

I paced around the apartment as my chest began to constrict. My breathing became shallower as adrenaline pulsed through my veins. I had no idea what to do. Heaven on Sheridan wasn't supposed to be a demolition site. This isn't how anyone rides off into the sunset. I told my landlord that I needed a moment, and I stepped into the hallway to call Heather. I told her about the flood. She reassured me that maintenance had solved this problem and that I should sign my lease before I hastily walked away from this incredible apartment forever.

A few moments later, I reluctantly signed the lease. My new landlord handed me the paperwork as I took out a pen. My hand shook as I scribbled my name across the dotted line, desperate to shut off my brain. Even though I was terrified, I knew I belonged in that apartment. And it turned out that my new building had an incredible in-house, 24-hour maintenance department. They conducted routine bed bug checks every six months. They had won awards for their pest control policies. Perhaps most people would overlook something like that, but of course I did not. If the plagues really were following me, I would need the best maintenance team I could find.

STOP RIGHT THERE

Mid-September 2018

During the second week of September, I moved into Heaven on Sheridan. I left Heather's house with a few duffle bags and some boxes filled with brand-new dishes that we had picked out together right after I signed my lease. The day of the flood, Heather forced me to meet her at the mall so we could decorate my new home. I walked around Crate & Barrel in a daze as Heather enthusiastically pointed to dishware. Willa ran through the halls of the store, lunging herself into expensive chairs. I attempted to play the part of someone who was excited even though acting had never been my forte. I went through the motions of purchasing a brand-new bed and all new bedding. I was willing to do everything in my power to move on.

Unfortunately, the first night in my new apartment was eventful in all the wrong ways. I lay awake in my new bed as I listened to the floorboards in the living room creak in the middle of the night. *What the fuck?* I threw off the covers and reluctantly made my way into the living room. As soon as I arrived there, the noises stopped. I turned on the light and glanced around the room. *Nothing.* Numbly, I headed back into the bedroom.

As soon as my head hit the pillow, the noises began again. *Creak, creak, creak.* It sounded like rolling thunder was moving through the floorboards. I had no idea what to make of it. Perhaps the floors in this building always creaked in the middle of the night. Even though the flooring was relatively new, the building itself was about sixty years old. I thought about texting my new landlord to ask her if this was commonplace. In the light of day, I decided against it.

Night after night, the floorboards continued to creak. I still had no idea what to make of it. I began to wonder if this place was haunted. Truthfully, I didn't know what I believed about the afterlife. But this was beginning to be too much for my brain to comprehend. Perhaps something out of this world was going on. *No, that's impossible.* I quickly pushed that thought out of my mind.

After I had been in my new apartment for a week, the maintenance department finished replacing the wall in my living room. I kept the workers company on their final day of repairs, begging them for an explanation of the leak. They couldn't provide me with one. The maintenance team told me that sometimes pipes just burst, but the pipes in my unit appeared to be in stellar condition. They didn't know why this flood had taken place either. *Oh, great. More uncharacteristic behavior.*

* * *

At the beginning of October, I received a written notice under my door from the building's pest control department. The bed bug patrol was set to inspect my unit on the morning of October ninth. This visit was part of their routine protocol. I was grateful that my new home paid such close attention to pest control. I was also petrified that they might find something. I couldn't even fathom going through another plague. I had gone to such incredible lengths to start over. I was officially begging the universe for a reprieve.

Tuesday, October ninth arrived, and I was home sick. I had a sinus infection that seemed impossible to cure. I knew the inordinate amount of stress I had been under was preventing my body from getting better. After a second visit to the doctor, I was ordered to stay home from work. I canceled my day of clients, and I sat in a blue armchair in my new apartment. Thus far, my apartment consisted of a new bed, a new desk, and a new blue chair. I waited for the exterminators to arrive. I felt a pang in my gut as I prayed for a clear result. The last thing I needed was another infestation. And I especially did not want bed bugs. I was secretly terrified of them.

As I drank my ginger tea, I heard a knock at the door. I sprung up to open it, forgetting momentarily that I was sick.

In walked two exterminators and a dog trained to sniff out the presence of bed bugs. They saw my empty apartment and said, "Piece of cake." I breathed a sigh of relief. I stood back as I watched the dog investigate the living room. I marveled at the fact that someone had taught this dog how to search for bed bugs. The dog sniffed the floorboards, my desk, and my chair. I quietly followed the team of exterminators into my bedroom. All I could think was, *one room down, one more to go.*

Next, the dog sniffed the perimeter of my bed. My eyes were fixed on the lefthand corner of my bedframe, though I didn't know why. I heard a voice from deep within me say, *Right there.* I shook my head, hoping to shake any negative thoughts loose. There was no way. This was a brand-new bed. I had only been in this apartment for a week. There was just no way.

The dog approached the lefthand corner of my bedframe and stopped. He clawed at the post. And then, I heard one of the exterminators say, "That's an alert." The demeanors of both exterminators abruptly changed. They began to radio for backup. They were shouting, "We got an alert in unit 3905, I repeat, that's a positive alert for bed bugs."

I burst into tears and fell to the floor. I buried my head in my knees as I began to wail at the top of my lungs. My voice shook as I confessed to the exterminators that I was at my brink. This couldn't be happening to me. Not now. *Not again.* I began to shiver uncontrollably, so much so that one of the exterminators took off her industrial gloves and placed her hand on the small of my back. She tried to reassure me that this wasn't a big deal. She told me I had so few belongings that it would be easy to get rid of the problem.

Her words did nothing to comfort me. I was back in hell. Actually, I had barely left. I was literally sick and figuratively broken in half by the plagues I had endured relentlessly for the last several months. I had survived swarms of angry ants and hundreds of moths. I had been forced to evacuate my home and relinquish control of my belongings. As soon as I signed my new lease, there was a flood. And now, *I had bed bugs.*

I excused myself and stepped into the hallway, slightly embarrassed by my public display of hysteria. I was unraveling all over again. I paced up and down the carpeted halls, trying to problem-solve with a brain that had been pushed well beyond its brink. My head began to throb. I stood in the hallway and stared at the wall in front of me until my eyes glazed over. I was officially trapped in the worst nightmare imaginable. There was no end in sight.

I stepped back into the apartment as the exterminators sprayed my entire bed, my blue chair, and the entire perimeter of the unit. They told me to begin washing all my clothing in hot water and to store everything I owned in airtight bags. They told me that I would need to continue this process for the next few months. The exterminators would come back weekly to spray my unit, and I was ordered to live out of plastic bags until I received an all-clear notice. It was official: the nightmare was continuing. I had moved into an entirely new apartment with all new belongings and the plagues had followed me. This couldn't be real. This couldn't be happening. *But it was.*

Robbed of my only recuperation day, I launched into action. I shut off my brain, just as I had done in order to vacuum dozens upon dozens of moth larvae less than two months earlier. I bagged the closet of clothes I had just bought and all my new bedding, and I shuffled myself down to the basement of the building to do multiple loads of laundry. I sat down in a folding chair and began to cry. *No.* I couldn't stop the tears this time, so I let them pour out of me. I was alone in the massive laundry room. The white walls had an institutional feel that was much different from the rest of the building. I cried until my nose filled with snot, and I could barely breathe. *How could this be happening? How.*

After I had done my laundry and placed all my clean clothes in fresh garbage bags, I unenthusiastically returned to my apartment. I threw the bags down in a huff. I couldn't even look at them. I had yearned for the moment when I could bring new clothes and a brand-new bed into my brand-new home. And now, it felt like everything was contaminated all over again.

Everyone has a limit, and I was quickly approaching mine. I walked over to my desk and sat in my new chair. My mind began to fill with darkness. I cried as the density of these dark thoughts permeated every inch of my brain. *No, no, no, Lauren.* But this time, I couldn't fight it. Everything was catching up to me. I began to break.

I don't know how much more of this I can handle. I just left my family. I lost everything I owned including my home. And now, I try to come over here, hoping for a fresh start, and the nightmare continues. I can't live like this anymore. I don't think I can do it.

Suddenly, I heard a voice deep within me begin to speak.

Yes, you can't live like this anymore. It's all too much. Maybe you should just end it. End it here. Maybe you aren't supposed to live beyond this point. Just go into the bathroom and take a razor. Draw a nice, warm bath and get in. That's all you need to do. Just get into the bath and slit your wrists. It will all be over soon.

I felt a wave of calm wash over me. Yes. I didn't have to live like this. I could just end it. I could put a stop to the hellhole that my life had become. It could all be over. It felt like such a simple solution. Why hadn't I thought of that? I began to cry.

The truth is, I don't think anyone will really care if I'm gone. I clearly don't have a family. Maybe I never did. They didn't care about what happened to me when I was right there. No one would care if they heard I was dead. And my friends will all be sad, but they will get over it. No one really loves me that much. Plus, they are all sick of how insane my life is. I know they are.

The voice from deep within began to take over.

Yes, that's right. No one cares about you. They won't miss you

when you're gone. You are nothing, you are invisible, you are not important. You should just end it right now. You can stop living in pain. There is a way out of this. Just a quick bath.

I sat up straight.

Wait a minute. Invisible and not important? I don't think I would go that far. It's easy for me to pretend that no one cares about me, but deep down, I know that's not the case. There are a lot of people who would miss me if I were gone. My clients might suffer the most. I don't know if I can leave them behind. Is it bad that the best part of my life is my work? That all I have to live for is my work? Whatever, that's the truth.

I loosened my shoulders and took a breath. I forced myself to think about how much I loved being a therapist. I knew I had found my calling. Social work was my lifeforce. And I truly loved my clients. I thought about them when they weren't around. What kind of message would I be sending to them if I killed myself? I couldn't let my clients down. No, I had to live. I had to live.

The voice from deep within returned.

No. End it here. You came far in this lifetime, but not all of us are supposed to keep going. This is your moment to give up. Give up now.

I tried to stand up. My head was throbbing, and my stomach was in knots. I clutched my gut in agony as I felt a sharp pain bowl me over. *What is happening to my stomach right now?* I sat back down in my desk chair and dropped my head between my legs. I felt the blood rush to my head.

No. I can't give up. This can't be how it ends. It just can't be. I honestly don't know how I am going get through all this, but I don't think killing myself is the answer.

I slowly uncurled my body and sat upright in the chair. I

was deeply at war with myself. But this moment felt strange and unfamiliar. I had never, *ever* experienced this level of suicidal ideation. I had been through so many horrific things over the course of my life, but I had never actively considered killing myself. I was about to move on when the voice deep within me grew louder and more pronounced.

Just go into the bathroom and do it. Don't think about this any longer. Do it. You can end all this pain right here. Right now. Do it.

Those words echoed through my bones. I felt like I was in a trance. I stood up …

STOP RIGHT THERE.

Then, I heard the voice of my heart.

There is NO WAY that I have come this far to end it now. I have so much more to offer the world. I know I do. And that's bullshit about no one caring about me. I know that my friends care. Hell, Heather would be devastated if I died. I know she would. And I don't even want to think about how Willa would feel. I can't do that to her.

Yes, this is a lot. Yes, I am in a constant state of hell that seems to be continuing for some reason. But I can't stop here. I can't stop now. If I killed myself right after leaving my family, I know that everyone would say that I was always sick so none of this was their fault. They would have an excuse. And I REFUSE to give them that excuse. NO WAY. It's time for me to live the life I just fought for. This is NOT how it ends.

I took a deep breath as walked over to my bathroom door. Then I shut it.

A HOME FILLED WITH RAINBOWS

I was in a state of shock as I stood facing the bathroom door. My eyes glazed over, frozen in time. I turned to walk away, but my body refused to move. It felt like my feet were encased in cement. Instead, I allowed my back to slide down the base of the door, until I was seated on the wooden floor facing the kitchen. I pulled my knees into my chest. *I was clearly testing myself.* I needed to make sure I wasn't going to change my mind and draw that bath. The longer I sat there, the more I became terrified of my own thoughts. *How had I come so close to slitting my wrists?* Nothing else in my life had ever driven me to that point.

I stared at the pile of white trash bags littering my living room floor. They were a stark reminder that the plagues were not over. There was just one problem: I was over them. I had reached the end of my capacity to handle all these crises. Something had to change. If it didn't, I knew I might not survive. I stared down at the floor as I took in the severity of that moment.

Soon my body began to ache from sitting too long in an upright fetal position. I hoisted myself off the ground as I clutched the bathroom doorknob behind me for support. I swayed for a moment, acutely aware that I had barely eaten that day. I made my way into the kitchen and grabbed a granola bar from one of the cabinets. I force-fed it to myself as I stared directly into the living room. I could see the lakefront view from every angle of this place. That view became the only redeeming quality of Heaven on Sheridan. A grief-filled rage engulfed my lungs. I threw the half-eaten granola bar on the counter as I ran over to the living room window. Shaking, I stood at the edge of the windowsill and screamed into the abyss:

"IF I AM SUPPOSED TO LIVE, I NEED A SIGN!"

I was about to storm away when a large, bold, double rainbow formed right in front of my eyes. The rainbow instantly appeared without a single drop of rain. It spanned the entire width of my lakefront view. It was the most beautiful thing I had ever seen. I burst into tears. I placed my hands into a prayer position at the base of my heart.

Thank you. Thank you. Thank you.

I didn't know who I was thanking, but it seemed like the only appropriate response. As I stared at this miraculous rainbow, my phone rang. I walked back to the kitchen island to retrieve it when I noticed the time. It was 4:44 p.m. I answered the phone, my voice shaking. It was Heather. She was driving right past Heaven on Sheridan on her way home from work. I asked her to pull over and come get me. Between the bed bugs and my brush with death, I couldn't bear the thought of spending the night alone in this place. Heather pulled off Lake Shore Drive and told me to be ready in five minutes.

I hung up the phone as I raced around my apartment. I ripped open a few garbage bags as I pieced together a pair of pajamas and something to wear in the morning. I grabbed my toiletry bag, still freshly assembled from my time spent living with Heather and Willa. I let the door to my apartment slam behind me as I headed down the hall to the elevator. I couldn't believe I was running away from a second plague-infested home.

I walked out of the elevator and into the lobby as I waved to my new doorman. He smiled as I threw on a pair of sunglasses, hoping to pass for Regular Lauren once again. I tore through the revolving doors and looked around until I spotted Heather's large white hatchback. I opened the passenger door and threw my overnight bag into the car as I let out an exasperated sigh. Heather stalled for a moment as she glanced at me, lovingly. I told her to drive. To drive us away from yet another place that had quickly descended into the pits of hell.

As we pulled away from Heaven on Sheridan, I disclosed to Heather that I was suicidal. I just blurted it out. I stared at

Heather as she continued to watch the road. She didn't seem too surprised.

I felt a sense of relief wash over me. I didn't stop there. I allowed the events of the past twenty-four hours to pour out of my mouth. I told Heather about the bed bugs. I told her that I had been pushed over the edge of my physical and emotional cliff. I told her that I couldn't do it anymore. I couldn't survive a scenario where relentless plagues seemed to stretch on forever. There had to be an end in sight. Otherwise, I was afraid I would create my own ending.

Heather was the first person I wanted to disclose to about my suicidal ideation, but she was also a complicated person to tell. She had recently taken a job as a therapist at a very well-known PHP (partial hospitalization program) in Chicago, and she worked on the intensive trauma unit. Heather's entire job consisted of delivering individual and group therapy to clients in crisis. All of a sudden, I felt a newfound comradery with all the clients I knew who had reached this level of hopelessness.

Every person is only a few traumatic life events away from rock bottom. That had always been my theory. I spoke about this concept in trainings and in supervision sessions with new therapists I mentored over the years. It quickly became one of my catchphrases. Now I knew it was true on a whole other level.

After listening to my entire story, Heather told me that she didn't believe I needed to be hospitalized. I agreed with her. Even though I was deeply suicidal and had a plan, I had prevented myself from carrying out that plan. I also knew that I couldn't be alone. These were all good signs. Heather admitted that she was glad I was coming back to her place for the night. We decided to take it one step at a time.

My body began to loosen in the passenger seat. I stretched my arms and legs out in front of me, as the seatbelt held my torso firmly in place. I rolled my neck from side to side as it began to crack. I stared out the window as Heather began driving toward Willa's daycare and not to the hospital. I let out a sigh of relief.

Heather talked about how understandable it was that the bed bugs drove me to my brink. She couldn't believe the plagues were continuing. *But I could.* I felt it in my gut. It was like watching a movie where the main character believes she has gotten through the worst of her troubles, but the moviegoer suspects that the worst is yet to come. That's how I moved into Heaven on Sheridan. Naively hopeful, but inherently distrusting.

As we drove to Willa's daycare, I couldn't shake the fear of how close I had come to my own death. Perhaps I didn't need to be hospitalized *tonight,* but I knew I was dangerously nearing that point. Things were getting progressively worse at my new apartment, and there was no foreseeable solution to all the madness. There's only so much repetition and complex trauma someone can take before it catches up with them. It had certainly caught up with me.

I decided to take matters into my own hands. I began to perform my favorite therapeutic intervention for suicidal ideation. This time, on myself. As I sat in Heather's car, I pulled out my phone and made a list of everything that was keeping me alive:

1. My work
2. Heather and Willa
3. My sheer force of will
4. The hope that this horror show is merely an acute moment in time
5. My refusal to give my family an excuse to blame the estrangement on my mental health
6. The possibility that I may fall in love again
7. An intense knowing that this is not where my story ends
8. The desire to contribute more to the world

Making that list satiated the parts of myself that were

absolutely terrified of my own brain. I read my list aloud as Heather smiled. She reminded me that part of the reason she didn't think I needed to be hospitalized was because I was a trauma therapist as well. I was particularly known for my crisis intervention skills and my impeccable clinical instincts. And now, I had effectively used those skills on myself.

Once I was reminded of my own therapist hat, I fastened it back on. I told Heather all about this training I had created for newly minted social service workers. The training featured a section where I provided insight into why someone might require a crisis-level response. In my opinion, crises happen when our risk factors around experiencing trauma increase and/or when our protective factors that provide a buffer from trauma decrease. Risk factors can be anything that adds danger or instability to a person's life. *For example, a series of violent plagues.* And protective factors are aspects of our lives that provide security and meaning. *For example, a family and a safe home.* I knew that I was in a precarious situation. My risk factors had undoubtedly increased and my protective factors were in the process of being stripped away, one by one. No wonder I found myself in this position.

* * *

Shortly thereafter, Heather and I pulled up to Willa's daycare. She smiled and reassured me that I was going to make it through this. I felt a newfound sense of trust in myself after reciting my own training material in the car, even though I had become the case study.

In an instant, I heard Willa's buoyant laughter. I waved to her from my passenger seat as her eyes filled with glee. Willa climbed into her car seat and exclaimed, "Auntie Lauren, you are back! Yaaaaaay! Do we get to have another sleepover?"

I looked at Willa and confirmed that I was back for another sleepover. Heather passed Willa a clementine as I squeezed her other little hand. Willa let out a squeal that rivaled the sound barrier. I laughed as I looked at Heather. We would later joke about the fact that Willa would remember this era as one giant party with Auntie Lauren. In my eyes, it was the darkest period of my life.

We pulled into Heather's garage and began to assemble ourselves. As we walked through Heather's perfectly curated backyard, I placed my hand on Willa's pink backpack. She began telling me about how much fun she had at her birthday party over the weekend. Willa had just turned four years old. As we walked into the house, my eyes grew wide. Apparently, Willa had chosen a rainbow theme for her party. There were rainbow streamers hanging from the ceiling. There was a tablecloth filled with rainbows in the kitchen. I moved my fingers over the laminated, rainbow tablecloth as a smile crept across my face. I had just screamed out the window of my apartment, begging the universe for a sign. And I had received a double-banded rainbow without the presence of rain. I felt silly hoping that my plea would produce a tangible result. But to my amazement, it had. And now, I was in a home filled with rainbows. Heather looked at me and smiled. "I know, right? When you told me about the rainbow outside of your apartment, I knew you just needed to walk in here and see this."

As I stood underneath a string of rainbow streamers, I whipped out my phone to show Willa the photo I had just taken of the incredible rainbow that appeared out of nowhere. Her eyes lit up with amazement. I explained that it was *totally crazy* that a rainbow formed without a drop of rain. I told her not to expect that sort of thing to happen again. But as I looked at Willa, I realized that she was unfazed by my reality check. She already believed that there was magic in the world. Perhaps I was the one who needed to believe.

I walked past the rainbow tablecloth and called my therapist, Marilyn. I left her a voicemail message with all the important key words: *emergency, bed bugs, extremely dark thoughts, I'm at Heather's again.* Marilyn called me fifteen minutes later. I went downstairs to the basement to speak to her privately. I certainly didn't want Willa to hear anything I was about to say.

I told Marilyn everything. I told her about the suicidal thoughts, and I told her I had a plan. She was relieved that I was with Heather, and she echoed that I did not need to be hospitalized. She told me that it was very important that I was not alone that night, and I agreed. We also planned to check in the following day.

* * *

I couldn't sleep at all that night. I tossed and turned in Heather's guest room as I began to wonder *why* all these strange plagues had been happening to me. I had tried to solve each of these plagues on the surface, but that had only resulted in a momentary reprieve. Now, I was suicidal. It was a life-or-death situation. If I had any prayer of existing beyond this evening, I would need to get to the root cause, once and for all.

I fumbled around in the dark as I searched for my phone on the end table. I unplugged my phone right as its bright light shot directly into my eyes. I winced. I turned down the brightness until my eyes had a chance to adjust to the glare. It was three o'clock in the morning.

I took to Google once again. But as I stared at the blank search page, I had no idea what to type. I decided to start with the biggest question on my mind:

Google: *What causes an ant, moth, and bed bug infestation at two different apartments?*
Result: *Infestations and how to get rid of them the natural way.*

Ugh.

Google: *Why do large-scale infestations happen?*
Result: *Large-scale infestations can occur during times of weather changes and when a home or building has been neglected.*

I threw my phone down on the bed as I stared at the wall in front of me. This wasn't getting me anywhere. None of these answers had anything to do with my situation. I began to panic. I absolutely had to figure this out, and I had to do it now. There was no more time to waste. I was clearly asking the wrong questions.

I felt my intuition begin to take over. I began to wonder if I was focusing too heavily on the infestations themselves. After all, the ants and moths had behaved quite strangely. I knew that for a fact; the exterminators had confirmed it. So perhaps the bugs weren't the main event. Perhaps they were merely a tool. A tool that someone or something was using to turn my life into a living hell.

I sat up in the bed. *But who? And why? And how?* My heart sank into my gut. There *was* something I had wondered about after each plague, but I didn't even want to say it aloud. All of a sudden, I had to find out if my deepest fears had any real merit. I had nothing to lose and everything to lose at the same time.

I opened Google once again:

Google: *Am I being punished for leaving my family?*
Result: *How to reconcile with a loved one.*

Nope.

Google: *Are curses real?*
Result: *Real-life stories about psychic attacks, black magic, and hexes.*

Oh shit.

Google: *What is a psychic attack?*
Result: *Energy attacks happen when a negative energetic vibration is directed toward us via other people's thoughts, feelings, and emotions. This often happens when someone is harboring anger toward us.*

I stared at this article from *Elephant Journal*[2] as my jaw hit the floor. Apparently, psychic attacks exist, and they don't require any malicious intent on the part of the person placing them. Words are quite literally spells. If someone speaks poorly of another person, they have the power to negatively influence that person's energy field and surrounding environment, even by accident.

After each plague, I had wondered if I was being energetically punished for leaving my family. I quickly dismissed that thought each time, since the mechanics seemed highly improbable. But it had crossed my mind. As I read about psychic attacks, my worst fears were realized.

However, I still had no idea *who* might be punishing me for the estrangement. For a moment, I wondered if it was my parents. I assumed they didn't believe in black magic or know how to use it, and frankly, I wasn't sure if I believed in it either. But if they were harboring any negative feelings toward me, I began to wonder if they could inadvertently fuck up my entire life. According to these readings, that was a possibility. It seemed far-fetched, but I wasn't willing to rule anything out.

Then I began to wonder if my ancestors were punishing me. My maternal grandmother Bess immediately came to mind. We had never gotten along while she was alive. She always felt that I was too outspoken, especially for a woman. She wanted me to fall in line and obey my parents, and I wanted my parents to treat me with more respect. We quarreled about that constantly. Without warning, I began to wonder if Grandma Bess was angry at me for ultimately leaving my family. For causing my mother pain. Could it be possible that she was conjuring up all this mayhem from beyond the grave? My stomach sank. *That felt extremely likely.*

A psychic attack grew more probable by the second. I opened a note on my phone and began to jot down the timeline of the past few months:

May: Estrangement
July: Ants

August: Moths
September: Flood, creaky floors
October: Bed bugs

A chill ran down my spine. The fact that all of this began taking place so shortly after my estrangement seemed a little too eerie to remain a coincidence. I had already tried the *normal* problem-solving route. Perhaps there was something metaphysical going on. At this point, I was ready to believe just about anything. I had experienced infestations at two separate apartments within the past few months. I had involved two different landlords and two teams of exterminators. There was no conceivable end in sight.

The common denominator was me.

I WAS A MUCH HARDER SELL

As soon as daylight broke through the blinds, I launched myself out of bed. I threw on a sweatshirt and made my way into Heather's kitchen. I put on a pot of coffee. I had about an hour before Heather's alarm would sound and the pitter-patter of Willa's footsteps would begin to fill the house. I stared at the timeline on my phone. *Estrangement, ants, moths, flood, bed bugs.*

Shortly thereafter, Heather walked into the kitchen, carrying Willa. She was surprised to find me there. Heather began asking how I slept, but I quickly interrupted her – "I THINK I KNOW WHAT'S GOING ON!"

Heather's eyes grew wide as she attempted to give me her undivided attention. This was challenging since Willa was dangling from her arm like a monkey.

"Heather, I think I am being punished for leaving my family."

Heather let out a deep sigh as she looked down at Willa. "Lauren, I was afraid you were going to say that."

I was shocked. I had no idea this might have already occurred to her.

"There's no way you are being punished for your estrangement," she said. "You did the right thing by leaving. You know you did. I don't want you to regret that decision for a single second. I don't think the universe is out to get you right now, and I really don't want you to think that way."

I began to feel slightly defeated. "Oh, I don't regret the estrangement at all. And I'm not sure that the universe is punishing me ... But someone might be. I wonder if my parents are placing negative energy onto me. Did you know that it's possible to cause a psychic attack just by having negative thoughts about someone? They might not even realize they are doing it! Or Grandma Bess might be haunting me because she's angry at me for leaving my mom. Those are my two hypotheses."

Heather looked visibly shocked. I began to read her everything Google had to say about black magic, curses, and psychic attacks. I watched Heather's expression closely as she took this information in and considered it. I couldn't tell if she was placating me or in agreement, but it didn't seem to matter. I finally had something to grab onto, and that brought me a huge sense of relief.

Heather drank the coffee I made for her as she packed Willa's lunchbox. I sat at the kitchen table and continued to relay my newfound conclusion that the root of all my problems might be metaphysical. Heather had always been open to all facets of spirituality. She had seen a psychic years ago who accurately predicted quite a few of the tumultuous events in Heather's life. Heather was also a natural believer in signs, fate, and gifts from the universe. I, on the other hand, was a much harder sell.

* * *

Heather raced around the house, vigorously changing into her work clothes as I wrangled Willa into a pair of leggings. I quickly grabbed my overnight bag, and we all walked to the car. As Heather began to drive toward Heaven on Sheridan, I opened my phone and began to cancel my day of clients. There was no way I could pretend to be Regular Lauren today. And besides, I felt like I was far too close to cracking this case.

Twenty minutes later, I walked into the front door of my apartment in Heaven on Sheridan and let out a sigh. Bags of clothing remained scattered all around the living room. My heart sank as I remembered the reason I had left. Bed bugs.

I sat down at my desk chair and opened my computer. I took to Google once again, prepared to go even deeper into the rabbit hole I had already fallen into. I continued reading about psychic attacks until I came across something even more frightening: spiritual possession. I laughed nervously. *Ok, Lauren, this isn't* The Exorcist. But I kept reading. Apparently, spiritual possession is quite common. Spirits join people all the time, especially when the host has experienced significant trauma. *Oh no.*

Still, a possession was at the very edge of what I was willing to believe. That seemed especially far-fetched, even for this moment. However, the topic led me back to the hypothesis that the spirits of my ancestors might somehow be responsible. It was highly possible that Grandma Bess was rolling in her grave after my estrangement. Or it could be someone I didn't have the chance to meet. After all, I was the descendent of a long line of Ashkenazi Jews. The Holocaust ran straight through our bloodline. We were well-acquainted with the concept of forced separation. And here I was, initiating a separation from within my family. There was an unspoken rule against that, and I had violated it. A chill ran down my spine.

* * *

I had no idea what I believed about the afterlife. Perhaps that's because I was raised in a reform Jewish household. In all the years that I attended religious school, there was never a single discussion of angels or spirits. That was especially true in my family. My parents felt that everything was far more concrete. You live and then you die. End of story.

A lot of my early religious beliefs were shaped by my father. He was agnostic, and he believed in rationality and concreteness. My father felt that angels and spirits were designed by humans who needed to be comforted by their presence. He believed that the afterlife was a fictional place that grief-stricken people create so they can rest assured that their loved ones are safe. He understood why someone would need to believe in these things. But he did not think any of it was real.

I wasn't sure if I believed in spirits, but I already knew that logic had its limits. I also had a few experiences as a child that stuck with me. For starters, there was something peculiar about the house I had been raised in. My childhood home was over a hundred years old. I was in kindergarten when we moved into that house. I remember skipping through the halls, overcome with a desire to explore every inch of that place. One day, a neighbor appeared at the front door holding a gift basket. I peeked around the corner as she told my parents that our house was rumored to be haunted. I watched as my parents laughed in response to that warning. The neighbor did not laugh and neither did I. And when I was about eight, I found a set of pearls in the attic. I remember picking up the necklace and hearing a voice shout: *Put that back.*

There was also something peculiar about the house that my mother was raised in. She grew up fifteen minutes from Salem, Massachusetts. Every summer, when we visited Grandma Bess, I felt extremely unsettled in that house. The interior was dark and drabby, with mud-colored carpeting and mahogany walls. It felt encapsulated in time. My grandmother had barely made any updates since the seventies. Now, I wondered if that was the only cause of the stale vibes.

When I walked through the halls of my mother's childhood home, I felt like they were closing in on me. And that basement was like being in a funhouse. One time, when I was about ten, Grandma Bess asked me to go downstairs to grab a case of sodas from the refrigerator. I descended the stairs by the front hall and made my way into the basement. At first, I thought nothing of it. But then I saw some paintings that my grandmother had been working on. I freaked out. I had come face to face with a painting of the most terrifying clown I had ever seen. And then, I heard creaky floorboards coming from the laundry room on the other side of the basement wall. My entire family was seated in the living room, on the opposite side of the house. There was no way any of them could create those noises. I ran to the fridge and grabbed the sodas as fast as I could. Come to think of it, those floorboards creaked the same way mine had in Heaven on Sheridan.

Despite all these examples, I still wasn't fully convinced that the spirit world existed. It was easier for me to make excuses for what I thought I saw and heard as a child. The voice shouting at me to return the necklace came from my own imagination. Perhaps someone had walked into the laundry room of Grandma Bess's house, and I just didn't know it. Maybe these stories were merely an example of confirmation bias. That's what I imagined my father would say.

Somehow I knew my supernatural encounters lived in a place that defied logic. I was terrified to journey to that place. But now I had no choice. I was engaged in a life-or-death situation. It was time to consider all the options, and I mean *all* of them. I could no longer do this on my own. If I was dealing with something metaphysical, I needed to turn to someone with a much deeper understanding of psychic attacks and the spirit world. I scratched my head as I cycled through an invisible Rolodex, desperately combing my mind for someone who could help me.

Suddenly, I knew exactly who to call.

THAT ONE

Summer 2010

On a sunny summer afternoon in 2010, I was sitting on Heather's living room couch staring off into the distance. My eyes were fixed on a ray of light as it entered through one of the bay windows and sliced through the coffee table. We were playing music from her computer as we drank herbal tea. Heather had just moved into a quaint one-bedroom unit in the middle of Lincoln Square. It had antique charm and rustic wooden floors. I loved this neighborhood even though Heather felt that it was too far north. After all, we were in our late twenties. We spent most of our time frequenting coffee shops and bars closer to downtown Chicago.

Heather asked me how I was feeling. Tears began to form in my eyes. I was a few months into a medical enigma that was equal parts frustrating and agonizing. I had been experiencing unexplainable chest pains along with an unrelenting cough. I had just taken a second round of antibiotics, which had failed to alleviate my symptoms. I had seen a multitude of doctors, one of whom performed a lung x-ray. Everything had come up short. There was no evidence of an ongoing infection, yet my body continued to scream in agony. The pain had become unbearable.

Heather looked at me and asked how my heart was doing. I frowned. I figured that I must have misunderstood her question. I reminded Heather that my heart was fine; the problem was my lungs. And that's when Heather told me she had just learned about the chakra system, and she thought it might be useful for me to read about it.

Heather handed me a new book she had just purchased on chakra healing as she flipped directly to the section on the heart chakra. I scanned the page initially, but the material began to pique my interest. I learned that the word *chakra* is Sanskrit for *disk* or *wheel*. There are seven chakras that span the length of the human body. They form a vertical line from the base of the sit-bones to the crown of the head. These wheels are meant to spin in a circular motion, but energetic blockages can jam up the gears. Untreated emotional pain is a common cause of an energy blockage. When the wheels stall, this can produce a physical and emotional imbalance in the body. If this blockage continues for long enough, it can produce a myriad of physical illnesses. There are practitioners who specialize in energy work, which unblocks the chakras and allows them to continue moving freely.

I sat on Heather's couch with my mouth wide open. I had never read anything like this before. I learned that the heart chakra encompasses the heart, chest, and lungs. It is the place where grief is stored in the body. And the lungs hold the deepest, darkest grief. The moments in our lives that fill us with despair and leave a palpable imprint. The kind of grief no one wants to talk about. I began to wonder if the grief I felt over my family in the past few months was leaving me breathless.

I had been through a lot of recent events that had the power to bring my heart chakra wheel to a grinding halt. Right around the time I began to experience chest pains, my relationships with both of my parents were heavily eroding. I cried to my friends. I cried in therapy. I walked around in shock and disbelief. But most of all, I walked around in pain. I tried to limit how often I let myself feel that pain because it was far too overwhelming. But one day, I brought my journal to the park, and I went there.

My journal was beautifully bound in mint green leather with white flowers. I didn't write in it very often because I was worried that my melancholic words would contaminate its beauty. I watched as the weeping willow trees swayed in front of me. Their leaves bent in the wind, concave and heavy. I was mesmerized by these slow and steady movements. But, as I continued to stare at the trees, I began to feel their pain until suddenly, I was filled with my own. And instead of shoving it back down, I decided to let the grief pour out. Tears streamed down my face. My pen shook in my hand. I opened my journal and scribbled down six words that changed everything: *My parents are breaking my heart.*

I stared at Heather as I told her about that day at the park. I began to cry uncontrollably as she sat with me on the couch. Heather knew everything. She knew that I felt that my parents had deeply betrayed me. She knew I was afraid that the damage was becoming irreparable. She knew I was shoving down a lot of pain and heartbreak so I could remain in my own family. Perhaps that motivated her to ask about my heart. I had ignored my own pain for so long, hoping I was wrong about it all. Now my heart was screaming through my chest, vying for my attention like a petulant child. Apparently it took a sky-high medical bill and an incurable cough before I began to listen.

Heather suggested that I find an energy healer; someone who might be able to unblock my heart chakra. I was skeptical, but curious enough to try it. After all, no one else could figure out how to help me heal my body. Perhaps energy work would provide some much-needed relief.

Heather and I walked over to her computer. She sat down at her desk as I bent over the back of her chair. We both stared at the screen as Heather began to type, *energy work, Chicago, north side.* We scanned the list of results in silence until I said, "That one." Heather smiled. She was always a champion of following one's intuition.

Heather clicked the link of the random profile I had chosen, and it took us to a website for an energy healer named Linda. As I stared at Linda's photo, my shoulders began to relax. She had thick, wavy, salt and pepper hair that fell slightly past her shoulders. Her bangs were effortlessly whisked to the side. I sensed an immediate gentleness exuding from her deep, green eyes. I also noticed that her maiden name was Jewish. I thought to myself, *Wow, she's a Jewish woman around my mother's age, but she seems so different.* I asked Heather to send me Linda's contact information immediately.

The following week, I walked into Linda's home for the first time. She greeted me with a warm smile and a deep hug. I almost cried in her arms. She continued to hold me as she let out a deep sigh. I began to pull away, slightly embarrassed that I had just projected the energy of an orphan looking for a replacement mother onto someone I had just met. But Linda didn't seem to mind.

Linda conducted her energy healing sessions out of the attic of her beautiful Victorian house, which was only a few blocks west of Heather's apartment. Her husband was a psychotherapist with a home office in their basement. *What a power couple.* As we made our way up the stairs to her attic office, I began to realize that I was in a home filled with the potential for tremendous healing.

I sat across from Linda as I watched her settle into a cozy armchair. I allowed myself to do the same. As soon as our eyes met, Linda began to well up with tears. She looked at me and exclaimed, "I don't know what you do for a living, but I know I am in the presence of another healer."

I looked back at her, astonished. I told her that I was a social worker, but it was more than that. I told her that I knew that I was also a healer. I felt like I couldn't say that very often without sounding conceited. But in that moment, I owned my power. There was more to my work than the education I received. I was a healer. I had a gift. I knew it then and I know it now. I just couldn't believe someone else understood that. At that moment, I knew Linda also had a gift.

The first time I lay down on Linda's healing table, my body began to relax immediately. She rolled a colorful blanket up to my chin and placed a lavender-scented eye pillow over my eyes. I don't remember very much from this session, but when I awoke, Linda told me that she felt my feet *whirling and twirling*. I gasped. I told her that I had been a competitive figure skater for a long time. She smiled and told me that my feet may always be at home on the ice. I smiled. I already knew that was true.

After a few visits to Linda's house, my chest pains began to dissipate. I didn't understand the mechanics of energy work, but I could tell that my body was responding favorably to it. I began to see Linda as often as possible. Sometimes, I was in her office weekly. Other times, it was monthly. No matter how much time had passed, I always felt grounded and grateful to be in her presence. She understood me in a way that few people did. She saw straight through to the center of my soul when we first met, and our relationship deepened easily with each session. I began to trust her implicitly. And trust did not come easily to me. Trust was delicate; it had to be earned. Linda earned my trust just as my parents were losing it. I became deeply aware of this stark contrast.

Linda ended each energy healing session by scribbling down notes that she received from her guides and ascended masters. I didn't know exactly what it meant to have a spirit guide, but I was curious about every aspect of Linda's process because her sessions were providing me with so much relief. On my way out, Linda handed me a piece of bright orange paper that always contained more accurate information about my body than I had ever received in a doctor's office. Sometimes, the orange paper had instructions for additional work I could do at home. Other times, there were mantras.

When I first started seeing Linda, I told her that my heart was broken. At first, I came to her because I wanted someone to *fix it.* But it didn't take long for Linda to reflect something much deeper. She told me that there was nothing wrong with my heart. And then she said, "The heart always breaks for a reason."

I began to tell Linda all about my heartbreak. I told her about the holidays where I ran out the door crying because my parents had betrayed my trust. I told her about the never-ending fights I had with my mother over the fact that I didn't feel safe around her side of the family. I told her about the way my father acted like this issue *didn't involve him.* And I told her that my heart couldn't go on like this for much longer. Linda encouraged me to let myself feel every ounce of that pain. The pain of yearning for my parents to take accountability so that we could move forward together. And the pain of knowing, deep down, that they never would.

HELP IS ON THE WAY

October 2018

I sat at my desk in Heaven on Sheridan and dialed Linda's number. I left an urgent voicemail message as I frantically ran my fingers through my dark, curly hair. I told Linda that I was afraid that someone might be using black magic to create havoc in my home. I told her that I needed help, and I didn't know who else to call. Linda called me back an hour later, and we booked an energy healing session for the following morning. At first, she thought it might be useful to conduct the session in my home. But after I explained that the plagues had followed me from one apartment to the next, she told me to come directly to her office. I hung up the phone, slightly relieved. *Finally, help is on the way.*

* * *

The next day, I walked through Linda's lush, overgrown backyard until I reached the client entrance to her house. I opened the black gate and buzzed the back door. I promptly entered the basement and began removing my shoes. I went through the familiar motions of entering Linda's home just as I had done for the past eight years, but I knew today was different. I felt hopeful and terrified at the same time. Linda waved to me from the top of the stairs as I ran up to meet her. She embraced me in one of her classic, deep hugs. I typically felt relaxed in her arms. This time, my body began to shake. We both pulled away simultaneously. Then we began to climb the steep staircase leading up to the attic. Neither of us said a word.

We were barely inside Linda's office when I blurted out the events of the past few months. I hadn't seen Linda since I estranged myself, but she knew that I had been on the brink of making that decision. I told Linda about the horror of the four plagues. I told her about the creaky floors. I told her that I had a bad feeling that I was being punished *by someone* for leaving my family.

I launched into my hypothesis that one of my ancestors might be using black magic to carry out a series of psychic attacks. I told Linda that I suspected it was Grandma Bess. Linda didn't flinch. Apparently she wasn't surprised by anything I had just said. I stared at Linda in disbelief. She was the only person who responded to the four plagues as if I was talking about my morning stroll through the park. And in that moment, I knew I had called the right person.

Linda paused for a minute, trying to think of an appropriate intervention to address this situation. Linda said that instead of doing our typical energy healing session, we should try something new. She suggested that we do hypnotherapy. I had never done hypnotherapy as a client or a practitioner. Honestly, I wasn't sure what I thought about it as a therapeutic tool. It felt like a lot of power to hand over to someone. But I trusted Linda. And besides, I was at my brink. I told Linda that I was suicidal. She cried as she begged me not to take my own life. I felt my chest begin to relax. Linda provided me with proof that I knew at least one person who didn't want me to die. And I needed as much evidence of that as possible.

Linda and I made our way down to her husband's basement office, which I had never seen before. He wasn't home that morning, so the room was available to us. Linda told me that we were going to conduct the hypnotherapy session there because she had more access to spiritual cleansing materials, like sage and crystals. I didn't know what that meant, but I took her word for it.

As we walked into the finished basement office, Linda directed me toward a long, beige couch in the center of the room. She sat across from me in an armchair as she advised me to lie down. I had no idea what was happening, but I did as I was told. I let my head fall back on the pillow as Linda instructed me to close my eyes. She began to put me in a trance. All I recall from that session is counting backward from ten.

I awoke from the session confused and disoriented. I glanced at a nearby digital clock. Over an hour had passed. I tried to sit up as my head began to throb. I fell back, allowing my head to hit the pillow once more. I pivoted my gaze slightly to the left as I studied Linda's body language and affect. I was desperate to know what had happened. But Linda avoided making eye contact with me. I could tell that she was holding her breath. I had become so accustomed to Linda's calm, peaceful demeanor over the years that her motionless expression caught me off-guard. A chill ran down my spine. That's when I looked down at my lap. I was gripping a large tennis racket in my right hand. *What the fuck?* I had no idea how it got there or what I was doing with it. Before I could ask a single question, Linda looked at me and said:

"Lauren, listen to me very closely. You have been possessed. This spirit is very dangerous. You need to go through a depossession immediately."

Everything came to a screeching halt.

My knuckles turned white as I gripped the racket even harder. I tried to open my mouth, but no words came out.

Linda sped over to her desk and began scribbling something down on a yellow sticky note. Apparently, I was not getting an orange piece of paper today. Linda handed me the sticky note as she said, "Possession is more common than many of us want to believe. I am not trained in this area, but I know someone who can help you. I am going to send you to the person I would trust if this was happening to me. Her name is Diane. I want you to call her as soon as you leave my house. Tell her that I sent you. Tell her it's a spiritual emergency."

I stared at the yellow sticky note as my vision began to blur. I had done my best to prepare myself for the reality of a psychic attack or even the presence of black magic. But believing in those things had required me to stretch my mind to the very edge. But a *possession?* That was way outside the limit.

I sat up and dropped the racket. I watched Linda move frantically around her basement. She threw a bunch of crystals and a bunch of white sage into a tan gift bag. *Lucky me, a parting gift.* Linda lit a piece of sage and instructed me on how to use it. She explained where each crystal needed to be placed around my home. Black tourmaline for the entryway; rose quartz for my bedroom. She told me to purchase pink Himalayan Sea salt and to pour it into cups. I was to position the cups in every corner of my home. I shut off my brain as I prepared to do exactly as I was told.

Finally, Linda told me that I needed to contact the Archangel Michael. I looked at her, confused, as I said, "Who is the Archangel Michael?"

Linda told me that the Archangel Michael was the most powerful archangel that existed. She told me that he had joined our hypnotherapy session. Linda explained that the Archangel Michael only comes when someone is truly in danger. Linda looked at me as she explained that my situation was incredibly serious. The spirit who had possessed me had become very angry.

I dropped the sticky note right next to the racket.

My body began to shake uncontrollably as my teeth chattered in fear. All of a sudden, I was afraid to exist in my own body. *Who else was here?* Linda walked over to the couch and wrapped me in a blanket. My mouth opened slightly as I tried to speak. I felt a lump growing in the back of my throat. I was too terrified to breathe.

Linda rubbed the small of my back. She comforted me gently. Linda told me that she knew this was a lot to take in, but there was a plan. There was a solution now. She took a few deep breaths as I attempted to mimic her.

When I had reached some semblance of equilibrium, we tried to close out the session. I placed my hands into a prayer position as I always did, and thanked Linda for the session. Though, this time, we both winced at each other in the process.

Linda told me to call Diane as soon as I got to my car. I stared at the sticky note once again, finally able to read it. Linda mentioned that Diane worked with a colleague who was a former Catholic nun. They had been performing these sessions together for years. If I was about to go through a depossession, at least it seemed like I would be in good hands.

Linda also instructed me to contact the Archangel Michael for guidance as soon as I got home. She told me that he would be able to help. After all, he was the leader of all the angels. I began to wonder why the head of all the angels would want to talk to me. I stared at my gift bag as a wave of skepticism tore through my mind. This was all becoming too much.

Linda could sense my hesitation. She reminded me that I had done the right thing by coming to her that morning. She told me to take this process one step at a time. First, I would call Diane. Then, I would use all my new spiritual cleansing materials throughout my home. And when I was ready, I would contact an angel for the very first time in my life.

I BENT MY MIND A LITTLE FURTHER

I left Linda's house and walked to my car, still hungover from everything that had just transpired. To my right, I saw two children around Willa's age playing with a set of sidewalk chalk. A little girl grinned at me as I walked past her. She was concentrating on drawing a large, pink heart. I looked down at her and forced a smile.

Twenty minutes later, I walked into the lobby of Heaven on Sheridan. I had already spoken to Diane. I called her during my drive home and mentioned Linda had sent me because I was having a spiritual emergency. Diane was kind, yet to the point. She spared me the emotional labor it would have taken me to rehash the events of that morning. Apparently, I had told her all she needed to know. We scheduled an appointment for the following Friday.

I rode the elevator up to my apartment on the thirty-ninth floor as I stared at the gold-plated elevator doors. I felt guilty that it had become impossible for me to enjoy the sheer beauty of this place. I walked down the hallway until I reached my corner unit. I opened the door and placed my gift bag of spiritual supplies on the kitchen island. I had no idea what I was doing, but it was time to try this approach. Perhaps it would work. Perhaps this was my answer to freeing myself from the never-ending cycle of plagues.

I removed a small piece of sage from the gift bag. I held it between my thumb and index finger as I lit it on fire. A line of delicate, white smoke rose from the grey branch. If *peace* had a smell, this would be it. I walked around my living room, fanning the smoke all over my apartment, just as Linda had instructed me to do. She also told me to speak an intention into the air as I smudged my home. I had no idea how to do that, but I decided to start anywhere I could.

"This is my home, and I want it to be safe. I am done with all this madness. I am done with all this negativity."

Slowly, I began to own my words.

"That's right, all negative energy must leave. And to the spirit who has possessed me: you need to stop. You need to stop doing this to me—"

I fell to my knees abruptly and burst into tears. Embers from the piece of sage began to blanket the floor in ash.

"How could you do this to me? How could you—"

I started sobbing uncontrollably.

"This ends here and now! I want you gone! Do you hear me? I don't know why you hate me so much, but you can't ruin my life anymore—"

I grabbed my head and buried it in my lap.

I cried until there were no more tears left in my body. My chest began to ache. I remained stuck to the floor for what felt like an eternity. The words I had just spoken felt so real and so completely surreal at the same time. *Was there really someone else living inside of my body?* I had no idea what that meant. But somehow, it began to make sense. It was the only way to explain why the plagues had followed me from the one place to the next.

Suddenly, my brain attempted to push all this away. *There's no way possessions are real, Lauren.* I took a deep breath as I stared at the black tourmaline I had just placed by my front door. Red solo cups filled with pink Himalayan Sea salt lined every corner of my apartment. It looked like spiritual frat party in here. Who had I become? I didn't know what to believe, but I forced myself to try this on. To *really* try it on.

So I bent my mind a little further.

CALL ON ME ANYTIME

The afternoon wore on, but I still had one more task left to accomplish. It was time to call on the Archangel Michael. I still had no idea what that entailed. Somehow I had managed to stretch my brain just far enough to accommodate the reality of a spiritual possession – and that had taken me most of the day.

Angels had always been a tough sell for me. I had considered Judaism to be a more practical religion. I wasn't deeply religious, but I did identify as a cultural Jew. I also appreciated some of the traditions. However, there was almost no discussion of the metaphysical world in my entire religious upbringing. I attended Sunday school and Hebrew school every week until my Bat Mitzvah[3] at the age of thirteen. And in all my years of formal Jewish education, no one ever mentioned the angels. Outside of popular culture references, I didn't even know who they were.

I had always associated angels with Christianity. But as soon as Linda told me that the Archangel Michael had come to visit me, I decided to look a little deeper. I turned to Google once again. And Google taught me that the Jewish mystics absolutely believed in the presence of angels. There was even a special relationship between the Jewish mystics and the Archangel Michael. I was floored. And then, I was angry. I was angry that all this information had been withheld from my formal educational experience. Especially because I desperately needed it now.

Earlier that day, Linda had told me to call out to the Archangel Michael naturally and then wait for him to respond. She told me that the Archangel Michael often makes a clear appearance with signs that are impossible to miss. I still had no idea what any of that meant, but I was curious to find out.

I walked over to the windows that spanned the length of my entire bedroom, and I looked out at the water. I steadied my gaze on a red lighthouse at the edge of the pier. For some reason, that felt right. The lighthouse felt like the kind of place where an angel would appear. I decided to go with it. And then, I just started talking:

"Hello, my name is Lauren. Apparently you called while I was at Linda's house. I'm sorry I missed your call. Anyway, I heard you want to talk to me. Here's the thing: I'm a Jew. I hope that isn't a problem. My understanding is that you have talked to Jews before, so hopefully you'll talk to me now. I need to be honest … I'm not sure I believe in you. I'm sorry if that's offensive. Before we go any further, I need you to show me that you are real. Please make it obvious because I am not going to stand at this window talking to myself like an idiot for very much longer. Ok, goodbye."

I laughed for a moment as I thought about the ridiculous voicemail message I had just left for the Archangel Michael. Was that even how it worked? Maybe I did it wrong.

Nevertheless, I stood at the window, bracing myself for just about anything to occur. Nothing happened. I began to grow more skeptical by the second. But then I remembered the double-banded rainbow that had appeared without a drop of rain. And I decided to stay, just a little longer. Just in case the Archangel Michael was real too.

I forced myself to remain at the window as my eyes scanned the entire room, looking for anything that I could fashion into a sign. Maybe that cloud looked a little like a rabbit. Perhaps that ray of light reflecting off the water was the Archangel Michael's way of calling me back. I sighed. It had been a few minutes. It was starting to look like my voicemail had not been received.

Just as I was beginning to grow weary, there was a knock at my door. I walked over the front door and peered through the peephole. There was someone from building security at my door. *Oh shit, what now?*

I opened the door and the security guard looked at me warmly. He said, "Hi, did you call me? I just wanted to check on you to make sure that everything is alright in here."

I looked at the security guard and told him I hadn't called anyone from his department.

The guard looked quite perplexed. He told me he was

certain that I had called him. He had been paged to respond to something going on inside my unit. I reassured him that I was fine. And then he said: "You can call on me anytime."

I smiled at the security guard and thanked him for checking on me. Just as I was about to close the door, I glanced at his nametag.

His name was Michael.

YOU CAN NEVER TRULY LEAVE YOUR FAMILY

October 2018

In the days that led up to my appointment with Diane, I had spent all my spare time filling my home with sage and screaming into the void as I begged the unidentified spirit to stop tormenting me. But my pleas weren't working. The floorboards continued to creak at night. And any time I was alone with myself, I was paralyzed in fear. The mere thought that someone else was living inside my body chilled me to the bone. I had no idea what a depossession would entail, but I was yearning to find out. I wanted this thing out of me.

Exactly one week after my hypnotherapy session with Linda, I got into my car and drove to my meeting with Diane. During our call, Diane had mentioned that she was in the process of renovating her home so we would be unable to convene there. However she had a close friend who owned an art studio with an office that we could use to conduct our session in private. When she gave me the address to the studio, it looked slightly familiar. Nonetheless, I thought nothing of it. I had far bigger things on my mind.

* * *

I wasn't paying attention to Google maps when I got into my car that morning. If I had, I might have noticed that the route to Diane's impromptu meeting place was about to take me on a tour of the neighborhood where I had been raised. I glanced down the road that led directly to our synagogue, where I had my Bat Mitzvah. Then I passed my father's favorite barbeque restaurant. Before I could think twice, I drove right in front of my parents' condo. I immediately pulled over as I began to hyperventilate. I had been so determined to get to this meeting with Diane that I had haphazardly driven right past the one place I never wanted to see again. *Fuck.* I was wholly unprepared to face this right now.

It had been five months since my estrangement. I hadn't

seen this building in almost a year. I glanced back at my parents' condo as a chill ran down my spine. I dropped my face below the headrest, periodically peering over the top of the seat as if I were engaged in a stake-out. It was eleven in the morning on a Friday; There was no way they were home. It didn't matter.

I stared at my parents' condo as a plethora of memories came flooding back to me. I saw myself standing in the kitchen on a summer evening as my father prepared salmon with all the right spices. I saw us laughing and smiling over dinner as I told them about how much I loved being a therapist. I saw all the times when I ran out of their building in tears. All the holidays that were ruined by one betrayal after the next. All the moments when I stood in their living room, begging my parents to repair our relationship. I saw myself try and try, until my tears overshadowed the moments when I had been happy. And then, last Thanksgiving, I saw myself run out of that building for good.

Now, I was back. And on this day, of all days. I was on my way to learn about a depossession, but apparently there was more than one ghost I had to face. What about the ghost of the girl I used to be? The girl who would run into her father's arms as he said, "Hi, sweetie." I wondered if it was possible to rid myself of all of it. Of all the memories that had nowhere to go. What happened to those ghosts? It seemed like they were trapped somewhere deep in the abyss. I supposed I would have to face them someday. At least I knew who they were. It was time to get rid of the one ghost who didn't belong here. The one who was currently wrecking my life from the inside out.

I started the car and began to drive again. For a split second, I strongly considered heading back to Heaven on Sheridan. Initially, staring at my parents' condo had seemed like a good idea, but it had quickly descended into darkness.

Nonetheless, a deeper part of me began to wonder if I had been sent back to my hometown for a reason. Ever since the Archangel Michael had appeared in the form of a security guard, I found myself questioning everything. Diane and I weren't even supposed to meet here. She was borrowing this space just for today. It began to feel like everything about this session had been designed just for me.

A few minutes later, I arrived at the art gallery and parked my car. I opened the large glass door and entered a quaint but beautifully curated art space. The gallery had crisp white walls and a smooth concrete floor. I began to show myself around, glancing at a series of modern impressionist paintings filled with vibrant colors. My mind blurred as I attempted to read about the artist. All of a sudden, I noticed a large, metal sculpture in the center of the room of a mother delicately holding her baby. It seemed out of place, but what did I know? I was hardly an art critic. Perhaps I only felt that way because I couldn't imagine a mother cradling her baby with that much care and attention. My throat began to close.

I was still staring at the sculpture when Diane stepped into the gallery and greeted me with a polite smile. She brought me back into a private room, and we sat down opposite each other. It took a moment for me to realize that we were standing in her friend's disheveled office. It felt very different from the meticulous gallery space I had just seen. The office was cluttered with yellow and green sticky notes that had been plastered all over the white cabinets. I almost laughed. I knew this vibe. I had worked for a dance company while I was living in DC, and I was acutely familiar with the juxtaposition of a clean performance space with a horribly messy office. It seemed to go with the territory of being an artist.

Diane gingerly took a seat at her friend's desk, careful not to touch anything. I sat in a folding chair directly across from her. Diane immediately apologized for meeting me this way. I smiled and reassured her that it was completely fine. Even in this disorganized office, all I could feel was Diane's warm competence. She had the energy of a true crone; I could see why Linda liked her so much. Somehow I knew she was going to help me.

Diane asked me why I had reached out to her. I launched into a twenty-minute monologue comprised of word vomit and an overflow of tears. I told her that I had recently estranged myself from my parents. And then I described the four plagues in great detail. I watched Diane's careful expression. She reacted in a similar fashion to Linda, nodding along with me as if I were talking about the unseasonably cool weather we were having. That was it. She wasn't shocked or shaken by anything I had just said. Apparently, I was the one who was having a hard time believing my own story.

I paused to take a deep breath. At that moment, Diane said: "Yes, this sounds like it could very well be a spiritual possession. We won't know until we really get in there and see if we find anything. I conduct these sessions remotely with my dear friend, Helen, who is an ex-Catholic nun. Together, we will conjure your soul and see if there is anything that shouldn't be there. We do this session without your body being present because it can be very traumatic for the person, and we don't want any interference from your fearful or egoic parts. So Helen and I will schedule a time to do this session together and then we will email you the written transcript from it. And if you have any guides or angels that you want to join this session for help, you can let me know and I will call them in as well – "

I immediately interrupted her: "Oh yes, you are going to want to call the Archangel Michael. Linda taught me how to make contact with him, and it's incredible. I can't believe it worked!"

Diane smiled. She reassured me that she was already well-acquainted with the Archangel Michael and that he often comes when someone calls him. I still didn't fully understand what any of that meant, but I was glad that someone else clearly did.

Diane leaned closer as she reassured me that we were going to get to the bottom of this. She asked me if I had any other questions before we scheduled the remote depossession

session.

Of course, I had many questions. But I narrowed them all down to one: "I want to know who did this to me."

I took a deep breath and continued. "Initially, I thought one of my ancestors was causing all the plagues because I thought she might be angry that I left my family. I thought it might be my grandmother Bess. But Linda told me that the plagues have been coming from somewhere else – somewhere deep inside of me. I just don't understand that. How could this be coming from me? Why would I try to ruin my own life? Are we going to find that out?"

Diane looked at me cautiously. "Helen and I will ask the spirit to identify itself, so hopefully, we will learn all about who has possessed you and when it happened. But I must warn you, this may be very difficult to find out. So you need to prepare yourself to hear just about anything. And it's almost never as simple as it seems. The spirit world is far more complex than we know. I can understand why you would think one of your ancestors was responsible for all this havoc. But something else may be going on. Something you haven't considered."

I hesitated as I glanced down at the concrete floor. "I don't know, Diane. I'm still convinced that my family is responsible for this, somehow. Why else would this spirit cause all this chaos right after my estrangement? There must be a connection between my family and this spirit. All I want to do is live my life separately from my family. I don't wish them any ill will, but I don't want anything to do with them ever again."

Diane looked at me as she became increasingly more serious. And then she said: "Yes, we can leave relationships with members of our family in this lifetime, but you need to understand that you can never truly leave your family. You can't renounce your ancestors without splitting off a part of who you are, and what made you who you are. Just remember that."

I felt my cheeks flush as my whole head filled with heat.

I avoided making eye contact with Diane as I began to speak: "From the moment I was born, I never felt like I belonged in my own family. It's been hell. Pure hell. I finally had the strength to walk away, and now you're telling me that none of that matters? The only way for me to heal is to completely sever those ties. It's the only shot I have at accepting myself."

Tears began to well up in my eyes. I wiped my tears away with my hand as I stared down at the concrete floor. I crossed my right leg over my left as my foot began to shake.

Diane looked directly at me and said, "Lauren, I understand. I can tell that this is all very raw. You recently estranged yourself and then you had all these strange problems occur in two different homes. There may be a connection, but it might be different from the one you are making now. I'm not saying you should reconcile with your living family members, but you should try not to sever your own root system energetically and metaphysically. I know all you see are the problems with those roots, but it's never that simple – "

I raised my voice: "Listen, you don't know how long I tried to hold onto my roots. It just made everything worse. Do you really think I would have gotten to this point if the entire system weren't toxic?"

I looked away again. I was officially yelling at someone whom I had just met. This was wildly out of character for me, but it was too late. I had already blown my lid, so I decided to keep going: "And another thing, Diane. This gallery is a few blocks from where I grew up. I know you had no idea, and we weren't even supposed to meet here, but still. I passed my parents' condo on the way here today. I made myself stare at it and all kinds of memories came flooding back. I haven't been there in a year. The last time I stepped foot in their home was last Thanksgiving. And they betrayed me so badly that I left in the middle of dinner. I really can't handle thinking about any of this right now. It's too painful. So excuse me if I am having an extreme reaction to hearing that I can never really leave my family as I sit blocks away from where they currently live. All I want to do is get away from these people and start over, but I can't seem to get away from any of it."

Diane's eyes grew wide. "You understand that none of this is a coincidence, right Lauren? Perhaps you needed to come back to your hometown so that I could deliver this message to you now. Perhaps all this needs to happen right here. Including the depossession. I don't know why I'm saying that, but it feels significant."

I dried my tears as I stared at Diane. I began to relax into my seat for the first time that day. "You know what, that same thought occurred to me when I was staring at my parents' condo. Maybe there's a reason I'm here right now. And a reason that we couldn't meet in your home, and we had to meet in this gallery. This neighborhood is the one place I never wanted to see again. I went through something similar ten years ago when I made the decision to move back to Chicago. This was the last place I ever wanted to live, but it was like my soul was beckoning me to come back here. I wonder if that's happening again now. The last place I want to be is the only place where the healing can happen. That's been true my whole life."

Diane smiled warmly. She seemed relieved that we were back on the same page. "Yes, Lauren. I absolutely believe that our souls call us toward certain places for a reason. Perhaps that's why you had to face your roots before you could have this meeting with me today. It seems that you are right where you need to be, even now. I know it's been a very challenging few months since your estrangement, but I believe I can help you. I know you are going to get through this. We are going to restore your soul back to you. And you are going to go on to do great things. I think you already know that."

I burst into tears as I nodded along with her.

Diane and I sat in silence for another moment as I felt the heat begin to leave my body. As I returned to reality, I was suddenly overcome with embarrassment. I turned to Diane and apologized profusely for my explosion. But Diane reassured me that I had done nothing wrong. Nevertheless, it was too late. The humiliation had already begun to seep into my bones. I had gotten angry at a few doctors and one therapist over the years, but I could count these emotional outbursts on one hand. This one had taken me by surprise.

My eyes glazed over as I watched Diane pull out some paperwork from her black messenger bag. She handed me a consent form. Diane smiled as I read over the consent form quickly and signed it.

We scheduled a remote depossession session for November seventeenth, which was still a few weeks away. I pleaded with Diane, asking her if there was any way she could fit me in sooner. But this was her first opening. Apparently, I would be returning home to an apartment infested with bed bugs and floors that creaked in the middle of the night for a while longer.

I left the art gallery and walked over to my car, still processing everything that had just taken place. As I drove away, I kept thinking about Diane's comment. The one that had triggered it all: *you can never truly leave your family.* I knew enough about defense mechanisms to know why I had gotten so mad at her. It was because I knew she was right.

Even if Diane helped me get rid of one ghost, there would still be others. And I certainly wasn't ready to face that truth. I had moved into Heaven on Sheridan, bought all new furniture, and blocked my parents on my phone. But clearly, my family continued to haunt my mind.

I couldn't even stare at a sculpture of a mother lovingly holding her child without having an intense emotional reaction. That sculpture could have been in the middle of France, and I still wouldn't have been able to look at it. This much, I knew. And my heart knew it too. It was the same reason I had forced myself to move back to Chicago in the first place. *Running away is not the same thing as freedom.* Diane had basically repeated those words back to me.

* * *

Each morning since my meeting with Diane, I arose ready and willing to face a new day. But as I walked into my bathroom and stared into the mirror, I saw my father's eyes and my mother's figure staring back at me. I couldn't outrun my roots, no matter how hard I tried. I would always be descended from people I chose to leave, and I didn't know how to reconcile that within myself.

I HAVE BEEN PRAYING FOR YOU

The three weeks until my depossession session proved to be the longest weeks of my life. During that time, I continued to live out of garbage bags as the bed bug patrol came back into my apartment for another round of fumigation. And every night, the floorboards in my living room creaked like I was in a horror film. I kept calling out to the Archangel Michael, and as soon as I said his name, the floorboards stopped creaking. Nonetheless, it was exhausting to be me.

The week before my depossession session, Mila and I went out for dinner. I wanted to tell her all about my newfound relationship with the angels, and I wanted her advice on my consultation with Diane. As the spirit continued to haunt me, I couldn't escape Diane's words: *You can't leave your family*, and *you may learn details about this spirit that are very hard to hear.* I didn't know what to make of it, or how to prepare myself for this session. But I knew that Mila was the only person I wanted to be around.

Mila was Serbian, and she had always been religious. She had grown up with a deep understanding and appreciation of the angels. I knew this because in middle school, she invited me over to her home to help her family decorate their Christmas tree. I had never done this before, and it was so exciting to be included in this ritual. I remember sitting in Mila's living room and unwrapping one of her delicate ornaments. I held the porcelain statue in the palm of my right hand as I examined the white figure with a blue robe. It was an angel. I asked Mila and her mother about this ornament, and they talked about how important the angels were to their religious beliefs. And that's when I told her that I didn't think Jews believed in angels, but I thought it was cool that other people did.

I ate those words as I considered the way that my relationship with the Archangel Michael had progressed over the period of just a few weeks. I had never experienced anything like this before. I needed to talk to someone who could relate. I needed to talk to Mila.

Before we had dinner, Mila and I went into a nearby store filled with incense, sage, and crystals. Mila wanted to buy some frankincense, and I had become very interested in all these things. As soon as I walked into that store, I almost fainted. I felt something deep within me constrict, and I ran outside to get some air. I crouched down outside this storefront, placing my hands on the cool concrete. My peacoat flew open as a gust of wind brushed up against my ribcage. I began to see stars. I felt a pang in my gut. Somehow I knew I had just agitated the spirit who was living inside of my body. Apparently it didn't want me in that store. I suppose that made sense. The store was filled with spiritual cleansing materials that were designed to get rid of something like this.

Mila bent down next to me and asked me if I was alright. For a split second, I almost told her what happened, but I kept that to myself. I stood up slowly as I fastened my peacoat. We walked around the corner to a small Vietnamese restaurant in my new neighborhood. We were the only people in the restaurant, which was perfect. I was about to disclose a whole lot of material that I certainly didn't want other people to overhear.

We sat down at a table near the window, and I stared into Mila's eyes. She almost teared up. I could tell that she was truly concerned. I hadn't seen Mila in a few weeks, and so much had happened. I blurted everything out before we had glanced down at our menus. I told her about the hypnotherapy session with Linda where I woke up holding a racket. I told her all about Diane and my outburst at the art gallery. I told her that I had made contact with the Archangel Michael and that he was here to help me. I told her about the security guard incident, half expecting her to laugh it off. But Mila looked at me, serious as ever, as she told me that she wasn't surprised by any of this. Then she said:

"Lauren, I don't want to freak you out, but I have been really terrified for you. When the moths came and we got rid of your bed, I had a feeling it might be a psychic attack. I know all of this is very, very real. The Archangel Michael is incredibly important and powerful. He has helped my family during our darkest times. And he only comes when someone is truly in danger. Like when someone's life is in danger. You need to be extremely careful with all of this. I have been praying for you."

My eyes welled up with tears. I knew she was right. I had broken down so many times over the past few weeks, but this felt different. I couldn't run from the way Mila was looking at me right now. She knew the severity of this situation, and so did I.

Mila and I began to eat our pho as I talked about the depossession session, and how Diane said that she needed to conduct it without my body present. Mila confirmed that this was a great idea.

I listened as Mila talked about the fact that possessions are real. I could feel her fear. Mila refused to hide it from me. At first, this made everything worse. But after a while, I was grateful that someone else had joined me in the terror of it all.

* * *

I survived the next week by smudging my house daily and contacting the Archangel Michael every night before I tried to go to bed. One night, I woke up because I felt like someone was strangling me. I saw a string of black smoke rise into the air. I felt the string of smoke begin to envelop my throat, tightening itself around the base of my neck. I shook myself in the bed, unable to get out of this imaginary chokehold. And then I called out to the Archangel Michael, and the string of smoke immediately vanished. I fell over on the bed, gasping for air. *Holy shit.* I turned over in my sweat-stained bed and began to cry.

The next morning, I frantically emailed Diane and asked her if there was any way she could do this depossession session as soon as possible. I told her about the string of black smoke that had placed me in a chokehold the night before. Once again, Diane told me that I would need to wait. She told me to continue conjuring the Archangel Michael and to smudge my home with sage every single night before I went to bed. I was officially terrified. It was becoming abundantly clear that waiting was dangerous.

At this point, I only had a few more days to go.

IT'S NEVER THAT SIMPLE

November 17, 2018

I woke up at 7:00 a.m. on the day of my depossession and stared idly at the ceiling. I could tell that my session was in progress, even though Diane had withheld the exact details from me. My brain abruptly brushed aside my intuition. Maybe I wanted to believe it was happening at this very moment. My gaze gravitated toward the large painting in front of my bed. I let my eyes blur as the outline of a wildflower dissipated into a swirl of blue and orange lines. I couldn't explain where this knowledge was coming from, but I knew I was right. It felt like I was waking up in the middle of soul surgery – groggy and only partially aware.

Luckily, Heather had offered to spend the day with me. She knew that I needed to be distracted as much as possible on the day of my depossession. Willa was off with her father, so Heather picked me up in the late morning for a day filled with brunch and shopping. Frankly, this wasn't indicative of how we spent time together. Heather and I were much more likely to sit in a quaint coffee shop or wander around a neighborhood park with Willa. Brunch and shopping seemed too basic for us. But on this day, I yearned to be basic.

Heather and I wandered into a fancy brunch spot in Lincoln Park, an area of town that was filled with soccer moms in Lululemon pants. The restaurant was large and overstated, with modern glass globes that hung from the ceiling as trendy music played in the background. I laughed. We never would have come here on a regular day.

As I sat across from Heather, I squirmed in the royal blue booth. I glanced at the menu, barely able to concentrate on the delicate cursive letters. I felt different, but I wasn't ready to say that out loud. I looked at Heather and I swore that I saw a halo of yellow light surrounding her entire body. *Fuck.* This phenomenon had been happening all morning.

An hour earlier, while I was waiting for Heather to arrive,

I parked myself on a bench in my lobby and people watched. But something strange began to occur: I saw flashes of color as each pedestrian walked by Heaven on Sheridan. I bent my head down and squinted my eyes. Maybe there was something wrong with my vision – I had recently gotten my first pair of glasses. Apparently, I had an astigmatism. Perhaps that was the reason I was seeing bulbs of color as each person passed by my building. I reached into my purse, searching reluctantly for my seafoam-colored glasses. But once my glasses were on, that only made it worse. The colors suddenly became more pronounced. I didn't understand what was happening, so I googled it. Apparently, I was seeing auras. *What the fuck?* This had never happened to me before. But on that day, they were everywhere. First a blue one. Then a red one. And now, a yellow one surrounding my best friend.

I looked up from my menu as Heather asked me what I planned to order. I blurted out that I had no idea; that I would just choose something when the waitress walked over to our table. After I quickly skirted past our small talk, I decided it was time to tell Heather what was really going on. So I looked into Heather's big blue eyes, and I told her all about my morning. That I had woken up at 7:00 a.m. knowing that I was in the middle of soul surgery. That I could see different colors surrounding people as they walked down the street. That I wondered why someone people had auras and other people didn't. Or why some colors were much brighter than others. And then I told Heather that her aura was yellow. She smiled. She didn't even seem surprised. I hoped that her warm gaze would calm my nerves, but it didn't work. I began to wonder why I was seeing auras on the morning of my depossession.

After brunch, we wandered into a small boutique. I tried to ignore people's auras as I focused my attention on a pair of overpriced, dark skinny jeans. I looked at Heather reluctantly. She laughed and said, "Let's get out of here and go somewhere more our speed." I put down the jeans and nodded. We left the boutique and promptly headed toward Nordstrom Rack.

Shopping ended up being the perfect distraction. And besides, it was the first time I had put any real effort into rebuilding my wardrobe after I lost everything to the moths. Heather and I wandered around Nordstrom Rack as she held up everything from large sweaters to frilly dresses. I thought back to that day in Target when my sole purchase was a tank top that said, *Livin' my best life.* I had come so far in just a matter of months.

As the sun began to set, Heather and I climbed back into her car. I piled my shopping bags by my feet as we drove toward my place. A wave of terror washed over me. I didn't want to go home. I couldn't go back to the creaking floorboards and the string of imaginary black smoke that had almost strangled me in my sleep. If the depossession had worked, would it have an immediate effect? I didn't know, and I wasn't ready to find out.

Heather immediately sensed that I was apprehensive to go home. At this point, she could read my emotional cues instinctively. Without skipping a beat, Heather invited me to stay for dinner. I quickly agreed. At least I could put this off for a few more hours.

Heather turned the car around and began driving toward the house where Willa was spending the day. We barely spoke for the next twenty minutes as I stared out the window. We pulled up to the house, and Heather smiled at me as she stepped out of the car. I took a deep breath and shifted in my seat. I pulled out my phone, attempting to distract myself by scrolling through Instagram. All of a sudden, I heard Willa's classic laugh, and I looked up. I waved to Willa as she got into the car. She exclaimed, "Auntie Lauren, you're here!" I smiled as I placed my hand on Willa's little knee and told her that I was coming back to her house for dinner.

As we drove away, the three of us talked about what we wanted to eat that night. I had a craving for good Jewish deli food, but I figured I would be the only one. Nonetheless, I decided to throw the idea into the mix. Heather enthusiastically agreed to it. After all, we were driving through

Skokie on our way back to Heather's house. I had grown up near these delis, so I knew exactly where I wanted to go. I typed my favorite deli into Google maps and promptly directed us there.

The best delis are always the ones that seem sketchy and unassuming from the outside. Kaufman's is no different. As we pulled up to the small storefront located in a generic strip mall, Heather looked at me as if I better be right about this place. I laughed and told her to trust me.

I left the two blondes in the car as I ventured into Kaufman's alone. As soon as I walked into the deli, a wave of nostalgia almost knocked me over. My father used to go here on a regular basis. He would wake up early on Shabbat so he could get to Kaufman's before a significant line emerged around the corner. All the best Jewish delis were busy on Saturday mornings. Luckily, my father had always been a morning person. And besides, the bagels were that good.

I loved Jewish deli food, but I had purposely avoided it since my estrangement. As a therapist specializing in trauma, I knew that olfactory memories often produce incredibly strong flashbacks. I had no idea what would happen to me if I smelled matzah ball soup simmering in a restaurant or fresh bagels right out of the oven.

When I walked into Kaufman's, the smell of freshly baked egg bagels and rugelach coated in cinnamon and sugar consumed me. In an instant, I was teleported back to the kitchen in my childhood home. I was standing next to my father. I had just woken up, and he was already back from his habitual trip to the deli. My father smiled at me as he sliced each bagel like a professional before placing them into the toaster, one by one.

I shook my head, attempting to push that memory out of my mind. I stood at the deli counter at Kaufman's as my eyes glazed over. The image of my father smiling at me in the kitchen was quickly replaced by the reality that I would never see him again. My mind flashed and swiftly, I was back at

FedEx mailing the estrangement letters to my parents. A chill ran down my spine. *How did we get here?*

I was catapulted back to reality as the Kaufman's cashier called out my number. I scrambled. A line of people had already formed behind me, so I was out of time. I went through the motions of replicating my father's regular order because I didn't know what else to do. I left out the pickled herring because, realistically, neither Heather nor I were going to eat that. A few minutes later, I emerged from the deli carrying two bags full of fragrant Jewish food. As I got back into the car, Heather remarked that it smelled amazing. I smiled.

It was up to me to make my own memories now. It was up to me to decide which traditions to release and which ones to carry into my new life. And in that moment, I was glad that Kaufman's was here to stay.

Once we were back inside Heather's house, I stepped into the kitchen and began to unload the bags of food. I instructed Heather and Willa to relax at the large, wooden table while I prepared our special meal. I fixed our plates without saying a word. Heather and Willa sat politely at the kitchen table as their eyes filled with anticipation. I took each bagel and sliced it in half, just as my father had done. Then, I threw the bagels into the toaster, one by one. As that was happening, I gathered all the crudités. When everything was ready, I took a bagel, smeared it with chive cheese, and then piled tomatoes, cucumbers, and lox as high as I could. Finally, I placed a slice of Swiss cheese on the top, closed the sandwich and threw it all in the microwave. This was a unique sandwich that I grew up eating. It was named after my mother's favorite aunt. We called it the Rosalyn Special.

I sat down across from Heather as I watched her bite into her very first Rosalyn Special. Her eyes lit up and she exclaimed, "Wow, this is delicious!" I smiled as I looked down at my own sandwich. The smell was intoxicating. As I bit into my Rosalyn Special, my body slowly relaxed into my seat. Diane's words flew into my mind: *I know all you see are the problems with your roots, but it's never that simple.* In that moment, I finally understood.

* * *

A few hours later, once we were satiated and Willa was in bed, Heather walked me to the front door as my Lyft driver approached her house. Heather asked me how I was feeling about going back to my apartment. I told her that I couldn't run from this anymore; I needed to know if the depossession had worked. She agreed.

Fifteen minutes later, I walked into my apartment, brushing through the front door with my shopping bags and some leftovers from Kaufman's. I turned on the lights as my hands began to shake. I placed the food in the fridge, avoiding looking around my home. Finally, I stared into my living room and placed another spiritual call:

"Hello, I am calling the Archangel Michael. It's me, your Jewish friend, Lauren. I want to ask for your protection tonight. I really hope the depossession was successful. If it worked, can you please give me a sign? I am afraid to go to bed. You know why. Ok, thank you. I am hanging up now."

I waited silently for a few moments. My shopping bags remained littered on the ground. Nothing happened. I retrieved my bundle of sage from the closet and began to smudge the entire apartment, just as Linda had instructed me to do every single evening before I went to bed. When I was finished smudging and pleading with the angels to get rid of this spirit, I brushed my teeth. I tried to be as quiet as possible since I was still waiting for the Archangel Michael to call me back.

Nothing.

I sulked around the apartment as I changed into my pajamas and climbed into bed. I was exhausted and wired at the same time. I switched on my table lamp and pulled out a book, but I couldn't concentrate on the words. I placed the book down and drew the covers up to my neck. I began to tremble in my bed. The floorboards had creaked every night since I had moved into this apartment two months ago. I had no idea if they were going to haunt me again.

Wide awake, I switched off my light, hoping to will myself to sleep. *No creaking floorboards.* My home was quiet and peaceful. I seemed to be the only living thing in my apartment. *Finally.* I let out a huge sigh of relief as I rolled over in my bed.

Just as I was about to drift off, I glanced at the wildflower painting in front of me. It was glowing in the dark. Right above the painting, a large, royal blue hexagon appeared. It looked like someone had projected it straight onto the wall. I glanced behind me, half expecting to see an overhead projector from my elementary school days. But there was just a plain wall, which remained pitch black in the dark. For a moment, I panicked. I wondered if I was being haunted again. But I felt my intuition tell me this was something different. This was a gift. The royal blue light felt comforting. Reassuring. Loving.

Always a skeptic, I grabbed for my phone in the dark. I opened Safari and sighed heavily. I didn't know what to type. Then I remembered that one month ago, I was at Heather's place wondering if there was a deeper connection to the four plagues. That night, I had finally stopped googling earthly infestation questions as I stretched my mind toward the metaphysical world. What would have become of me if I hadn't taken that leap? I didn't even want to think about it.

I decided to trust my intuition, just as I had when I googled *psychic attacks* for the first time. The blue light in front of me felt like a gift. I knew it did. What if I was right? I typed the only sentence that came to mind: *is blue an angel color?* My jaw hit the floor.

The Archangel Michael's color is royal blue.

IF YOU DON'T LEAVE, YOU'RE IN FOR A BATTLE

Two days later, I received an email from Diane. She told me that the depossession had been successful. Then she provided me with the full transcript from the session:

Diane: Helen and I are thankful for this wonderful opportunity to assist in your healing.

Diane: The session began with Helen and I inviting the Light to be in and around you as we prepared to engage in this healing work. Helen received permission from your higher self … to enter your field.

Helen: I called your name and I saw you sitting cross-legged at a [bonfire] outside. The fire was being fed by you … as a fire in your belly. You said you could not leave this place because if you moved away, you felt you would be destroyed.

Diane: I asked for a name, and Mary Frances was given. She said she was twelve years old, and she joined you when you were eleven. She was attracted to you because she thought you were interesting, but also, she noted there was a big emptiness inside of you.

Mary Frances: I told her I could help her.

Diane: I then asked how she was affecting you mentally, emotionally, and physically.

Mary Frances: Things were ok for a long time … she took my guidance … but then she wanted to strive on her own … to be more independent … she wanted to go in a direction I did not think was good. So, I created things in her environment that caused her stress. She would be more cautious, and I would insert, "You are nothing, you are invisible, you're not important." I created stress in her body, discomfort, and pain, especially at her stomach area.

Diane: I often inquire about the history of these entities to get the backstory. So, I asked about her life when she was living on this Earth.

Mary Frances: I did have a family. We lived in a time when there was a lot of depression, hunger, and famine. And many people died. My parents tried to give whatever they could to us, however, when they died, I didn't know what to do. One day I just collapsed into the great darkness. I had to learn what to do.

Diane: I then called upon Archangel Michael and Rafael as well as the light workers to surround you and to keep Mary Frances contained. I invited the light workers to connect with her to send messages that only light workers could influence the entities. After a while, Mary Frances remarked that the light workers are reminding her of things that happened to her. They are telling her that she is taking her frustration out on Lauren and creating a lot of chaos. And they are blaming her.

Mary Frances: They say I intentionally created the chaos in your environment. I told the light workers that I wanted Lauren to learn about her own abilities. But the light workers asked me why that would be helpful. I feel like they are being confrontational with me.

Diane: I then asked you, Lauren, to step forward and talk about what you are learning from this session.

Lauren: I find myself very irritated by Mary Frances when I hear her talk about what she has been doing to me like I am some kind of experiment. What's been happening recently only exemplifies my issues with my parents. I wonder how much she has been involved in all of that. All of these distracting things happening around me – I want them to stop. I want all of these things to stop now. The fact that I have your name means I will call you out in a more conscious way. You need to leave me and go into the light. If you don't leave, you are in for a battle.

Diane: I encouraged Mary Frances to continue listening to the light workers for they ultimately have the power to convince her to leave. As the light workers continued to communicate with her, I reminded her that there is probably someone amongst the workers who she has known in the past. After a short while, she noted that her siblings, Joey, and Jim, came forward. They're telling her to go into the light so they can all be together. They tell her it's been a long time and they have been waiting for her.

Mary Frances: Okay, I will go into the light enjoying my family.

Diane: Before Mary Frances left, I asked her to take back any negative thought forms or different energy blocks that have been impacting you mentally, physically, and emotionally. She agreed to do that.

Mary Frances: I'm sorry I created such chaos in you, Lauren. You were such a great beacon of light. Be well.

Diane: She then took her siblings' hands and was escorted into the light. And that is the same time golden violet light came in and repaired all the damages and filled in all the areas where Mary Frances had been. We then did a soul retrieval to check on whether any parts of you split off during the time Mary Frances joined you. You said you felt that sense of spontaneity was hidden from you, and you became more cautious as a child. So, we called those parts that split off from your body and brought them back into your body. I then asked if there was any energy which took over and wasn't yours.

Lauren: I took the energy of being overly industrious, getting overly involved in situations and conflicts and creating a lot of resentment.

Diane: I then asked you to release that energy out of your body and send it up to the light. The session concluded with prayers that released you from all contracts, vows, and agreements that were made with the darkness. As we recited our Shamanic prayers, you were surrounded by Healing Light.

Diane: It's with much love and gratitude that Helen and I have this opportunity to do healing work for you. We hope this brings you much peace and tranquility.

WE WERE BOTH SO YOUNG

November 19, 2018

It was 6:00 p.m. on a Monday, and I had just wrapped up a successful day of therapy at my office. I walked over to my desk so I could gather my things and head home. I opened my laptop and refreshed my browser one last time. And that's when I saw the email from Diane.

At first, I told myself to wait until I got home to read it. But I couldn't wait any longer. I had been anxiously awaiting this moment for the past two days. I opened the email and began scanning Diane's words. I clicked the attachment without thinking twice. My eyes grew wide as the breath left my body. I forced myself to read the entire transcript, but as I neared the end, I began to hyperventilate.

I stood up and began pacing around my office.

"Mary Frances? Who the – what the fuck? Wait – I was eleven when this happened?"

I couldn't contain my shock. I was convinced the possession took place around the time of my estrangement, right when the plagues began. Apparently, I was wrong. Very wrong. In actuality, I had been walking around possessed for over twenty-five years. How could this be possible? *How?*

I paced back and forth in my office. My hands shook as I continued to speak aloud:

"Mary Frances was a child? Wait. I think I'm going to throw up."

I bolted over to the teal garbage can next to my sofa. I hovered over the bin for a second, as I closed my eyes and reluctantly parsed open my mouth.

Nothing.

"Ok … maybe I won't say her name."

Slowly, I lifted myself upright. I made my way back to the center of the room, walking between the couch and my desk as I rubbed my clammy palms together. I took a sip of water from a cup on my desk.

"She was twelve. I was eleven."

I continued to repeat myself.

"She was twelve and I was eleven. We were both so young."

I froze and keeled over again – this time, resting one hand on my back and the other on a cream-colored accent chair. I took a deep breath.

"That was such a horrible time in my life. So many bad things started happening to me. I can't think about it. I don't want to say it."

I felt my chest rip open.

"I had to grow up way too fast. My parents should have protected me. They should have known. But no one did anything. No one cared."

Tears streamed down my cheeks.

"And she was just a child when she died. I don't even know if I am crying for me or crying for her."

Suddenly, my brain came back online. *Wait, what the fuck, Lauren? You got possessed. Exorcist-style. Don't make her into anything else. Don't even try to make her human.*

I dried my eyes as the confusion began to set in.

"But she didn't seem so evil. She didn't seem like a demon at all. She was just a little girl. What the fuck am I supposed to do with that?"

My mind went blank again. There was no blueprint for something like this. I had no frame of reference. I didn't know anyone who had gone through a real-life possession. In that moment, I felt confused and alone.

"She seemed like an orphan just looking for a family. She lost her whole family, that's what she told Diane. I was so alone at that age too. I didn't feel like I had a family either."

I stood upright, still grasping my cream-colored chair.

"Oh my God. She was an orphan. Maybe that's why she got so mad at me for leaving my family. All she wanted was to have a family, and I robbed her of that. I bet that's why she caused the four plagues. Wait, didn't she admit to that?"

I scrambled as I raced back over to the computer. I scanned

the transcript until I found this line:

Mary Frances: Things were ok for a long time ... she took my guidance ... but then she wanted to strive on her own ... to be more independent ... she wanted to go in a direction I did not think was good. So, I created things in her environment that caused her stress.

I gasped as I thrust my hands onto my head.

"She punished me for leaving my family! That really happened! But it's not what I thought. I thought I was being punished by one of my ancestors. I was convinced that black magic was coming from inside my own family, but it wasn't. It came from some random orphan girl ... Inside of me."

I felt the empathy drain out of my body. My cheeks grew hot.

"Oh my God. She caused the plagues. She just said she did it. She said she created stress in my environment."

I backed away from the computer.

"Fuck this. Seriously, how could she do this to me? She ruined my life for the past few months. I lost my home and all my belongings. For what?"

I ran over to the couch and grabbed a pillow. I began throwing it against the wall as I screamed at the top of my lungs. I didn't care if anyone heard me. I couldn't contain my rage. I grabbed another pillow and punched it until my lungs ached and my arms grew weary. I threw the pillow onto the floor as I let out an audible sigh.

Slowly, I slid down the edge of the couch until my back was resting firmly against its base and I was seated on the floor. I drew my legs into my chest and buried my head. I stayed there for another minute, waiting for my thoughts to catch up to the rest of me.

"Didn't she say something else that stood out? I think she called me a bunch of names ... names I wouldn't have called myself."

I rose to my feet entirely too fast. I began to see stars. I placed one hand on the couch and the other on my pounding forehead. I walked back over to my computer and sat down at my desk. I took a deep breath and scanned the transcript once again:

Mary Frances: She would be more cautious, and I would insert, "You are nothing, you are invisible, you're not important." I created stress in her body, discomfort, and pain, especially at her stomach area.

I froze.

"She said I was not important. She said I was invisible. I think she called me those names when I was suicidal. I knew something about that situation felt off. I wouldn't have used those words to describe myself. I wonder if she told me to slit my wrists, because frankly, that wasn't even on my mind. I remember feeling extremely low that day. But I didn't think I was invisible. Even that day, I knew people cared about me who would be sad if I was gone."

I burst into tears.

"I can't believe this is happening right now. Wait – she said she caused pain to my stomach area? I had the worst stomachache that day."

The breath left my body. I sat in silence as my hands went numb in my lap.

I think she tried to get me to kill myself.

I stared straight ahead, listless.

That means I didn't try to kill myself.

A wave of relief washed over my body.

Wait – someone tried to kill me.

My lungs became dense and heavy. My eyes glazed over.

My brain came back online again.

Wait, is this even real? This is almost too convenient to be true. How could one transcript seriously answer everything? Maybe this whole thing is bullshit.

I stood up as I closed my computer. It was getting late, and

I had stayed in my office for a full hour trying unsuccessfully to make sense of this situation. I decided to go home. I grabbed my coat and my messenger bag as I headed toward the door.

Then I stopped cold.

Mary Frances. I think I've heard that name before.

I lingered by the entrance to my waiting room, sieving through my Rolodex of memories until I found it:

It was eleven years ago, and I was twenty-five years old. I had just moved back to Chicago. It was late at night, and I had just finished watching a documentary about the supernatural world. I brushed my teeth and climbed into bed. Right as I was about to go to sleep, I decided to try a little experiment. I said: "Is anybody here? If someone is here, you can come visit me."

I awoke a few hours later as my bedroom grew colder by the second. My body began to shake violently as my entire torso was lifted into the air. It rose and fell against the bed. And then, I saw a figure emerge directly in front of my face. She was a young girl with long, straight, brown hair that reached her ribcage. She was dressed in a white nightgown with a delicate, blue ribbon in the center. The nightgown hung down to her knees with a small frill at the bottom. She looked like she was from another time.

She said her name was Mary.

DANCES WITH WOLVES

Twenty minutes later, I walked into my apartment in Heaven on Sheridan. Somehow, I had managed to get myself home. I closed the door behind me and fell to the ground bawling. It was all hitting me. I had been possessed at the age of eleven. I had *met* that spirit before. She took responsibility for the plagues. She took responsibility for the dark thoughts I had about myself. She took responsibility for everything.

I had spent the past hour pacing around my office, trying to make sense of that transcript. But I continued to feel scatterbrained during my entire commute home. Clearly, I wasn't done analyzing this situation. I needed to know *when* Mary Frances joined me. And *how*.

I walked into my living room and settled onto the floor. I sat cross-legged as I lit a candle. I stared into the flame for a moment, trying to decide how to best retrieve this information.

My heart told me to call the Archangel Michael. After all, he had helped Diane during the depossession, so perhaps he could tell me more about what he had seen. I closed my eyes and fanned the candle's flame as I drew my fingertips toward my eyelids. This was the customary way to pray in Judaism. I figured that it was best to stick to what I knew as I ventured even deeper into more unknown spiritual territories.

Slowly, I began to speak:

"I call upon the Archangel Michael to join me. Hello, it's me, Lauren. Thank you for showing up to my depossession. Thank you for encouraging Mary Frances to leave my body. I am so grateful for all you have done. I just have one more question. I want to know when Mary Frances joined me. That wasn't a part of the transcript, and I really need to know. Please show me the moment it happened. Don't be afraid to reveal the whole truth. I need to see it with my own eyes. Thank you."

I remained seated on the floor as I waited.

All of a sudden, the Archangel Michael appeared in my mind's eye. His blue and white robe fluttered in the wind as he held his sword in one hand and a large shield in the other. He stretched out a hand, and I grabbed it. We began to tumble through a black spiral until a portal opened at the bottom. The Archangel Michael led me through the portal, calmly. We arrived in the living room of my childhood home just as the black hole closed behind us.

1993

My parents and I were seated in the living room of our house in suburban Chicago. I sat in the center of the large, wraparound blue couch. I playfully tugged at one of my tight, dark brown curls. My mother sat on one side of the couch as my father settled into his favorite black leather reclining chair, which once belonged to his father. There were at least four feet of space between each of us. I watched as my father pulled the lever on the side of his chair, kicking his feet onto the footrest. He placed his hands behind his head and smiled.

My mother jumped to her feet and walked over to the VCR. She began to remove a VHS tape from a blue and yellow Blockbuster container. She sighed as she placed the video into the VCR to rewind it. She was clearly irritated that the last patron didn't do us that courtesy.

My parents had rented *Dances with Wolves.* The movie was rated PG-13. I was eleven – still a few years away from being old enough to watch it – but I begged my parents to let me stay. They glanced at each other, ultimately deciding that I could join them.

I beamed with pride as I adjusted my posture. I sat completely upright, hoping to mimic someone older. *Is this how thirteen-year-olds sit?* I clasped my hands in my lap as I rolled my shoulders back. I felt very impressed with myself.

Partially through the movie, my body began to grow tense. *I think this is a romantic part.* My eyes expanded as the breath left my chest. *I hope it's over fast.* I stayed completely silent as I tried to blend into the background. I watched my mother as she watched Kevin Costner climb into his lover's teepee. I winced as Kevin Costner began to caress his lover's face. My brow furled. *Wait, she likes that?* I began to squirm in my seat. Kevin Costner and his lover began to undress each other. Slowly. With intention. With care.

Without warning, I bolted out of the living room. Tears

began to well up in my eyes. I ran up the stairs and into my bedroom. I shut the door and climbed under my bed. I was shaking. I curled myself tightly into a ball as I began to cry. I kept repeating, "No, no, no, no."

A few minutes later, there was a knock at the door. Both parents had arrived. I heard my father's voice: "Hi sweetie, can we come in?"

I cowered under the bed. My father spoke again. "Lauren, can we please come in?"

I peeked my head out as I quietly said, "Ok." I watched as the door cracked open, revealing a sliver of light from the hallway. I glanced at the tops of my parents' feet as they entered my bedroom. My father bent down as he locked eyes with me. Neither of us said a word.

Then I heard my mother's voice: stern and firm. She requested that I come out and sit on the bed. I didn't want to leave my hiding place. I retreated further under the bed, lying face down on my belly. I pressed my cheek against the pale, pink carpet and stayed there. My mother called out to me, again. I began to sense the impatience in her voice. *Ugh, I don't think they are going to leave.* I reluctantly slid my body out from under the bed. I rubbed my eyes as they adjusted to the light.

Slowly, I sat at the edge of my bed with my hands clasped together and gazed down at my feet. My parents flanked me on either side, sitting entirely too close to me. I was still shaking. Neither one of my parents looked at me. We sat in silence for another moment as we all stared down at our toes.

My mother broke the silence by launching into a speech about sex. She told me that sex is what happens when two people love each other and they are already married. I frowned. *Um, Kevin Costner is not married to that lady.* My father quickly cut off my mother, as he urged her to try again. My mother took a moment to regroup herself. Then she said that sex is what happens when two people love each other. I hunched my back and folded my arms. *Well, that isn't true either.*

Suddenly, I was catapulted back to my apartment at

Heaven on Sheridan. I opened my eyes and backed away from the candle. I looked around the room, trying to reorient myself. A part of me wanted to be done. This memory was entirely too painful. But a part of me knew that I still hadn't received my answer. My voice shook as I asked the Archangel Michael to show me the exact moment when Mary Frances joined me.

I closed my eyes once more. The Archangel Michael appeared before me once again. He took my hand as we fell back into a deep spiral. We arrived at the scene we just left. He told me to keep watching.

I saw myself sitting on my bed, while my parents flanked me on either side. The Archangel Michael asked me to step into my eleven-year-old self so I could hear her.

So I did:

My parents are way too close. I wish I could run away again.

HE looks at me the way that guy just looked at the lady in the teepee. But HE is so old. Not like that guy in the movie. It's so gross. We're family. Well, sort of family. I want holidays to be just us, but they're not. Why does HE always have to be around?

But why did that lady like it? I guess some people like it. Well, I don't. Maybe I should try harder next time. Ew, Lauren. That's super gross. Ok, ok, I take it back.

Why is Mom talking to me like I don't know about this stuff? I wish she would stop saying the word, sex. It's bad. She looks like she doesn't want to be here right now. That's fine. I just want to play with my Kirsten doll. I like her braids. I want to do my hair like that someday.

Wait, someone else just got here. There's a girl standing next to Mom. I don't know if Mom and Dad can see her, but I can. I want to know who this girl is. She seems nice, like she's around my age. She's smiling at me.

She just started talking. She says I shouldn't talk to her yet. She wants me to pretend I'm still listening to my parents, even though I'm not. She says her name is Mary. She wants to be my new friend. I think she can see how sad I am right now. She wants to help.

She says I just need to let her in.

THAT FATEFUL NIGHT

November 2018

I opened my eyes and stared at the dimly lit candle. I had no conception of how much time had passed since the Archangel Michael took me back in time. I glanced out the window, desperately trying to reorient myself. It was pitch black outside. The sun was just beginning to set when I first asked the Archangel Michael to show me the scene of my own possession.

I rose to my feet and made my way into the kitchen. I glanced at the clock and realized it was almost 9:00 p.m. I opened the fridge and whipped together a pathetic salad. I wasn't even hungry. I sighed as I poured a bag of wilted romaine lettuce into a large purple bowl. I grabbed a handful of baby carrots and a few cherry tomatoes and threw them in, attempting to liven up my meal. I stared at my dinner and shook my head. *Whatever, just eat it.* I leaned my elbows against the black granite countertop as I shoved a forkful of lettuce drenched in ranch dressing into my mouth. My mind continued to wander uncontrollably.

* * *

I could count on one hand the number of times I let myself recall the *Dances with Wolves* story. And I had never seen that memory in as much detail as I did with the Archangel Michael. When it first happened, it was far too much for my little brain to comprehend. So I shoved that night into the depths of my subconscious, hoping never to face it again.

But the memory came regurgitating back up a few years ago. The first (and only) time I ever told someone the *Dances with Wolves* story, I was in therapy. Marilyn asked me when I first realized that I had been a victim of incest. Truthfully, it had taken me decades to even call it that. I kept insisting that what *HE* did to me didn't qualify as incest. But every therapist I saw from my early twenties to the present day pushed me to see that it did. And as I sat on Marilyn's dark leather couch, all I saw was Kevin Costner delicately undressing his lover as I ran out of my own living room.

* * *

I threw down my fork, splattering ranch dressing across the counter. Tears began to well up in the corners of my eyes. I walked into my living room and resumed the position of sitting cross-legged on the floor, in front of the candle's deep orange flame. *Dinner would have to wait.* I buried my head in my hands as I began to weep.

That fateful night when I was eleven was so much worse than I initially thought. I cried into my lap as I let myself break open. *Dances with Wolves* was the first consensual sex scene I had ever watched. And it flabbergasted me. It was overwhelming. Overpowering. It was the moment I first realized that *HE* was sexually abusing me. Until that point, I told myself that no one liked *that kind of thing.* But the moment I watched Kevin Costner make love to his costar, I could no longer hide beneath that lie. So I hid under my bed instead. Something very bad was happening to me. And that was the first time I knew it in my bones.

But apparently, there was even more to that fateful night. It was also the scene of my possession. I had no idea that Mary Frances joined me right as I sat on my bed, flanked by my parents on either side. My brain tried to push this knowledge away. Once again, all these answers seemed a little *too* convenient. Before logic could take over, I felt my chest rip open. *I know what I saw.*

But why would Mary Frances join me in that moment? I thought hard as I stared back into the candle's flame. In an instant, I knew. When I ran out of the movie and hid under my bed, I thought about telling my parents *why* I left the living room. I just needed them to ask me if something was wrong. If they had asked, I might have told them.

But that's not what happened. My parents sat on my bed

as they delivered a generic message about sex without ever asking me a single question. They didn't ask me why I ran out of the room. They didn't ask me why I was hiding under my bed, shaking. And they certainly didn't ask me if something was wrong.

In fact, they didn't talk *to* me, they talked *at* me. It felt like they were checking off a page from a parenting book. Discuss sex with your child: check. There was just one problem: I already knew way too much about sex. Because of what *HE* did.

Since no one was planning on asking me anything that night, I began to disappear. And that's the moment when Mary Frances appeared. Unlike my parents, she saw me. She knew that I was lonely. She knew that I was sad. She was the only person in that room who said she wanted to help me. And it felt so good to be seen.

So I let her in.

SAY THAT TEN TIMES FAST

It's time to talk about who *HE* is.

Ever since I completed the genogram of my own family back in 2008 during graduate school, *HE* became known as the Black Square. When I drew that pair of red, jagged lines between my black circle (code of cisgender female) and the Black Square (code for cisgender male), I knew there was no turning back. I had used the code for sexual abuse to define our relationship.

Frankly, I'm surprised *HE* even made it onto the genogram. The Black Square was not technically related to me by blood. He was my mother's brother's wife's cousin's husband. Say that ten times fast. Somehow, the Black Square was always around. Our families lived within a half hour of each other on the north shore of Chicago, so we spent most major holidays together. I can't think about the Jewish holidays without thinking about him.

I hate that.

The Black Square had always creeped me out. I felt that he was rude and overly boisterous. I watched him make inappropriate sexual comments at the dinner table. Nothing and no one were off limits. He did it in the middle of Rosh Hashanah. And Thanksgiving. And Passover, which he frequently held at his house.

One time, he made an outrageous comment about a relative's breasts while she was seated right next to him at my parents' house. She stormed out of the house and vowed never to be around him again. After she left, I watched a few of my family members rip *her* to shreds. My parents didn't partake in the roast, but they sure didn't stop it either. Instead, my parents continued to sit at either end of their dining room table as they allowed this charade to unfold.

The Black Square was also one of the most religious members of our family. The moral injury of being sexually abused by someone who claimed to be pious forced me into a very complicated relationship with my own religion for decades. As a child, I sat in temple during Yom Kippur and watched as all the adults around me began reciting the *Al-Chet* (the Jewish prayer for forgiveness)[4]. The older I got, the more this holiday filled me with rage. It became very hard for me to exist in a family that seemed to be full of hypocrites. Year after year, I watched my family sit in temple as they prayed *to someone* for forgiveness. And year after year, I sat there wondering if anyone would ever apologize for all the terrible things that were happening to me.

Everything got worse by the time I entered high school. Developmentally, this was the age when my peers began to experiment with sex. But I felt like I was a salmon swimming upstream. I had been oversexualized by the Black Square for most of my childhood, and I was desperate for a break. So when boys my age began to take an interest in me, I avoided all contact with them. I couldn't handle the thought of someone else touching me.

By sixteen, I was already done with all the unwanted sexual attention. At first, I tried simply rejecting this attention, but a few of the boys became threatening and coercive. *I couldn't handle any more abuse.* I felt like I was dodging bullets from every angle. So I invented an imaginary boyfriend and ran with it. My pretend boyfriend remained dutifully committed to me for the entire junior year. He went to a different school. He was my age. He was kind and attractive. He was gentle and sweet. He was everything I yearned for in a boyfriend and was afraid I might never receive.

Parading around with my faux boyfriend worked for a while. The guys at school largely left me alone. But in my senior year, a friend caught me in one of my lies. And the shame seeped into my body like molten lava. Soon the people I cared about began to distrust me. I had lied to just about everyone so I could maintain the validity of my story. That broke me. It was awful to mislead my own friends. I was becoming the exact opposite of the person I wanted to be. On top of that, the very thing that began as protection became my inherent downfall. So I had no choice but to break up with my imaginary boyfriend.

I had been desperately afraid to be single, and for good reason. Without the shield of a faux boyfriend, I felt like I had no choice but to begin dating. Most encounters with guys my age quickly morphed into reenactments of my childhood trauma. I was terrified to be naked. I was terrified to be touched. Moments that were supposed to be full of curiosity and experimentation left me flooded and split off from my own body.

And that wasn't all. The Black Square set the standard for all my romantic relationships since he was all I knew. As result, I was raped by multiple partners. I was stalked, threatened, and emotionally abused. I had no idea how to exist in my own skin. I developed an eating disorder to survive one of these abusive relationships. Every time he belittled me, I starved myself. I lost so much weight that I didn't menstruate for months. I remember standing in a dressing room at Old Navy as I tried on a mini jean skirt. I pulled the skirt up to my waist and zipped it closed. The skirt immediately fell to the ground. It was a size zero. I cried.

Clearly I was caught in an endless web of sexual abuse, anorexia, and emotional abuse. I needed to find a way out. During my sophomore year of college at the University of Michigan, I went on a sabbatical from dating. Slowly, I began to eat again. My period returned. I banned my friends from talking to me about boys so that I could finally have the break I had been yearning for since high school. And it was pure bliss. I felt liberated. I felt free. I felt safe for the first time in my entire life.

There was just one problem: The Black Square was always waiting for me at home.

After college, I moved to Washington, DC. And I went home less and less often. I began to heal by staying away from my family. During that time, I even entered my first healthy long-term romantic relationship. But that proved to be deeply challenging. It took me an entire year to have sex with my boyfriend. He was in therapy. I was in therapy. We practiced exercises designed to help me stay present in my own body. It was a long and arduous road, but we got there. Together.

Every time I think about what he did for me, I get extremely emotional. He was the first person who resembled the faux boyfriend I had invented in high school. He was patient. He was kind. He was committed. Apparently, I knew exactly what kind of partner I wanted, even back then. It took me almost a decade before I met him.

Despite how great my life had become, memories of the Black Square haunted me throughout my time in Washington, DC. I was constantly plagued by flashbacks and nightmares from the abuse, even as I shared a bed with my kind, compassionate boyfriend. And while I had come extremely far in my healing journey, I knew there was only one thing left to do. I had to go back home.

In 2008, I moved back to Chicago for good. And I was immediately forced to be around the Black Square repeatedly for the first time since high school. He wasted no time. A month after I moved back to the city, the Black Square did it again. And again. And by Passover, he was giving me unwanted backrubs and licking his lips from across the table. That was the night I changed into a hot pink tank top with white stars and was almost raped all over again.

There was just one problem: I was different now. I had experienced a healthy relationship. I had been to therapy. I had spent seven years living away from my family, and that had given me a ton of perspective. Even though the Black Square wasn't done with me, I was done with him. So when I drew sexual abuse lines on my genogram and turned that assignment in to my professor, I knew there was no turning back.

NOW OR NEVER

Spring 2008

It had been two days since my fight with my grandmother, Coco. It had been two days since we sat across from each other in silence at our little French bistro, while neither of us were able to finish our chocolate ice cream with chocolate sauce. I sat in my apartment and thought about our one and only argument, still haunted by Coco's words. She was adamantly against my decision to tell my parents about the Black Square. Coco was thoroughly convinced that my father wouldn't defend me if I came forward. I still disagreed with her. And even though she knew her son, I also knew my father. I knew that if he heard what the Black Square had done to his one and only daughter, he would be completely outraged. And besides, after that night at the house party, I couldn't afford to keep this secret in the vault any longer. It had to come out.

I was still thinking about my fight with Coco when I received a text from my parents, inviting me over for dinner that evening. I decided this was my chance to tell them about the Black Square. I promptly accepted their invitation for an early Sunday night dinner and jumped in the shower.

A short while later, I left my apartment in the city and drove thirty minutes to my childhood home, where my parents still lived. As soon as I walked into the foyer, I smelled the aroma of fresh salmon and grilled asparagus. I made my way into the kitchen as I announced my arrival. My mother greeted me with a polite hug as my father waved from beyond the refrigerator.

Soon after, we sat down to dinner and began a lively discussion about politics. For many families, politics can be taboo and divisive. For us, this would be the easiest part of the evening. I thought about the way that dinner with my parents began just like dinner with Coco. We talked about current events and caught up in a surface-level way. But dinner with my parents never ended like dinner with Coco. When the plates were cleared, that was it. There was no chocolate ice cream with chocolate sauce. There was no *dish it.* I tolerated light conversation with Coco because I knew that at some point, she would ask me what was really going on. She made me feel seen. She could always tell when something was wrong. And even on the night when we had our first fight, there was real love between us. I knew that she confronted me because she cared.

I excused myself after dinner, and I went upstairs to the bathroom that I had shared with my brother when we were children. I stared at myself in the mirror as I said: *It's now or never.* I returned to the kitchen and sat back down at the table, facing both of my parents. My father continued to make small talk, and I smiled awkwardly. I looked under the table and realized that my palms were beginning to sweat. As soon as I pressed them together, both of my arms began to quiver. My parents both looked at me, confused. My father stopped talking.

Suddenly, the words began to pour out of my mouth:

"There's something that has been going on in this family since I was a young child, and it is still going on. It started happening when we would go over to his house for the Jewish holidays. But it has also happened in our house. He did so many disgusting things over the years, there are almost too many to count. I have no idea how young I was when it all started. It was definitely going on by the time I was eleven. He noticed when I wore a training bra for the first time. He's actually the first person who ever looked at me in a sexual way. That has affected all my romantic relationships. I hate that it's something I have to live with forever."

I shifted in my seat.

"I know you think he's just rude and harmless, but I'm telling you that it's a lot worse than that. When I went away to college and then to DC, I didn't have to deal with it as much since I wasn't around for the holidays. I was really hoping that when I moved back here, he would stop. But he did it again.

When we were all at his house this year for Passover, he licked his lips when he looked at me from across the table. Maybe you saw that, I don't really know. Oh, and this year, at Rosh Hashanah, I was standing next to him in the front hall of this house. I had only been back here for a month. He asked me what I was doing in Chicago, and I told him that I was in school to become a therapist. Then he interrupted me and said that he had stopped listening because he was too busy picturing me naked."

I finished my monologue and stared straight ahead. I deliberately avoided making eye contact with my parents. Out of my periphery, I watched my father sink into his chair, listless. He remained completely silent. He looked like a defeated little boy. I stared straight into my mother's sharp, blue eyes. The silence between the three of us was deafening. One of my parents needed to say something, and fast.

My mother stood up and placed both palms on the table as she leaned toward me. She tapped a finger as her gold wedding ring clanged against the lightly colored wood. My mother sighed as she exclaimed that she didn't know what she was supposed to do with this information. She didn't understand why I was bringing this up now. Then she told me that I needed to find a way to exist alongside the Black Square, just as I had done for all these years.

I rose to my feet and walked out of the house.

SALEM IS HAUNTED

November 2018

The week after my depossession, Diane offered to be available by phone in case I had any lingering questions. Despite the many hours that I spent pacing around my office, I still had questions. *Lots of them.* And I was reeling from the vision the Archangel Michael had shown me, revealing the night of my possession. I needed to talk to Diane about all of it.

I also needed someone else to confirm that all of this was real. My mind was beginning to question everything. I tried my best to crack a door open for the possibility that my possession had taken place the same night I ran out of *Dances with Wolves.* But it was becoming increasingly more difficult to quiet my rational brain.

I started pacing in my living room. The voice of my rational brain launched itself into the role of devil's advocate:

Maybe I wanted to see the Archangel Michael so badly that I conjured him up in my mind. There's nothing wrong with that. When someone wants something to be true, the brain can find a way to make it true. That's the root of confirmation bias. But that can be a dangerous place to live. I don't want to live there.

The voice of my rational brain resembled the kind of lawyer I certainly didn't want to go up against. But once it quieted down and I was alone with myself, another part of me began to emerge. A part of me that knew what I had seen. Despite my brain's best efforts, my intuition stayed in an unshakable place. And in that moment, I became even more terrified.

I walked over to my computer and emailed Diane. I told her I wanted to talk as soon as possible. Diane wrote me back immediately, and we scheduled a phone call for the following afternoon. As I placed the event on my Google calendar, I glanced at the date: Wednesday, November 21. I realized that I was set to process the results of my depossession the day before Thanksgiving. *Well, that seems fitting.*

* * *

The next afternoon, Diane called promptly at the time we had arranged. I was still at my office, but I had finished seeing clients for the day. It felt good to hear Diane confirm that the depossession had worked. I expressed my unrelenting gratitude to her and Helen for rescuing me from everything Mary Frances had done.

Diane asked me how things were going in my apartment, and I told her that the plagues had magically cleared up. The floorboards no longer creaked in the middle of the night. The bed bug patrol had come back for another round of fumigation, and they found no sign of bed bugs. The string of black smoke that had tried to strangle me in my sleep was no longer a problem. Everything seemed to vanish on the day of the depossession.

Diane was not surprised. She asked me if I had any follow-up questions, and I blurted them all out at once:

"How did this happen? When did Mary Frances join me? How common is this shit? Could it happen again?"

Diane did her best to answer all my questions. She told me that the possession happened when I was eleven years old. She said that she didn't know the exact moment when the spirit joined me. Then she told me that Mary Frances seemed to be hanging around my mother.

I gasped. "Oh my God, Diane. I tried something the other night where I asked the Archangel Michael to show me the moment the possession happened. He took me to a scene from when I was eleven, and I was sitting on my bed with my parents on either side … It was a very traumatic memory, and one that I pushed down for ages. In the vision, I saw Mary Frances standing next to my mother. I can't believe you just said that."

Diane quickly clarified. "Sometimes we find spirits hanging around certain people. I don't want you to read too much into that, Lauren. We don't always know the backstory, and sometimes, there isn't one. The fact that Mary Frances was standing next to your mother might not mean anything at all."

But I couldn't let it go. "I need to know more, Diane. I need to know why she would be hanging around my mother. There has always been something loaded about my relationship with my mother. I have always focused on that relationship more than any other relationship in my life. I understand that there may not be a connection. But if there is one, I need to know."

Diane asked where my mother was from. I told her that she was a from a small town, right on the ocean, about fifteen minutes from Salem, Massachusetts. She let out a long sigh. And then she said: "Well, Salem is haunted."

The breath left my body as my phone began to shake in my palm. My mouth was agape.

Then I found words: "Good God. How could I not realize that? Of course, Salem is haunted. I remember going to the Salem Witch Museum with my family when I was a child. It was terrifying. And there was always something strange about the house my mother grew up in. Grandma Bess never left that house. Every time we visited her, we stayed there. There were parts of that house that I avoided because they creeped me out so much. I think a lot of bad things happened there. My mother refused to talk about the way she grew up, but I could feel it. Even as a child."

Tears began to well up in my eyes.

Diane said, "It's very possible that your mother grew up in a house that was haunted. Spirits sometimes travel with a person, but not always. I still don't think we know for sure if that's how Mary Frances got to you. What about the house you were raised in?"

I took a moment to compose myself. "Well, our house was over a hundred years old; I know that much. We moved into our house when I was in kindergarten. One time, I was exploring the attic, and I found a string of pearls hidden in the back of a trap door. As soon as I picked up the necklace, I heard a woman shout, 'Put that back!' I looked around, but I didn't see anyone. I avoided the attic after that."

I could feel Diane nodding on the phone. She told me that between my mother's house and the house I had been raised in, there were multiple opportunities for me to encounter a spirit like Mary Frances. I couldn't tell if this made me feel better or worse. I cleared my throat as I changed the subject. "Ok, now I need to know why Mary Frances made my life hell as soon as I estranged myself."

Diane took a moment before responding. "Mary Frances told us that you took her guidance for a long time, but that you went in a direction that she didn't want you to go in. That's not surprising because spirits like to be the ones in charge. Perhaps your decision to leave your family came from a place Mary Frances couldn't influence."

My eyes grew wide. "Yes, Diane. When I woke up on Mother's Day and decided to estrange myself, I felt alive in a whole new way. It felt like I made that decision from an empowered place, maybe for the first real time."

I could feel Diane smiling on the phone. "The other possibility," she continued, "is that since Mary Frances was an orphan, it's likely that she didn't want to remain in the body of another orphan. She was very distraught when we found her. She had lost sight of her own family in the afterlife. It's possible that she wanted to join you in part because you were a little girl who had a family."

A chill ran down my spine. "So when I estranged myself, I orphaned Mary Frances for the second time – " I couldn't finish my own thought. A wave of nausea rippled through the back of my throat. I stared at my teal garbage can as I promptly changed the subject: "Diane, I also want to tell you that I think I saw Mary Frances once before. It happened about a decade ago when I was twenty-six. I had just watched a documentary about spirits, and I got curious. I asked if there was anyone who wanted to visit me. And then, I felt someone shaking my entire body, *Exorcist*-style. I saw a young girl appear before me. She had long, brown hair, and she was wearing a white nightgown with a blue bow in the center. The nightgown had ruffles on the edges. Her outfit was very old-fashioned. She told me that her name was Mary."

Diane wasted no time before she responded. "Yes, Lauren. That's the same girl we saw in our session. This is why I love doing this work. That's an incredible story."

I laughed. "Well, I'm glad one of us thinks that's an incredible story because I'm scared shitless right now."

Diane encouraged me to let this sink in.

I changed the subject again. "How common are possessions? Could this happen to me again? I have been walking around downtown Chicago afraid to make eye contact with just about everyone. I don't want to accidentally catch another spirit."

Diane paused. Then she said: "Spiritual possessions are a lot more common than people realize, but that doesn't mean they happen easily. It's not like catching the flu, Lauren. For someone to get possessed, they must experience a tremendous amount of soul loss first. And in your case, you must have experienced a lot of soul loss before the age of eleven. It's also possible that you experienced past-life trauma."

I tilted my head. "What do you mean by soul loss?"

Diane responded quickly. "Soul loss is exactly what it sounds like. When we experience trauma, parts of our soul sometimes sever off and leave our bodies. Especially if the trauma is incredibly severe. We can only handle so much, you know."

I sat up straight. "Oh, I think I understand that from a therapeutic perspective. When people experience chronic trauma, they can undergo a split where they sever parts of their consciousness off so they can continue to survive. This is especially common in complex trauma survivors when someone is continually exposed to their abuser with no way out. Is that what you're talking about?"

I waited for Diane's response like I had just answered a *Jeopardy* question.

"Yes, Lauren. That's exactly what I'm talking about. Splitting is another way to describe soul loss. It's rooted in the same concept."

I glanced down at my knees, which were beginning to shake. I wondered what had happened to my soul during all those years when I couldn't escape from the Black Square. When I was forced to sit at his dinner table during Passover, year after year. When he walked through the hallways of my house on Rosh Hashanah, looking for me. Deep down, I already knew.

I changed the subject once again. "You said something about past-life trauma? What the fuck is that?"

Diane laughed. "Past-life trauma is the result of unfinished business that follows us from a previous lifetime – "

I interrupted her. "Well … I'm not sure I believe in all that stuff."

Diane continued, unfazed by my reluctance. "I would suggest looking into past-life work, Lauren. It's very possible that you experienced a tremendous amount of soul loss in this lifetime before the age of eleven. But in order for a spirit like Mary Frances to take up residence in your body, a lot of space is required. It is possible that you came into this world with a part of your soul already missing. And then, you lost even more of your soul through childhood trauma. If I were you, I would remain open to that possibility."

I nodded, somewhat reluctantly.

Diane spoke again. "I have to go in a moment, Lauren. But I want to make sure I tell you one last thing. You may experience a lot of fatigue in your body now that the depossession is complete. After all, Mary Frances had been living inside of you for over twenty-five years. We just removed an entity that was taking up a lot of space. Think of it like soul surgery. Be very gentle with yourself in the coming days."

I promised Diane that I would take it easy over the Thanksgiving holiday. It's not like I had any plans. Over the past decade, I had spent so many holidays alone. This wouldn't be my first Thanksgiving watching *The Real Housewives* while I ate a can of soup.

THANKSGIVING AND A CAN OF SOUP

As soon as I got off the phone with Diane, I left my office, desperate for a change of scenery. I was running late to meet Danny at a bar in Andersonville on my way home. We had known each other for a very long time. Danny was in town from Michigan, and I really wanted to see him. I made my way down to the lobby of my office building and ordered a Lyft. My head began to pound as I swayed back and forth. I placed my hand on the cool, stone wall inside the lobby of my office building, trying to steady myself. *What the hell is happening to me?*

I ignored the signs from my body as I texted Danny to let him know that I was on my way to meet him at the bar. I also texted Heather: *CALL ME.* My thoughts began to race as slivers of my conversation with Diane slid back into my mind. She had seen Mary Frances standing next to my mother, just as the Archangel Michael had shown me in that vision. Diane's confirmation was enough to quiet my rational brain. At least for now.

I made my way outside as I waited for the Lyft to arrive. The weather was beginning to turn colder in Chicago. I smelled the cool, crisp air as I wondered if it might snow. I fastened the belt tightly around my burnt orange peacoat, trying to stop myself from shivering in place. The bright lights of the city block blurred together until they formed one massive ray of light. I shook my head. I was beginning to feel a little strange. I had scarfed down a small salad for lunch in between therapy sessions. Perhaps that hadn't been enough. I stared down at my phone and opened the Lyft app. My ride was quickly approaching. I glanced up as I waved to the driver. He pulled in front of my building as I climbed inside his sedan. It felt so good to sit down.

Suddenly, my phone rang. It was Heather. I picked up the call and immediately blurted out that I had just debriefed with Diane. Heather gasped and begged me for details. I didn't want to say too much. There was no way I was about to talk about a spiritual possession in front of my Lyft driver. I told

Heather that I couldn't get into it now, but that I would tell her everything later. She could sense that I was slightly out of sorts. Heather asked me what my plans were for the rest of the evening. I told her that I was on my way to Andersonville to meet Danny for a drink. Heather urged me to reconsider. She told me that I needed to go home and take care of myself. She reassured me that Danny would understand. I knew she was right. And besides, my head was really beginning to pound. I canceled on Danny and gave the Lyft driver my home address. I looked out the window as the Lyft driver spun the car around.

Shortly thereafter, I walked through the front door of Heaven on Sheridan. I made my way up to my apartment and shut the door behind me. The room began to spin as I collapsed onto the ground. *I'll stay here for just a moment.* I curled my body into a ball on the light wood floor. The wooden plank felt cool and comforting against the heat emanating from my right cheek.

I wrapped my peacoat tightly around my body as I continued to lie on the floor. I pulled my legs closer to my chest, trying desperately to swaddle myself. I could tell that I was moments away from falling asleep. It was still so early in the evening; I had no idea why I was so tired. But this was a type of an exhaustion I had never experienced before. Even my bones were tired.

I buried my head deeper into the panels of my coat. It began to grow darker and darker inside of my apartment. I remained on the floor, thoroughly immobilized. At some point, I reached for the light switch directly above my head. I could barely lift my arm. I felt like I had just finished an intense session of weightlifting. All of a sudden, my entire body began to ache. *Oh no, I think this is what Diane warned me about.* I think I had soul surgery.

I peeled myself off the floor and turned on all the lights. It took all my energy to change out of my work clothes and into sweatpants. I was moving at a glacial pace. I glanced at my phone. My head pounded as I squinted my eyes. Danny had texted back. He wanted to know if he could come over on his way home. He said he really wanted to see me. *That's sweet.* As I considered letting Danny come over, I began to see stars. I leaned against the wall as I sighed audibly. Then, I told him it was best if he just went home. Danny could tell that something was wrong. I told him that I was fine, and I just needed to take it easy. That felt like a lie. In the end, I suppose it was true; I just left a hell of a lot out.

I stretched my aching body onto the couch and turned on the television. *The Real Housewives* was on. Perfect. I dozed off before I could watch the characters get into another one of their epic fights over nothing. When I woke up, it was the middle of the night. All my lights were still on, and an infomercial was blasting through the television. My head pounded uncontrollably. I could feel my heartbeat pulsing through the veins in my temples, keeping the beat going like a metronome.

I sat up, slowly. My whole body felt like a ton of bricks. I stood up and began to ping pong myself against the walls of my apartment until I made my way into the bedroom. I threw myself onto the bed and curled into a tight ball. I let out a huge sigh of a relief. The journey from the living room to the bedroom had felt long and arduous. I pulled the covers up to my chin as the pain penetrated every cell in my body.

The next day, I woke up in the middle of the afternoon. It was Thanksgiving, and I could barely get out of bed. My body continued to ache in ways I couldn't even place. It wasn't quite the flu, and I had never had surgery, so I didn't know what that might feel like in my body. But I guessed that Diane was right. Soul surgery was the analogy that fit the best.

Heather had wanted to celebrate Thanksgiving with me. Willa was spending the holiday with her father, and she was all alone. I knew that was going to be difficult for her. Heather wanted us to go shopping downtown and then to a fancy dinner. I called Heather and told her that I was completely comatose. I felt so guilty. But there was no way I was going anywhere. I would be lucky if I made it back into the living room.

It was Thanksgiving, and all I could eat was a can of soup. Luckily, I had a spare can of Progresso minestrone in the cupboard. I tended to keep one in the cupboard for holidays and emergencies. For the past decade, holidays and emergencies had equated to the same thing.

But everything felt different this time.

THE REAL HOUSEWIVES AND A CAN OF SOUP

After I told my parents about the sexual abuse, I spent the next decade watching my relationships with them completely erode. Most of our problems centered around holidays and other family gatherings, since these were the events where I was most likely to see the Black Square. After I stormed out of my parents' house on the evening of my disclosure, I felt brave enough to tell them I didn't want to be in the same room with the Black Square ever again. Unfortunately, they had a hard time respecting this boundary. And the rift between us began to grow.

My parents continued to spend time with the Black Square as if I had said nothing at all. Shortly after my disclosure in 2008, they had the Black Square over for dinner and called me afterward. I can still hear the way my mother talked about how nice it was to see him. There was a lightness in her voice as she casually told me about their evening. She talked about what they had for dinner. She talked about how funny the Black Square can be; how I just didn't understand his sense of humor. I sat on the phone, no longer breathing. I felt like I was living in an alternate reality. How could this have happened? How could they have listened to me describe decades of disgusting, vile sexual abuse and then proceed to cook dinner for this man? My parents appeared to be living their pre-disclosure lives. Meanwhile, for me, everything was different.

It meant something that I had come forward after decades of silence. I had freed myself in new and valuable ways. I was no longer carrying the burden of this secret and all its consequences. I even told some of my closest friends about the abuse. That night at the house party came back into clear view, but this time, I felt sure of the fact that it would not be replicated. After I ran out of that house party dressed in a white tank top with pink stars, I knew I was done. And even though Coco had warned me about the consequences of coming forward, I had spoken up. I had said it. And now, a part of me had been liberated. I felt a congruence that was starkly unfamiliar and incredibly comforting. I was finally living in alignment with my own story. There was no going back.

There was one other person who seemed to be affected by my disclosure. Ever since I had come forward, the Black Square couldn't even look at me. When Thanksgiving rolled around that year, I explicitly asked my parents not to invite him to our house. It had been a few months since my disclosure, and I was looking forward to spending my first holiday without the Black Square. But, against my wishes, my parents decided to let him come for dessert. I was not told about this. So when the Black Square walked into our house, my stomach sank. I felt like I had been ambushed.

Thanksgiving 2008

I was seated on the radiator ledge in the middle of our formal dining room talking to my cousin when the Black Square walked into our house. Our dining room had an archway that opened into the front of the house, so I saw him enter immediately. I watched the Black Square arrive as I stopped talking to my cousin. The breath left my body. My mother greeted the Black Square lovingly as she took his coat. He smiled back at her as he thanked her for extending him an invitation.

Then the Black Square marched right up to me and asked if we could talk. His whole demeanor shifted as he began to shake. He could barely look at me. For the first time in my entire life, I felt our roles reverse. To my surprise, the Black Square was the one cowering in front of me. He was the one who was afraid. I marveled in this moment. I stared at the Black Square and proudly told him that I was not going anywhere with him in private. I told him that it was completely inappropriate that he was here, and that he shouldn't be trying to talk to me at all. He looked particularly defeated as he banished himself to our nicely finished basement. I felt strong. The Black Square had displayed the affect and body language of someone who had been caught. And I had held my ground.

I truly thought all of this would work to my advantage, but I was wrong. Instead, everyone spent the remainder of the evening shaming me for setting a boundary. My mother talked about how sorry she felt for the Black Square, as he sulked alone downstairs. She tried to pressure me to go *fix it*. I was enraged. What planet was I living on? Why would my mother be telling me to venture into our basement alone with my perpetrator? Either she didn't believe me, or she didn't think what he did was that bad. I couldn't bear to stomach either of these options.

The Black Square continued to sulk in our basement for the remainder of the evening. Meanwhile, I held firmly to my boundary. I planted myself in the center of our large dining room table as I attempted to enjoy a slice of my mother's perfectly cooked pumpkin pie. I dodged glares from her as I scooped a second dollop of whipped cream onto my plate. I shoved a forkful of pie into my mouth and told myself to enjoy it.

But it would never taste the same again.

2009–2014

As time wore on, I struggled to make sense of what was happening (or not happening) in my family. I couldn't believe that my parents pretended it was business as usual. It was all too much for me to bear. I never considered that Coco might have been right. I never considered that I could lose my family over my own sexual abuse disclosure. Frankly, I wasn't ready to imagine that thought. I tried to shove down all the freedom and growth that I felt right when I came forward so that I could attempt to belong to my family. At times, I even tried to induce a sense of amnesia around my story. What disclosure? Maybe I hallucinated it. Maybe I hallucinated all the abuse. I must be the one who got it all wrong. Perhaps my mother was right, the Black Square wasn't *that bad* after all. Everyone knows what kind of person he is. No one can argue with the fact that the Black Square is overtly sexual and inappropriate. The problem must be me. Maybe I'm *too sensitive.*

When I told myself this version of the story, I got to stay. I was integrated back into family gatherings and holidays. I was allowed to belong. But when I told myself the *other* story, the one about the Black Square sexually abusing me, everything changed. Suddenly, I was not accepted anymore. If I interrogated my parents about why they continued to see him, they would respond by simply asking me if I planned on attending Thanksgiving at their house. Which of course was the house that I grew up in. It became abundantly clear that I would need to make the ultimate, impossible choice. My parents were asking me to choose between having a family and feeling safe. The problem is, that is not a real choice. That is what I call a *traumatic choice*. A traumatic choice is two bad choices that are presented as a free-will decision. I didn't feel like I had been given a choice. However, I did feel that my parents had chosen. It felt like my own parents had chosen the Black Square, *who was not even a blood relative*, instead of their own daughter.

* * *

During the years that followed, I tried to weave my way through the never-ending maze of this traumatic choice. At first, I chose to have a family. To do that, I shoved down all the liberation and internal alignment I had just worked so hard to get. Instead, I got dressed in my apartment, just like old times, so that I could attend more Jewish holidays alongside the Black Square. I fell into the familiar pattern of rationalizing how silly it was that I couldn't seem to choose an outfit for Passover. I tried to convince myself and all my friends that I was fine, that I wanted to go to these gatherings. But I could see the disapproving looks in their eyes. No one was ready to say it, but everyone knew the truth. I was not alright. Nothing about this was alright.

I desperately tried to continue down this path. But as the leaves turned brown each year and the holidays began to approach, my heart would sink into my stomach and stay there. The lead-up to the holidays was always the worst. I would ruminate over what would take place. Would I need to use one of my lifelines and phone a friend? Would I need to give myself permission to walk out if the Black Square were there? I devised so many exit strategies ahead of Passover that I felt like I was reenacting the story of the Jews escaping from exile all over again.

Logistically, it seemed like I had thought of everything. I believed this was the key. I truly believed that if I covered all my bases ahead of time and if I had the perfect plan, I would be fine. But I learned one very important lesson. You can pack an emergency bag to use in the event of a tornado, but if you need to use it, that means you are fleeing from a tornado. Well, I packed that bag. I packed it so many times. And while my life would have been much worse without it, I did not escape unscathed. That's because I essentially walked headfirst into a tornado, year after year.

At first, it took me hours to get out. I would text my friends from every holiday table, looking for support. Everyone always told me to leave, but it was so hard. These events felt like witnessing a car crash that I couldn't peel my eyes away from. I sat there year after year, as I watched my parents interact with the Black Square. I watched my mom laugh at his ill-timed and inappropriate jokes. I watched my dad talk business with him. Being forced to sit through my own betrayal was the worst part. And soon, it rivaled everything the Black Square had done to me.

After a while, I couldn't tolerate these conversations anymore. So I began to leave earlier and earlier. All this exit planning was so that I could stay in my family. Yes, I had to keep leaving so that I could ultimately stay. I realize, in retrospect, that makes no sense. But that's how I felt. Year after year, I would leave my apartment in the city to drive to the suburbs for yet another holiday, feeling hopeful and naively optimistic. I would walk through the front door, scanning for the Black Square. If he were there, I would leave immediately and drive straight home. Once I was home, I would wait by the phone, expecting my parents to call me. I would wait for them to beg me to attend the next holiday; to tell me how badly I was missed. But none of that ever happened. Every time I walked out of a holiday, that was it. I was effectively shunned and seemingly forgotten.

Sometimes I fantasized about walking out in a huff and seeing my parents run down the street, begging me to stay. But no one ever chased after me. They continued to have an overt relationship with the man who abused me for half my life. Then they let me leave our family gatherings alone.

Sometimes I would ask my parents ahead of time if the Black Square would be in attendance. But the truth is, I stopped doing that after one particularly devastating tornado. My uncle was hosting a weekend brunch at his house. I asked my mother whether the Black Square would be there, and she said no. So I felt better. I got dressed with far less effort, and

I headed to the suburbs. But as soon as I walked through the foyer of my uncle's house, I saw the Black Square standing in the kitchen. I felt incredibly betrayed. And so I promptly deployed the use of my emergency bag, and I left. After this incident, I was forced to institute a new protocol: what to do in the event of an emergency when I cannot trust my parents.

* * *

Eventually, it became worse to exhaust all the energy that it took to attend these holidays, only to leave exasperated after a few minutes. I began to feel severely abandoned and betrayed by my parents. They sent a clear message that no further action was necessary after my disclosure. They had proved their point over the past six years. Somehow I still couldn't believe it. I couldn't believe that my parents weren't planning to fight for me. I was heartbroken and alone. And leaving in the middle of one too many Yom Kippurs drove that stake into my heart even deeper. So I started to stay home.

The first time I spent Thanksgiving alone, I remember standing in my kitchen and crying over a lukewarm pot of Progresso minestrone soup as I waited for it to boil into something edible. Then I turned off my phone and hurled it into the bedroom. At least I had the foresight to know that the only way this evening could get any worse would be to go on social media. I couldn't scroll through everyone's gratitude posts. I couldn't bear to see photos of folks sitting around tables filled with food and love. And worse yet, I couldn't take the chance of accidentally seeing a post from someone in my own family, showing off a table comprised of my mother's stuffing and my father's perfectly cooked turkey. A meal that, year after year, I had helped them prepare. One of my friends suggested that I try to eat some of the traditional Thanksgiving foods that night, but I knew that would make everything worse. I needed to pretend that I was home on a regular Thursday night. I needed to pretend it was not a holiday. And that's how I ended up with *The Real Housewives* and a can of soup.

There was just one problem: I couldn't trick myself into forgetting. I sat on my couch, eating my oversalted soup and watching Bravo. At least I was watching a show about a group of women who were pretending to like each other but who kept erupting into fits of ridiculous dysfunction over fancy dinners. I could relate. That's what my holidays had become. I usually loved indulging in the drama of *The Real Housewives*, but that night, I was barely there. My gaze kept drifting out the window. Even though this Thanksgiving felt far safer than the alternative, it was not my choice. And just like that, I found myself on the other end of the traumatic choice: safe, but alone.

Thanksgiving 2015

In the fall of 2015, I began to go low contact with my parents. All those years of holiday betrayals had finally piled up. The summer before, I had tried to force my parents to take accountability for maintaining a relationship with the Black Square, thereby ousting me from my own family. But I slowly began to realize that I couldn't orchestrate my own apologies from my parents. The repair process would have needed to come from them. And clearly, that wasn't going to happen. So I began to listen to my heart – and my heart needed space.

I called my parents less often. I began spending holidays with my friends. I invented excuses when my parents invited me to their condo for Sunday dinner. I didn't know what else to do. During that time, I vacillated between months of not speaking to my parents and periods of time when I launched myself back into pleas for repair. But these attempts proved to be futile. No one was planning to budge.

The only person I spoke to with any real regularity was my grandmother, Coco. And Coco was in the process of leaving this Earth. I struggled immensely to cope with that. I knew I needed to let her go, but I was terrified of what would happen to me in a world without Coco. In a world without our evenings at the French bistro. In a world without *dish it.* She held on for so many years, and I think that she held on for me.

The last Thanksgiving that she ever had, we spent together. It was the fall of 2015, and somehow I knew it would be her last. I wasn't speaking to my parents, and for some reason, they weren't planning to see Coco either. So she was alone. I remember calling her and asking if she would like me to come over. Coco enthusiastically agreed. And when I asked her what I could bring, she, in true Coco fashion, asked for chocolate ice cream with chocolate sauce. This time, it would be our dinner.

I picked up some chocolate ice cream with chocolate sauce,

as well as some of Coco's favorite flowers, and I headed to the nursing home she had reluctantly moved into a few years prior. Coco hated it there. She always complained that there were *too many old people*. I think Coco believed that she was immortal. She would pull out photo albums during those years as she told me the same stories repeatedly. She pointed to the people in black-and-white photos as she yelled, "Dead, dead, they're all dead." I think Coco felt that she deserved an award for outliving them all.

* * *

Later that evening, I walked into Coco's room, holding our ice cream in one hand and flowers in the other. I sat down next to her and immediately burst into tears. Coco leaned over and grasped both of my hands. Her blue-green veins shimmered in the warm light of her table lamp. Then she said: "I knew they weren't going to side with you, Lauren. I just knew it. It's disgusting, everything that has happened. And for all this time. Part of me still can't believe it. It's just disgusting. I can't believe you sat home all by yourself for so many holidays. It breaks my heart. I told you years ago that it would go this way if you came forward about the abuse. I know that was hard to hear. I really didn't want to be right. I'm so sorry, Lauren."

We both cried. Coco talked about wishing she could make this better for me. I talked about how deeply she had been right all those years ago at the French bistro when we got into our one and only fight. And that's when I turned to her, and I said, "Coco, I can't believe you were right about my father. I really thought he would back me up. But you were right. I feel so abandoned by him. I can't even look at him anymore. He used to be my biggest role model. But now, I don't respect him at all."

Coco began to cry. I watched a tear trickle down the side of her cheek as she said, "I know, Lauren. It pains me so much to be right about your father. But I know my son. He has a huge blind spot when it comes to your mother. He just won't go up against her. And she was never going to support you. So I'm not surprised that he didn't either. I hate that it's gone this way."

We continued to hold each other's hands as we cried together. Then I said, "Coco, I need to tell you something. I am almost at my brink. I don't know how much longer I can stay in this family. It's clear that Mom and Dad aren't going to repair any of this with me, and when I try, everything just gets worse. They are breaking my heart. And I need you to know that I have a bad feeling that I am going to end up estranging myself."

Coco looked at me and said, "This may feel like an odd conversation to be having on Thanksgiving, but that's our family for you. Do what you need to do, Lauren. You've tried everything. No more looking to the past. It's time for you to live your life. I just want you to be happy."

We ate our ice cream in silence. Finally, Coco asked me to tell her something good that was happening in my life. So I began to tell her all about my work as a therapist and how I felt that I had found my calling. Coco smiled as she listened to me talk about how much I loved helping my clients empower themselves.

We began the evening with something heavy, and we ended with something more uplifting. It was the first time we had done *dish it* in reverse.

By the following summer, she was gone.

Thanksgiving 2016

After Coco died, I felt my place in the family shift once again. She had been the only person who truly understood me. She had felt like my one true ally. I didn't know how to exist in my family without her. I didn't know if I even could. Without Coco, I felt even more like an outcast. I would have traded all that fancy food my parents liked to cook for a bowl of chocolate ice cream and one more session of *dish it*.

In the aftermath of Coco's death, something surprising happened. I began to grow closer to my father again. He had just lost his mother, and that broke something open inside of him. He also knew how close Coco and I had always been. I could feel how deeply my father appreciated the relationship I had with Coco. I was truly grateful for that. I could also feel us trying to hold onto each other. Neither one of us wanted to experience another loss.

That fall, I tried to spend more time with my parents. But Thanksgiving was quickly approaching, and frankly, I had lost so much trust in my parents over the years that I was extremely reluctant to attend a holiday with them ever again. And with good reason.

The day before Thanksgiving, I received a text from my brother, Peter. He had just flown into town from Montgomery, Alabama, with his girlfriend. They were both newly minted lawyers who were employed at an organization that worked tirelessly to release wrongly convicted people from death row. Peter was built for that job. He was extremely principled and dedicated to his work. And he excelled at it. I told him that I was considering attending Thanksgiving that year. Peter couldn't contain his shock and his excitement.

* * *

Peter and I had been cordial as kids, except for the times when I treated him like he was my annoying younger brother. I regret

232

those times. As we got older, we became exponentially closer. Peter and I even went to the same college, and since I was three years older than him, we overlapped there for a year. We backpacked through Chile and Greece together. And we were known to spend hours on the phone talking about our crushes and what to do about them. I cherished the time I spent with Peter. We talked about work. We talked about where we each wanted to live. We met each other's friends and partners. But there was always an unspoken rule between us: we were fine if we didn't talk about our family.

Peter and I did well when we could pretend that we weren't related. Over the years, we had developed vastly different ways of coping with the way we had been raised. My approach had been to move back to my hometown so that I could confront everything and everyone. Peter openly told me that he would never understand why I made that decision. Instead, he made a concerted effort to distance himself from the stress and conflict that appeared to be built into the fabric of our family. In this way, I felt that he took after our father. I sometimes wondered if my father's avoidant tendencies provided an entryway for my brother to follow suit. Even though there were many times when Peter supported me in private, I was the only one who took a public stand against the toxicity that we had both been born into. Nonetheless, I accepted our different methods of coping for many years. But in the aftermath of my sexual abuse disclosure, Peter's absence was becoming more difficult to condone.

When I began to go low contact with my parents, I had a long conversation with my friend Sarah about the dynamics in my family. I met Sarah in graduate school, and we had been close friends for the past nine years. One day, she mentioned that it was odd that she didn't know very much about my brother. I admitted that Peter and I had been close during certain points in our lives, but that he avoided coming home as much as possible. I told Sarah that Peter had joined the Peace Corps after college and had limited contact with all of us for two years. I told her that Peter had chosen to live all over the country, and in places that were each a solid plane ride away from Chicago. I told her that Peter only visited a few times a year and was only in town for a few days at a time. I joked about the fact that Peter had been the first one to go low contact with our family. Sarah nodded along with me as she exclaimed, "So basically, you don't have a real brother, you have a *holiday brother*." I laughed. Then, I felt the poignancy of that statement hit me squarely in the chest.

According to Sarah, a holiday brother was someone who stepped into the role of a brother during special occasions but abandoned that role for the rest of the year. I couldn't believe how accurate that term felt to me. At this point, the only time I saw Peter was when he flew into town for the holidays. And that was quickly becoming the worst time for me.

* * *

During the years when Peter was busy embodying the role of Holiday Brother, I was building a genogram of our entire family and connecting the dots. Going low contact with my parents helped me step back and look at my entire family tree with a lot more clarity. I began to realize that the Black Square didn't exist in a vacuum. For him to exert so much power and influence, the whole system had to allow it. As I stepped back from my parents, I began to distance myself from other family members too. Specifically, my mother's brother: Uncle Ron.

My uncle had always been good friends with the Black Square, and when they were in the same room together, I felt that they were worse than two frat boys hazing a freshman recruit. Uncle Ron was part of the toxic culture I had decided to go up against. So, earlier that year, I made it clear to my parents that I didn't want to have a relationship with my uncle anymore either. That proved to be an even more substantial problem. This time, I was telling my mother that I didn't want to speak to her only brother.

Donald Trump had been elected a few weeks before Thanksgiving and it was all anyone could talk about. Most of my family members were staunch Democrats. Uncle Ron, on the other hand, was a card-carrying, gun-toting Republican. Everyone (besides Uncle Ron) was overtly horrified that this man had been elected. All I could think was this: the Black Square appeared to be the Donald Trump of our family. And Uncle Ron resembled a loud, belligerent Trump supporter wearing a MAGA hat, yelling about how we were all snowflakes who couldn't take a joke. I knew exactly how Donald Trump got elected. It's the same way the Black Square and Uncle Ron seemed to rule over our entire family uncontested. Until I stood up and said: enough.

I didn't want to spend my first Thanksgiving without Coco alone. Since I had been in a relatively good place with my parents over the past month, I agreed to attend Thanksgiving at their home. This time, I was certain the Black Square wouldn't be there. I also knew that Uncle Ron was out of town. If there was ever going to be a time for me to safely celebrate Thanksgiving with my family, it was now. I got dressed in whatever the hell I felt like wearing and drove twenty minutes north to my parents' condo.

* * *

There's a reason that I knew the Black Square wouldn't be at our Thanksgiving this time. Two years prior, my parents made the decision to cut the Black Square out of their lives after six years of prioritizing just about everything else. I was so grateful that my parents finally distanced themselves from the Black Square. I was also deeply hurt that it took them so long to do it. Once the boundary had been set, I felt like my parents expected me to be immediately happy. They expected me to move on. Before I could do that, I needed them to acknowledge how painful the last six years had been. I needed them to acknowledge all those holidays when I stayed home with a can of soup while everyone else congregated together. And all those years when I felt forced to choose between safety and belonging. It was imperative that my parents understood the impact this situation had on me.

By the summer of 2015, it was clear that I couldn't move forward without a repair process. So I confronted my parents, separately. My father and I had an incredibly enlightening conversation where he broke down on my couch and took accountability for everything. He told me that he deeply regretted his inaction after my disclosure. He told me that he was broken over what I had endured in the family in silence, and for so long. I forgave him on the spot. We cried as we embraced. I was hopeful for the first time in years.

The following week, my father took his apology back. He yelled at me on the phone as he accused me of trying to be the therapist for our family. He called me arrogant for attempting to confront him. My father had undergone a complete metamorphosis and I felt absolutely blindsided. I had no idea how he had backslid so far and so quickly. All I knew was that the man who sat on my couch crying the previous weekend was gone.

During the confrontation with my mother, she never once took accountability for anything I had endured. She refused to acknowledge the abuse, except by continuing to poke holes in my story. I expected this reaction from her, so I didn't experience the same blowback I had felt when my father rescinded his apology. Nevertheless, the verdict was in: the repair process I desperately needed was unlikely to occur. As I prepared to go to Thanksgiving at my parents' condo for the first time in years, I did so with the understanding that we had already hit a wall.

* * *

When I walked into my parents' home, the aroma of my father's turkey and my mother's stuffing filled the air. I almost teared up as I realized how much I had missed their food. Peter and his girlfriend were in the kitchen, preparing an overly ambitious dessert. I gave everyone hugs as my father poured me a glass of white wine. This felt good. Really good.

My parents had invited their college friends to join us for Thanksgiving, and I was excited to see them too. It would just be us and them, and I felt so much comfort in that. Finally, a holiday without the toxic influences of the Black Square and Uncle Ron.

Right after we sat down to dinner with our plates piled high, Uncle Ron called, ruining the moment entirely. My father stood up from the table to retrieve his iPad as he accepted the FaceTime call from California. *I froze.* My father returned to the table with the iPad, and I heard Uncle Ron's famous wild hyena laugh. I tried to continue eating, hoping that I would simply blend into the background. Uncle Ron barked an order through the screen, "Who is there? Show me who is there tonight?"

My dad flipped the iPad around and began to scan the room as each person reluctantly waved. I was seated directly next to my father, so I knew I would be last. As my father brought the iPad closer to me, I looked at him out of the corner of my eye and mouthed, "NO." I shook my head vigorously as I held my hands in an X over my chest. I was doing my best to simulate *NO* with my entire body. I was so clear in that moment that I could have been a professional mime.

Everyone at the table saw me do this. My father hesitated. He was about to take the iPad down and conclude show-and-tell when my mother yelled, "Lauren is here too!" And just like that, my father picked the iPad back up and shone the screen directly into my face. I felt like I had been involved in a full-frontal exposure. I placed my palm in front of my face like I was shielding myself from the paparazzi. And then I ran out of the room without saying a word.

I slipped into my parents' home office and closed the door. I burst into tears. My father knocked on the door, and I sent him away. My mother didn't even try to check on me. I sat there alone for a few minutes, reeling from yet another holiday betrayal and boundary violation when Peter knocked. I told him he could come in.

Peter entered my parents' home office and sat down in my father's desk chair. He waited for me to say something. I told him that I felt betrayed by our parents all over again. Peter said he fully understood my boundary with the Black Square, but he didn't understand why I had extended that boundary to Uncle Ron.

I looked at my brother, perplexed. *Is he seriously asking me this right now?* I felt as though I had just been gaslighted. Peter was well aware of the fact that I had never gotten along with Uncle Ron. That was no secret. In fact I had spent most of my life fighting with Uncle Ron over everything from politics to whether I was *too sensitive* for ending up in tears each time he hurled an abrasive insult in my direction. At one point, my uncle told me that he loved me, but he didn't like me. The entire basis of our relationship was friction. I was shocked that my brother needed me to produce a single defining reason to cut Uncle Ron out of my life. But there we were.

* * *

Peter and I continued to sit across from each other in our parents' home office. This time, in silence. I watched as he crossed one leg over the other, attempting to reposition himself in our father's swiveling desk chair. The warm light of the desk lamp cast a thin shadow across his face. I could tell that Peter was patiently waiting for me to respond to his question. I stared back at him, suddenly unable to find the words to tell Peter why I didn't want to speak to Uncle Ron anymore. There was clearly no point.

I began to sob as I grabbed a decorative throw pillow and drew it close to my chest. As I cried, I stared deeper into my brother's unassuming brown eyes. I scanned his face, hoping that he might redirect himself once he realized how much his question had upset me. But he held firm. I began to realize that this situation was a direct consequence of having a holiday brother instead of a real one. He had been absent during so many critical moments, especially lately. I no longer had the mental or emotional fortitude to catch Peter up to speed. I also felt that he knew better. Over the years, Peter and I had so many discussions about Uncle Ron's problematic behavior that I had assumed that we were on the same page. But Uncle Ron had always liked my brother. He had taken him golfing. He had granted Peter permission to join the good ol' boys club of our family. Apparently, that membership carried more weight than I had expected.

Peter's critique of my decision to stop speaking to Uncle Ron felt like the second betrayal of the evening. He had stepped into our parents' home office under the guise of support, only to immediately question my boundaries along with everyone else. He sounded just like my parents. Until that moment, I had tried to place Peter in a different category. I would never make that mistake again.

My only option was to let the distance between Peter and I continue to grow. My heart began to break. I yearned for our college days when Peter was more than just a holiday brother. I cried in that room while Peter dropped his gaze to the floor. His abandonment became all-consuming. I missed Coco even more in that moment. She would have been angry right alongside me. She would have been a real ally, not a superficial one. I began to sob harder. All of a sudden, I was overcome with the grief of it all. Of losing Coco. Of only having a holiday brother. And of the night that would forever be known as the iPad Thanksgiving.

* * *

Peter and I sat in our parents' home office in silence for what felt like an eternity. He stared at his feet before awkwardly turning his body toward my father's desk. He let out an audible sigh. I realized that we had both given up on having a real conversation about our family. A part of me was relieved. Another part of me knew there was nowhere to go from here.

I pulled out my phone and began to text my friends, furiously. Tears welled up in my eyes as I let my friends know about my father's iPad betrayal and that Peter could no longer be trusted. Messages began to pour in as my friends responded with anger and disgust at the series of events that had just transpired. I couldn't believe that everyone was taking time away from their respective family gatherings to respond to my SOS message. I felt a pang of guilt. I stared at the flurry of incoming text messages that had been sent in all caps. Everyone was urging me to leave. My eyes glazed over. I desperately wanted to get out of that room, but I felt like my entire body had been superglued to the sofa.

This time, I had been wholly unprepared for another Thanksgiving incident. I hadn't even packed my emergency bag or alerted any of my lifelines until it was a full-blown crisis. None of my friends even knew that I had spent Thanksgiving with my family until it was too late. I couldn't believe that I was immersed in another holiday from hell. The Black Square was out of the picture this time. Uncle Ron was in California. But the ambush took place anyway. From the sexual abuse to my parents' repetitive betrayals, to the profound disappointment of Holiday Brother, I was sick and tired of everyone blowing through my boundaries.

* * *

I began to grow increasingly more uncomfortable sitting across from Peter. I didn't understand what compelled him to stay in that room with me for as long as he did. *Did he think he was providing any real support?* If this was the best he could do, I knew I would be better off alone. My legs began to shake as I gripped my phone in my hands. I needed to get out of that room.

I broke the silence by telling Peter that I was not going back to that dinner table and that I needed to go home. He understood. It felt good to be back on the same page with Peter until I realized that all we had agreed upon was that neither of us wanted to be stuck in our parents' home office any longer.

Nevertheless, we began to devise an exit plan. First, Peter would walk out of the office and declare to the room full of people that I would be leaving and there would be no time for questions. I felt like he was my public relations representative. As he did that, I would sneak into the kitchen and steal some of the Thanksgiving food that I was once again robbed from eating. We rose to our feet as we made our way toward the door. I hugged Peter reluctantly as tears welled up in my eyes. He whispered in my ear that it would be alright. But I knew better. None of that was true.

Peter followed protocol as he walked back into the open kitchen/dining room where the rest of my family were still seated. I heard him recite the pre-planned statement we had crafted together in my parents' office. I knew it was now or never.

Without warning, I stormed into the kitchen. A ball of rage grew inside my stomach as my cheeks filled with heat. I couldn't even look at my parents as they remained seated at the table. Instead I grabbed all my mother's favorite Tupperware containers and began to pile mounds of turkey, stuffing, and green beans into them. Then I sliced through her perfectly round pumpkin pie, demolishing it in the process. In the end, I stole a third of the turkey, two containers of stuffing, and half a pie. My mother glared at me as she lifted a finger to object. I glared back as if to say, *Try me.*

Everyone sat in silence, upright and no longer breathing. They looked like they were in the throes of a hostage situation. I tore through the kitchen, slamming cabinets until I found a shopping bag large enough to contain my bounty. I began shoving large Tupperware containers into the shopping bag as I looked around the room for my coat. I hauled my shopping bag all around the apartment as it burned a red line into my forearm. Finally I found my peacoat hanging politely in my parents' front hall closet. I threw the coat over my arm and slammed the door shut behind me.

Twenty minutes later, I walked into my apartment. I threw the shopping bag onto the floor as I began to cry. I changed out of my cute, burgundy romper and into some sweatpants. And I stood over the microwave, sobbing uncontrollably as I warmed up a plate of my contraband dinner. Somehow, the slow-cooked turkey and stuffing tasted just like a can of Progresso soup. A decade later, it felt like nothing had changed.

That was the last time I saw my parents.

I BELIEVE YOU

New Year's Eve, 2018

Danny returned to Chicago just in time for New Year's Eve. We hadn't been able to see each other over Thanksgiving since I was too busy convalescing from my recent soul surgery. Of course, Danny didn't know that. He barely knew about anything that I had experienced over the past six months. Nonetheless, he was back in town, and this time I was determined to see him. Physically, I had recovered. Emotionally, I was still a wreck.

I felt bad about blowing Danny off the night Diane and I processed my depossession transcript. I still had no idea what had come over my body on the evening before Thanksgiving, which was an entire week after my depossession. I began to wonder why the soul surgery had taken so long to catch up with me. And just when my brain was about to return to a place of skepticism, I remembered everything I knew about trauma.

Until I spoke to Diane, my body had undoubtedly continued to exist in survival mode. Even though the plagues had completely disappeared, I remained suspended in a state of fear. I paced around my apartment nightly, bracing myself to go into battle with Mary Frances if she dared to return. I tried re-reading the transcript; hellbent on convincing myself that the nightmare was over. But my body remained hypervigilant.

And there were signs. The day before I spoke with Diane, I was standing in the office of Heaven on Sheridan as I waited to retrieve a package when I heard someone say the word *moth*. My eyes grew wide as the breath left my body. In an instant, I abandoned my place in line and bolted back up to my apartment. I began patrolling every crack and crevice of my unit with the weak flashlight from my phone. I peered under my couch. My eyes darted around the dark underbelly of the couch as I waited for an army of mealy, white moth larvae to reemerge. *Nothing*. There were no signs of any more plagues.

Still, my body refused to relax. I backed away from the couch and continued to scan the room, determined to catch the next plague before it started. But nothing ever happened. The war with Mary Frances was over, but now, I was at war with my own brain.

And that's trauma. Once the acute threat dissipates, an entirely new battle begins. The battle to convince the mind and body that it is over. That it is safe now. Unfortunately, I know that battle all too well.

Growing up, I constantly felt the need to flee my family. As a result, safety always remained elusive. Even before my life was turned upside down by the plagues, safety felt like a theoretical concept that existed for other people. I had only experienced it a few times in my life, and those moments had always been short-lived. Usually, those moments involved Coco. When I spent time with Coco, I felt safe. But Coco didn't live in our house. So, at some point, I always had to return home. And I never knew what would be waiting for me when I got there.

Trauma, however, was a constant. There was always more of it. There was always a new threat, another betrayal, and more chaos lurking around every corner. I lived that life for so many years. I knew it in my bones. And the plagues had driven me back there once again. Back to the place filled with shallow breath, tight shoulders, and a clenched jaw.

I suppose it's not surprising that I needed Diane to confirm that my nightmare was over. Once she had, I felt my nervous system begin to retreat from high alert. But the road from high alert to comatose was extremely short. That's how my body works. It's the same reason that I always managed to get sick as soon as I took a vacation. Any time my body received a much-needed time out, it took full advantage. And that's how I arrived at the place where I spent yet another Thanksgiving with *The Real Housewives* and a can of soup.

Now, I was feeling a little better. And Danny was on his way to see me. I glanced down at my phone and realized that he would be at my place shortly. I began to wonder what it would be like to be in his presence again. I was excited, but nervous. Danny knew about my estrangement, but he didn't know about anything else. The last six months rolled around in my head like a tidal wave. *Should I tell him?* A part of me yearned to shove everything about Mary Frances into a vault. Another part of me knew that I was done with vaults.

Danny and I made plans to go to a Vietnamese restaurant near my apartment for lunch on New Year's Eve, before we both ventured off to different places to say goodbye to 2018. I made my way down to the lobby of Heaven on Sheridan as I waited for Danny to arrive. As soon as I saw his car, I ran out of my building, eager to see him.

* * *

Danny and I had a long and winding history together. We first met at a social event for liberal Jews over eight years ago, and we immediately clicked. Danny and I exchanged numbers and decided to meet for a drink the following weekend, right after the Thanksgiving holiday. I wasn't sure what to expect. I didn't know if it was a date or something else. Danny was six years younger than me, and he was only in Chicago for the next month before he moved to Jordan. My brain told me that all these things were a problem. My heart told me that none of it mattered.

Our timing was precarious for another reason. Danny and I met shortly after I told my parents about the decades of sexual abuse that I had endured in my family. We met during the era when I began packing emergency bags to get through another Passover seder, seated directly across from the Black Square. My life was in shambles, but I began to wonder if it might help to be around someone new. Someone who *didn't know*. Besides, Danny was only in town for a short time. I could probably get by without telling him very much (if anything) about the desecration of my own family.

Danny and I met for a drink at a local pub in Evanston. As

it turned out, we were on a date. And from that moment on, Danny and I were inseparable until he left for Jordan at the end of December. I don't think either of us expected that to happen, but it did. I grew accustomed to meeting him for dinner after work. He spent many evenings at my place. And before we knew it, our time had come to an end.

After Danny left for Jordan, I truly believed that I would never see him again. So when Danny moved back to Chicago the following year, I honestly didn't know what to do. We struggled as we tried to figure out how to remain in each other's lives authentically and in a way that made sense for both of us. We both knew from the start that we weren't supposed to be together. But we also knew that we had something special. Something unique. Something that didn't fit into a socially constructed box. We weren't partners and we weren't really friends. We were something else.

Over the years, we both dated other people. We met each other's partners, and we continued to find ways to stay connected. The physical side of our relationship ebbed and flowed, but the warmth we initially felt for each other remained constant. I didn't know it was possible to go through so many iterations of a relationship with the same person. And for that, I will always be grateful.

* * *

Danny pulled up to Heaven on Sheridan and waved eagerly at me. I opened the passenger side door and climbed into his car. We smiled at each other as light rain began to hit the windshield. He drove us to the Vietnamese place around the corner from my apartment, and we caught up a bit. I could feel my heart beating quickly. It was nice to see Danny, but I was acutely aware that so much had happened over the past few months and that he had absolutely no idea about any of it. I wasn't about to text Danny about my depossession while he was at graduate school in Ann Arbor. Besides, I didn't know if he would believe a word of this story. I always felt that Danny was more religious than me. He often wore a kippah[5] and observed Jewish holidays. I, on the other hand, identified with my cultural identity as a Jew, but was not very religious. And now I was communicating with the Archangel Michael. Frankly, I didn't know how that would go over.

Danny and I arrived at the restaurant and got two orders of vegetarian pho in bowls as large as our heads. I really needed a good bowl of soup after my weeklong stint of eating oversalted minestrone from a can over Thanksgiving.

I asked Danny to tell me about school and his plans post-graduation. He had just attended a silent meditation retreat, and he seemed incredibly relaxed. I looked at him, hoping it wasn't too obvious that I was hoping to feed off his peaceful energy.

At some point, I decided to tell Danny what had transpired in my life over the past few months. I immediately apologized for canceling our plans over Thanksgiving. I told him that a lot had gone down that evening. He asked me what happened that night, and I just blurted it out. I blurted it all out. We sat in that crowded restaurant as I told him about the four plagues. I told him about my near suicide attempt. I told him about Mary Frances. And I told him that on the evening I was supposed to meet him, I debriefed with the woman who ripped Mary Frances out of my body.

Danny sat there, barely able to continue eating his soup. His eyes grew wide as my story progressed. I could feel him attempting to process the string of metaphysical details I had just catapulted his way. My entire story felt like gibberish as soon as it left my mouth. I couldn't even begin to imagine what he was thinking. I stared down at my soup, which had become cold and unsightly. I swirled my spoon around the edge of the bowl, accidentally catching a piece of tofu. A wave of embarrassment washed over me. I looked up as my eyes met his. I was yearning for Danny to say something, but he was deep in thought. He also looked like he had just taken a bullet.

We left the restaurant and headed back to my place. I invited Danny to come inside for a cup of tea. We walked into my apartment, and I took his coat, still cold and wet from the rain. Danny told me that he needed a moment. He walked into my bedroom alone and sat down on the long, blue ottoman that faced my bed. I peered from around the corner and saw that he was meditating. Or trying to meditate. His palms shook in his lap as he attempted to steady himself. He was working hard to regain his composure, but I could tell that he wasn't getting very far. I felt a tinge of shame run down my spine.

I left Danny alone and walked into the kitchen. I shook my head as I began to fill with regret. *Dammit. I knew I shouldn't have said anything.* I began to make some tea as I waited for Danny to return.

A few minutes later, he met me in the kitchen. Then he said, "Ok, wow. Lauren, I am really trying to take this in. Your story challenges so many of my own spiritual beliefs. But I need you to know that I believe you."

I let out a huge sigh of relief that filled the entire room. I reassured him that all of this was very hard for me to believe too. It felt so good to talk to someone else who was Jewish— someone who could relate to what I had been taught about the world. And I was so grateful that I was also in the presence of someone who cared about me enough to take this seriously. I watched as he worked incredibly hard to process my story. And I knew he was doing that for me.

I told Danny that I had lost a few friends since the depossession. Some of my closest friends just couldn't get on board with such a huge paradigm shift. I understood that, but it was also very painful. I felt like I had left the regular world and entered the metaphysical world overnight. And not everyone was coming with me. So when two of my closest friends told me that they just didn't believe *in all this stuff,* I felt like my entire life had been invalidated. I didn't need everyone close to me to start a relationship with the Archangel Michael.

However, I did need everyone to believe *me.* Danny stood there and told me that he did.

* * *

Danny and I made our way over to my couch with two cups of herbal tea. We slowly inched closer to each other. Danny looked at me lovingly. He asked if he could hold me. I said yes. He wrapped his arms around me as we lay back onto the couch together. I allowed my body to sink into his as my shoulders began to relax. I closed my eyes. I felt the rise and fall of his chest as my cheek settled in right beneath his collarbone. My jaw softened. My body was starting to come down.

In that moment, I realized that no one had held me in years. *Years.* I had lost my entire family, been through a series of psychic attacks, and survived a depossession. And during that time, no one held me. Not like that.

Suddenly, I began to weep. Danny held me tighter as he contained my body and all the emotion that had been stuck inside of it. My tears stained his navy-blue shirt. I tried to slow my breath, but the floodgate had already opened.

Danny whispered into my ear as he ran his fingers through my hair. He told me that I was incredibly strong. He told me that he was so glad I made it. That he was so glad I was still here. We both cried. And then, I told him that I was grateful that we had found a way to remain so connected, even after all these years.

Day morphed into night as Danny and I sustained our embrace. I think we both needed to hold each other exactly like we did. We remained truly present with each other as we allowed ourselves to feel the power of such genuine care and affection.

I gazed into Danny's warm, brown eyes. My neck regained its full range of movement as the breath returned to my chest. A smile melted across the corners of my face. And that's when I realized that I could add this moment to the very short list of times when I felt safe.

THROW IT ALL TO THE FIRE

I walked Danny over to the front door of my apartment, and we stared into each other's eyes once more. I hugged him deeply for the last time. He smiled at me as I handed him his coat. I watched Danny walk down the hallway and press the elevator button. I lingered at my door. For some reason, I needed to watch him leave. Danny continued to smile at me as he waited for the elevator to arrive. I heard the doors open, and then, he was gone.

I closed my front door and pressed my back up against it. A smile crept across my face. I paused for a moment as I began to realize exactly why I had been so comforted by Danny's presence. Perhaps it was because Danny and I had never tried to possess each other. Not once. Not ever. No matter where life took us, we managed to reunite at the exact moment when we needed each other the most. This type of connection was so refreshing, especially after everything I had just survived. All of a sudden, I yearned to feel a sense of freedom in all my relationships. Perhaps that would be a prerequisite from now on. After all, I never wanted to be possessed again.

* * *

I wanted to continue basking in the moment that Danny and I had just shared, but I glanced at the time. *Shit, I'm going to be late!* I began rushing around the apartment. I threw on a bright red sweater and reapplied my lip gloss. I slipped into a different pair of jeans and grabbed a pair of boots from the front hall closet. I was going to a highly anticipated New Year's Eve party, and I had been looking forward to this event for weeks.

Sarah had invited me to join her at a friend's house to ring in the new year. There would only be a few folks in attendance, and this party had a very specific theme: 2018 was a dumpster fire, it's time to let it burn. Apparently, everyone at this party had something in common: we all had a horrible year. I thought I was the only one. Granted, I'm not sure that anyone else experienced a depossession, but it was nice to know I wasn't alone. As the end of the year approached, I joked with all my friends that I had never been so excited for the clock to strike twelve. I was extremely ready for 2018 to come to an end.

Sarah told me all about the folks who would be at this party. Apparently, they were well-versed in tarot, astrology, and crystals. This seemed like a sign that I was going to the right place. As my relationship to the Archangel Michael continued to deepen, I had become increasingly interested in all kinds of witchy things. So I decided to bring some of my new spiritual cleansing materials with me to this party. I grabbed the gift bag full of sage and crystals that Linda had given me, piled the contents into a large, maroon tote, and sealed it shut.

I was a little late to the party, but I didn't mind. My time with Danny had been well worth it. When I walked into the host's living room, everyone was already seated around the dining room table. They were drinking champagne and reading tarot cards. Tarot was still very new to me, but I was very much intrigued. I had just purchased my first deck, and I was beginning to create a ritual around pulling cards for myself. Of course, the card I pulled the most was the Tower.

* * *

The Tower is a frightening card to receive. In most decks, it depicts a light grey tower that is built on the side of a cliff. It closely resembles the Leaning Tower of Pisa. But that's not all: a bolt of lightning is often seen striking through the top of the tower as people jump hastily out of every window, falling into the deep water below. When I first pulled this card, I screamed. I didn't even want to read the description. In all honesty, this card looked like everything my life had become since my estrangement. Each plague had caused me to jump out of a burning tower as I prayed for a safety net. Despite all odds, I had survived. I had managed to conquer the deep waters and pull myself ashore.

Still, I continued to receive the Tower card. Each time, I

cried in agony. It took me a long time to realize that the Tower brings deep medicine along with its terrifying imagery. While the people in the card appear to be plunging to their deaths, in reality, they are escaping from a burning building that is about to crumble at any moment. The water below is scary and unfamiliar. But they certainly cannot afford to remain in a tower that has been set on fire. No one wants to be trapped inside a home that is about to come crumbling down. I understood that better than anyone.

The Tower accurately reflected my journey over the past six months. Everything I had lost was built on shaky ground. I had accumulated so many losses over the years, but I could never have imagined that my estrangement was only the beginning. Apparently, there was a crack in the foundation of my life that was so deep, so core shattering, that I never would have found it on my own. Lightning struck my tower four times: the ants, the moths, the flood, and the bed bugs. Until finally, the Tower revealed the deepest crack in the foundation: Mary Frances.

* * *

Midnight approached as we concluded the tarot portion of our New Year's Eve celebration. I managed to avoid pulling the Tower. And for that, I was truly grateful. Perhaps I had reached the end of all the shedding that needed to happen in my life. Perhaps the last thing that needed to go was 2018. And I was very ready to say goodbye to the worst cumulative year of my life.

We decided to begin the ritual we had been highly anticipating all evening. It was finally time to create an actual dumpster fire to bid farewell to 2018. We threw on our winter coats and began to congregate in the backyard around a large fire pit. The host lit a fire, and I watched as the flames began to grow. Yellow and orange flames began to build steadily at the base of the fire pit. I closed my eyes as I imagined lightning striking through the tower one last time. This was the final shedding, the big release. I was ready to throw it all into the fire.

I brought out my sage and lit a piece as we cleared the energy around us. The host of the party passed around slips of colored paper and thick Crayola markers. We each took a moment to write down everything we wanted to release from the year. Everyone took turns speaking to the group as they cleansed themselves of their colored paper. I looked around at these people, most of whom were strangers. I felt an immediate affinity to them. We all had a terrible year, and this was how we wanted to say goodbye to it. That was enough for me to feel the rustling of a new kind of spiritual community forming in my life.

When it was my turn, I looked around at these faces as they glimmered in the light. I rubbed my palms together, feeling the warmth of the fire and the community we had created. I imagined the tower once again. Slowly I said, "I lost a lot of things this year. Things I thought defined me, but none of it really did. I think I lost it all so that I could find myself."

Then I looked down at my only piece of orange paper, and I threw it into the flame. I watched the piece of paper disintegrate as it morphed into black ash.

It was short and concise:

Goodbye, Mary Frances.

ONE WHO DOES THESE THINGS WILL NEVER BE SHAKEN

February 2019

I don't know what I expected 2019 to bring. I had hoped that a new year would somehow provide me with a completely clean slate, though that never happens. New Year's resolutions are often made, and they are rarely kept. That's because life doesn't magically shift in January. My process was no different. I still had work to do. I still had to face the truth of everything that 2018 had brought crumbling down to the ground.

After I threw Mary Frances into the fire, I thought I would wake up different. I had been waiting to *start my new life* since May of 2018, when I left my family. I desperately needed that energy to shift now. I had waited long enough. There was just one problem: the tower had stripped away so many defining elements of my life that I had no idea what to do next. I was more comfortable taking a wrecking ball to everything that wasn't working than I was drawing up a blueprint for the new life I wanted to live.

One day I went to brunch with my good friend, Liz. She was from the same network of Jews where I had originally met Danny. I decided to tell Liz the truth about all the metaphysical elements of my story. Since Danny had taken my story like a pro, I was hopeful. Liz digested my story with a lot of care and consideration. Then she suggested that I go through a Mikvah.

A Mikvah is very special Jewish ceremony typically done to honor important passages in someone's life. It is often referred to as a ritual bath. People perform Mikvahs ahead of getting married, and they can also be performed during most other periods of sacred transition. I had never been through one before, but I had always been curious about the process. Once Liz offered to go with me, I wholeheartedly agreed.

I decided that I wanted my Mikvah to double as a renaming ceremony. I had recently embarked on an expedition to change my name. Most elements of my birth name felt wrong at this point. I wasn't ready to change my legal name, so I started with the easiest transition: a new Hebrew name.

The Hebrew name my parents chose for me at birth was Leah. I assumed they had chosen this name because it was the closest Hebrew name to Lauren. However, after I left my family, I began to wonder about the origins of that name. As a result, I started researching the Hebrew name Leah and what it meant.

I turned to Google once more. My mouth was agape as I read the story of Leah. In the Torah, Leah had been married to Jacob, but he never loved her. She pined after him, yearning for Jacob to pay more attention to her. I could feel Leah's desperation and heartbreak. In my experience, it's hard to be alone, but it's worse to be partnered with someone who doesn't love you. Jacob never returned Leah's affection. She bore multiple children and was the perfect wife. But in the end, Jacob left Leah for her sister Rachel, whom he had always loved. I read this story and then I read the direct translation of the name Leah. It meant *delicate and weary.* It also meant *the unloved one.*

Everything began to register. The unloved one. *My parents named me the unloved one.* I couldn't believe how visceral that felt. I had always felt unloved. As a child, I chased after my parents' love, but it always felt out of reach. The night of my possession illustrated just how far I was willing to go to be seen. My parents missed all the signs I was throwing their way. But Mary Frances came swooping in at just the right moment. She saw me. She chose me. And that was all it took for me to let her in.

I went on to chase after the love of so many partners, but it never came. I felt like I had been cursed. I shrunk myself way down, attempting to appear agreeable and desirable in all my early romantic relationships. I became the partner who smiled and nodded. I became someone who pretended to like the same things as my love interest. I became someone unrecognizable to myself, all in pursuit of being seen. And each time a relationship ended, I felt like I had failed to become loveable once again. That's when the shadow side of my fawn response began to creep in: If my own parents didn't really love me, who else would? I became increasingly convinced that I was destined for a lifetime of heartbreak. That I was destined to end up like Leah.

Everything was different now. I was no longer willing to seal my fate in the Hebrew name my parents had haphazardly chosen for me. By leaving my family, I sent myself a very strong message: I was done showing up for people who refused to show up for me. I gave my parents an entire decade to prove that my sexual abuse story mattered to them. That I mattered to them. There were only so many holidays I could spend pining after their support and ending up alone with a can of soup. I didn't want to continue down the path that had been paved by Leah. So I left. The day I mailed the estrangement letters, I went in a new direction. And just like that, my Leah days were over.

I sat in my apartment in Heaven on Sheridan as I began to draft an entirely new blueprint for my life. I decided to start by changing my Hebrew name. In search of a new one, I looked at names that began with "C" because I wanted to name myself after my grandmother, Coco. In Judaism, it is also commonplace to name someone after a deceased relative to honor them.

I scoured lists of Hebrew names that began with "C" until I landed on Chava. I couldn't take my eyes off this name. I didn't know what Chava meant, but it resonated deep within my soul. I began to research it and I came across a video by Rabbi Aaron L. Raskin. It was seventeen minutes long. I watched the entire thing.

The beginning of this video took my breath away. Rabbi Raskin said: "A Jewish name is a very powerful thing. A Jewish name is not only a word that distinguishes one person from another, but a Jewish name represents the combination of the life force that the soul gives to the body as it enters the body. Therefore, we are told that the name that a child is given at birth, based on the father and the mother, is really based on prophecy."[6]

My eyes grew wide. A Hebrew name is the name of the soul. And my parents named *my soul* delicate and weary. Because of this decision, my parents *prophesized* that I would be unloved. That made my blood boil.

I took a deep breath as I resumed the video. The rabbi continued: "Chava was the wife of Adam. And why was Chava given this name? Because Chava means the mother of all life. The word Chava means 'one who speaks.' And from here we see that every single woman was given the power of speech. However, we find that the name Chava also means 'the power to reveal by telling.' There's an even deeper meaning. We find that Chava also means 'to reveal secrets, to reveal the unknown teachings and the mysteries of the universe. To reveal, and to bring down all the secrets that happened in Exodus. And to make it known to the entire world.'"

I burst into tears. I knew with certainty that Chava was the correct name for my soul. That's when I realized that I had always been Chava. I had been given the power of speech from the time I was a young child. People were heavily affected by my words, in both positive and negative ways. I was an Aries sun and an Aries moon. I had a natural power with words and boldness in my blood. I also had a lot of opinions, and I freely shared them. When I spoke my truth, I was often met with dissent from the adults who surrounded me. Except for Coco. She loved the truth-teller within me.

* * *

I began to recall moments in my life when I had felt like Chava. Most notably, my Bat Mitzvah at the age of thirteen. I had been given a Torah portion in Leviticus since my Bat Mitzvah took place in April. One of the tasks of my Bat Mitzvah was to write a d'var Torah[7] where I analyzed the Torah portion I had been given. In the verses that corresponded to my Bat Mitzvah, God banished everyone who had leprosy to a separate island, exiling them from the greater population. I had a serious problem with this portion as soon as I read it. I felt that God had discriminated against his own citizens, and he was delivering the wrong message to everyone by sending these lepers away. I also felt that we shouldn't be reading this portion and simply going along with it. I wanted everyone to think about what it was really about. Accordingly, I wrote a very "Chava" speech.

When it was my turn to stand in front of the entire congregation and give my speech, I used the power of my words with great intent. I stood at that podium with my hot pink braces and my cream-colored dress, and I disagreed with God. I told everyone in attendance exactly what I thought of this Torah portion. I said it was problematic. I also said that God's decision reminded me of the current messaging around HIV/AIDS. I felt that we were discriminating against people with HIV in a similar fashion. By the way, I wasn't having that either. It was the nineties, and the movie *Philadelphia* had a strong impact on me.

I looked out onto the crowd. It seemed like my speech had upset a lot of people. I felt a sense of rage begin to burn inside of my little body. And I remember thinking: *I am an adult in this building today, and this is my truth. And you are going to listen to me. I don't care if it makes you uncomfortable.*

* * *

After I watched this video, I formally decided to become Chava. I talked to Liz and told her that I wanted to go through with a Mikvah and that I was changing my Hebrew name. Later that week, we went in search of the right place to perform this ceremony. Unfortunately, my options were limited. Not all synagogues have Mikvahs; they are often attached to conservative and orthodox congregations. I knew that I wouldn't be allowed inside of an orthodox Mikvah, mainly because of my tattoos. I hoped that there was a conservative Mikvah that would accept my liberal, tattooed body. Luckily,

Liz knew exactly where we could go. Apparently, there was a Mikvah associated with a conservative synagogue that was located in the same suburb where I was raised. That felt like fate. We had another liberal, tattooed friend who had gone there before her wedding. As a result, I knew they would accept me. I called the rabbi and made an appointment. Due to strict rules around menstruation, the first available time I could go was Sunday, February 17 at 6:15 p.m.

On the evening of my Mikvah, Liz picked me up outside of my apartment, and we drove to the suburbs. We were both truly excited. I told her that I was very ready to become Chava. Liz told me that I had chosen the perfect name, and that Chava fit me a lot more than Leah ever had. We talked about how I had just released so much from my soul that didn't belong to me. Now that Mary Frances was gone, I wanted to fill that space with my own soul. And my soul was Chava.

The snow began to fall as we approached the Mikvah. I watched as small, white snowflakes began to blanket the parking lot of the synagogue, which was located just ten minutes down the road from the house where I had been possessed. There was a pale yellow light shining through the main door, which confirmed that we were in the right place. The Mikvah was in a smaller, separate brick building that was on the same property as the synagogue. We walked up to the door, rang the bell, and waited.

After a few minutes, the rabbi opened the door and let us in. I let out a sigh as I entered the warm lobby of the Mikvah building. It was small, but cozy. Liz and I sat down in identical black folding chairs, and the rabbi sat across from us at her small, wooden desk. It was littered with pamphlets from the temple. The rabbi asked me why I wanted to perform this Mikvah, and I told her that I had just gone through a very transformative time and that I was looking to celebrate my rebirth by changing my Hebrew name. Liz and I had unanimously decided that I should leave out the details of my estrangement, as well as virtually everything else that had happened. In retrospect, I think that was a good call.

I asked the rabbi if Liz would be allowed to come into the ritual bath area with me, but the rabbi said no. She told us the Mikvah was private, and it was to happen between me and the rabbi only. However, Liz would be permitted to stand at the slatted wooden doors and listen to the entire ceremony. The doors were thin, so thin that I knew she would be able to hear everything. This was critical since I had asked Liz to recite a very important psalm that I had chosen as an entryway into my life as Chava.

The psalm was called Walking with Integrity, and I first heard it at Coco's funeral in June of 2016. When the rabbi read it that day at the gravesite, I burst into tears. I had just been hired to teach a course in social work at the University of Chicago, in the same program I had attended years back. I had decided to call my course Practicing with Integrity. I had named that course immediately before Coco died. I didn't even get the chance to tell her. As soon as the rabbi read that psalm, I knew it was for me. Coco was showing me that she was still there.

In the years that followed, I revisited the psalm so many times that I decided to create a tattoo out of it. I tattooed the last line of the psalm on the small of my back in Coco's handwriting in December of 2017. That line became my guiding light. It reads: *one who does these things will never be shaken.* In fact, I called my parents the day I got that tattoo to tell them all about it. That was the last time I ever spoke to them.

I waved goodbye to Liz as the rabbi escorted me to the back of the Mikvah. We shut the door behind us. I looked directly in front of me and realized that we were in a bathroom, complete with a shower. The rabbi told me that I needed to take a full shower, which included brushing and flossing my teeth. Then I had to comb all the tangles out of my hair to the point where she would be able to run her fingers through my hair without a problem. I thought to myself: *This will be the toughest part.*

I did my best to bathe according to all the rules, paying careful attention to every crevice of my body. I also conditioned my hair. Twice. Wrapped in a brown towel, I met the rabbi outside the bathroom. The rabbi walked over and examined me. She ran her fingers through my long, dark, curly hair, as I stood motionless. She smiled. *Phew.*

The rabbi told me that I passed the preparatory portion of the evening. And as a reward, she opened another slatted wooden door, unveiling the Mikvah for the very first time. My eyes grew wide. It was the most beautiful thing I had ever seen. It looked and felt like an ancient bathhouse. Beige tiles lined the floor and the walls. In the center of the room, there was a large pool with water that glistened in the dim light. The water was greenish blue, the color of the Caribbean Sea.

The rabbi asked me to remove my towel. I had never been naked in front of a rabbi before. I handed the rabbi my towel as I turned toward the pool in front of me. And in that moment, I realized that the rabbi would be staring directly at my tattoo that said *one who does these things will never be shaken* as I descended into the pool to be reborn as Chava. All of this was in honor of my grandmother, who was the only person who had accepted me wholeheartedly. It was perfect.

My ankles brushed up against the cool water as I approached the top step of the Mikvah. I took a breath, allowing my body to adjust to the temperature as I made my way down each layer of the pool. The rabbi advised me to wade all the way to the base of the Mikvah where the water reached my waist. I stood in the center of the pool with my arms held out at either side, as was the custom.

The rabbi began the ceremony. She told me to recite the first prayer in Hebrew, which was written on a laminated sign directly in front of me. I sang the prayer as I stood in the water. And then the rabbi advised me to dunk my entire body into the pool. I lifted my feet off the ground, and I allowed my body to fall back into the cool, clean water. I held my breath for a few seconds, and I felt the water cleanse everything that didn't belong to me. I stayed underwater as I said goodbye to my family, to Mary Frances, and to Leah. We repeated this cycle two more times.

Then the rabbi asked if there was anything special that I wanted to add. I asked Liz to step over to the slatted wooden door so she could read my special psalm. I heard her rise from her chair and draw closer to me. And then, I heard Liz's voice:

Psalm 15: Walking with Integrity

A Psalm of David
Adonai, who may dwell in Your tent?
Who may live on Your holy mountain?
The one who walks with integrity,
Who does what is right,
And speaks truth in his heart,
Who does not slander with his tongue,
Does not wrong his neighbor,
And does not disgrace his friend,
Who despises a vile person in his eyes,
But honors those who fear Adonai,
Who keeps his oath even when it hurts,
And does not change,
Who lends money without usury,
And takes no bribe against the innocent.
One who does these things will never be shaken.

I fell back into the water one last time. And when I emerged, I felt different. I knew I had been reborn. I was no longer Leah: the unloved one. I had become Chava: the one who brings down secrets and reveals them to the entire world.

THE MAZE OF MY LIFE IS MINE

February to March 2019

The Mikvah proved to be a rite of passage. I became Chava in that pool of sparkling green water and never looked back. I felt the transformation begin to take shape as soon as I left the synagogue that evening. I glanced at Liz as we both climbed back into her bright orange hatchback. My hair was wet and fastened into a messy bun at the top of my head. A string of dark brown curls escaped from my hair band, brushing up against the base of my neck. A smile crept across my face. I was glistening.

As we drove away from the town where I had been born and then reborn, I stared out the window, deep in contemplation. We swung onto the highway ramp, barely avoiding a drive-by of my childhood home. I breathed a sigh of relief. I hadn't been back there in years. It was the house where the Black Square abused me. Where Mary Frances possessed me. Where I disclosed to my parents and then stormed out of their kitchen. I never wanted to see it again.

As I continued to stare out the window, I felt myself thank Leah for all she had done to survive the lifetime of pain she had been given. And then, I felt myself pass the baton over to Chava. The one who brings down secrets and reveals them to the entire world. The first woman of her kind.

* * *

By the end of March, it was time to celebrate my birthday. I had always relished throwing myself a birthday bash, but this time, the novelty was gone. Ever since my estrangement, I didn't feel like my birthday belonged to me. I knew that day also belonged to my parents, and that fundamentally changed how I felt about it. My birthday would always be the day I left the womb of a woman I had struggled to connect to for my entire life. The day my parents named me Lauren, a name I had always failed to appreciate. It was also only a few weeks before my parents branded my soul Leah: *the unloved one.*

But I chose to leave. And in leaving, I chose to live a life that was separate from the one I had been given at birth. I chose to be reborn on the night of my Mikvah, with a new name and a new perspective. I felt the cool waters of that pool receive my naked body. The pool felt like another womb, especially as I tucked my body underneath the light waves, simulating a newborn baby's journey out of the birth canal and into the world. I had been given a second chance. A do-over. I planned to take full advantage of it.

Overall, it felt so right to be Chava. Slowly, I began to realize that Chava wasn't a new identity, rather, she was a reclamation of the person I had always been. I had been the *revealer of truth* many times over the course of my life. Perhaps my Mikvah ceremony hadn't been a renaming; it had been a homecoming. I had finally come home to myself.

I wondered how Chava had gotten so lost over the years. I would come to learn that Chava had been buried under layers of social conditioning and other people's projections. Reclaiming Chava was just the beginning. I had made so many changes to my external world. It was time to turn the tower moment inward.

* * *

I don't know how I expected to just move on from the wreckage, but that's the opposite of what happened as soon as I had a chance to slow down. I entered another phase of grieving the loss of my family, my home, most of my belongings, and a part of my soul that never actually belonged to me. Even though I had thrown Mary Frances into the fire, the memories of all she had done haunted me to the bone. I had no idea how to come back from that. How could I even begin to piece together a new life and a new identity when the world I had been living in was suddenly rendered obsolete? I had endured so much change that facing it became insurmountable. There was no blueprint for what came next after everything had crumbled to the ground.

Yet somehow, I forged ahead: blindly determined to build a new life. The path forward was an unlikely combination of rainbows and landmines. That's the best way I can describe how it felt to be in both liberation and in mourning. My emotions seesawed between two extremes, almost daily. One minute I was looking out the window of my beautiful apartment in Heaven on Sheridan and basking in the glow of my own survival. The next I was curled into a ball crying on the floor. Tears stained my teal rug. I missed having a family. My heart ached for my parents while I simultaneously never wanted to see them again. My grief was like a valve that wouldn't shut off. Night after night, the tears poured out of me. I held myself tightly in the dark as I whispered, "It's ok, it's going to be ok." I did my best to act as my own parent. To fill in. To replace what I had lost. But I felt like a pinch-hitter who had been thrown into a baseball game with no training and no preparation.

Traumatic memories from the past year began to flood my brain. The four plagues contaminated my dreams, making it impossible to sleep through the night. I would wake up, drenched in fear and sweat; gasping in horror as I realized that my nightmare had been real. I missed the days when I woke up from a nightmare and breathed a sigh of relief. Not this time. Now my nightmares were actual memories of all the events I had barely survived.

April to September 2019

Over the next few months, I continued to question everything. I examined every inch of my former life like a detective looking for clues. I was desperate for answers. I yearned to find anything that would help me to understand how this could possibly be my story. *A possession? How did I manage to end up in* The Exorcist*?* There was no way to make sense of it. My brain continued to buck and refute that storyline. I thought back to the day when I first read the transcript of the depossession in my office, and I almost threw up in a trash can. Logic seemed completely out of reach.

After a while, my mind grew quiet as the voice of my heart stepped forward. I have absolutely no recollection of when I allowed the voice of my heart to take over with so much force. My guess is that it happened slowly, especially as the evidence of metaphysical interference began to pile up. But once I heard my heart, I absolutely knew it was all true. This was my story, whether I liked it or not.

Still, it was wholly overwhelming to come to terms with it all. I wrapped myself in a cocoon and shut almost everyone out. I didn't know what else to do. I kept my network small: Heather, Mila, Marilyn, and Linda. After all, they had been there for everything. Even though they were all haunted by my story, they didn't run from it. They didn't run from me. I don't know what I would have done without each of them. Even though I knew these were my people, I kept many aspects of my inner world hidden from them. I just didn't think anyone would truly understand.

Besides, my path was mine. No one else could walk it for me. Nevertheless, it was incredibly isolating to walk through it alone, and I sank into the deepest depression of my life. On the weekends, I refused plans and slept until the middle of the afternoon. My whole body ached with grief. I barely ate. I stared out the window of my beautiful apartment and cried. I was slowly wasting away.

One day in therapy, I was talking to Marilyn about how I had been feeling. I told her that calling this stage "depression" didn't even begin to cover it. And that's when Marilyn asked me if I had ever heard of *a dark night of the soul.* I hadn't, but I was immediately intrigued. I left her office and pulled out my phone. I took to Google once again.

I learned that a dark night of the soul can sometimes feel like depression, but that's not quite accurate. A dark night of the soul is often referred to as *ego death*. It happens when the soul begins to step forward as the ego steps back. While this may sound positive, experiencing it is completely terrifying. The ego holds most of the material that comprises our identity, or at least who we think we are. It can be everything from the role we play in our families to who we are at work. In short, we often believe that the ego *is* who we are.

The ego is severely threatened by a dark night of the soul. The ego fights to remain relevant, as the soul continues to reveal a deeper truth. What follows is an epic internal battle. And if the soul wants to reveal to us that we are quite different from who we thought we were, the result is a period filled with extreme confusion, loss, and uncertainty. That is what happened to me.

* * *

My dark night of the soul lasted for a total of eight months. During that time, I was plagued by two questions that cut through my bones and penetrated every cell of my body:

How will I survive without my family?

Who am I without my family?

I didn't know.

I didn't know.

Slowly I began to realize that I didn't know how to survive without my family. During the dark night of the soul, I was in a strange place. I started grieving my parents with such ferocity that it almost broke me. My ego was wholly unprepared for that. She fought against any storyline that involved me having empathy for my family and all that had transpired between us. She liked the simple version where I was the perpetual victim. Where I was the one running out of Passover and eating cans of soup alone on Thanksgiving. But apparently, my soul believed that there was more to this story.

In the end, my soul won. My soul forced me to grieve my parents. I spent many days alone in my apartment, crying over the loss of my father. I cried so hard that my chest began to burn. I even developed an unrelenting cough, just like the one that brought me to Linda over eight years ago. Once again, I went to the doctor multiple times and even had a chest x-ray. Each time, they found nothing. This time, I knew what was going on. Linda's words echoed through my body. *I was sick with grief.* Soon, I began to own it. I coughed up every memory of my father that had gotten lodged in my chest. I stared at the lime green mucus as I watched it disappear down the drain.

Cough, rinse, repeat. I said goodbye to my father this way. I coughed for five straight months. I washed him down the sink at work and at home. I washed him down the sink at Heather's house. Each time I coughed up a new memory, my chest began to feel lighter and heavier at the same time. Even now, as I write this, I can feel my chest burning all over again.

I grieved the loss of my mother, too, but it felt different. That loss was much more complicated. I cried *for* my mother more than I cried *over* her. I thought about who she could have been if she had been loved more when she was child. I thought about the fact that she treated me just as she had been treated, and I knew that wasn't solely her fault. I imagined the parallel lives we could have led if everything had been different. *I mean, everything.* In that life, we enjoyed each other's company and looked up to one another with unconditional, positive regard. I mourned that imaginary life. I mourned that imaginary mother. I cried over all the love that was never exchanged between us. I cried over that love like a child crying over a spilled ice cream cone. It was so close I could almost taste it.

Instead, it had splattered all over the floor.

* * *

I also didn't know who I was without my family. During the dark night, I came to realize that I had developed much of my identity in opposition to my family. I seemed to exist *because* of that tension. Ultimately, I didn't know what kind of person I would be without that fight. This was a harsh reality I was not ready to face.

In my family, I had always been the outspoken one. The inconvenient one. The one who fought back against things that didn't seem fair or right. After I came forward about the Black Square, that role was heavily amplified. But for years, I wasn't ready to leave. I wasn't even ready to understand how desperately I needed to leave.

Before I started working with Marilyn, I had another therapist whom I saw for five years. I saw this therapist during the height of all the tension that arose in my family after I came forward about the Black Square. She watched me pack every holiday emergency evacuation bag. She listened as I recounted all the fights I had with my parents over their relationship with the Black Square. And together, we created an archetype for the role I was playing in my family. We called her the Wounded Warrior.[8]

My therapist described the Wounded Warrior as an extraordinarily burned-out version of the Tin Man who stood in an empty field in rusty gear flailing all over the place. We both agreed that the Wounded Warrior was completely exhausted by all the fighting. Soon, she was fighting all the time, regardless of the threat level. She desperately wanted to retire her sword, but there was never an opportunity to do that. The hits just kept on coming.

I thoroughly identified with this archetype. I was the Wounded Warrior for many, many years. In truth, I felt like I had been born into that role, and then learned how to play it out of sheer necessity. Even though I desperately wanted to put my sword down, I didn't know what would happen if I did.

Obviously, there was no way to retire my sword while I remained connected to my family. There was no question about that. It wasn't safe to remove my armor amid all those active threats. Besides, there was always another holiday betrayal. There was always another fight with my mother over whether the Black Square *really was that bad*. And as the leaves turned brown every year, I began to stockpile cans of soup for the upcoming holiday season. Ultimately, all these hits began to accumulate in my tired body. Until Mother's Day, when I left for good.

Now, during my dark night of the soul, my ego continued to play the part of the Wounded Warrior. She didn't seem to realize that I had left my family. I must have forgotten to tell her that she could remove her armor and go home. The Wounded Warrior continued swinging her sword in an empty field, exhausting herself to the bone. I tried to get through to her numerous times; to tell her it was all over. But something else was clearly keeping her going, and I didn't know how to stop it.

It almost felt like she *enjoyed* being in that role. I didn't understand how that could be possible. I desperately wanted to eat something other than a can of soup on Thanksgiving. After all, a key attribute of the Wounded Warrior archetype is that she doesn't want to be fighting so much. Or so it seemed. My soul began to peel back the layers of this archetype, and it was a big reveal. One that I wished I could shield my eyes from seeing.

I began to slowly understand why my ego was drawn to that role. She had played the Wounded Warrior for so long that there was a comfort that came along with it. She knew all the lines. She knew how to convey the perfect tone. She had mastered the retelling of a Wounded Warrior Thanksgiving. It was like a trusted party trick. My ego clung to the Wounded Warrior with all her might. She continued to fight for its relevance.

My soul helped me understand why this was happening. I realized that fighting against my family made me feel strong. It gave me purpose. It won me instant empathy. And admittingly, it also allowed me to feel like a victim. All these things were very attractive to my ego. My friends were routinely horrified by all the holiday betrayals. But a part of me relished telling them these stories, and watching them look at me with unequivocal sympathy. Over time, I began to realize why this was so attractive. I wanted that exact response from my own parents. I wanted them to be horrified by everything the Black Square had done. I wanted them to be horrified by their own tacit consent to all that toxicity. So the Wounded Warrior continued to stockpile other people's sympathetic responses, hoping to fill the wound created by my own family. Of course, that's not what happened. Not even the Wounded Warrior could help me fill the gaping wound that each holiday betrayal left behind.

The dark night of the soul came in like a wrecking ball and took all that novelty away. I knew it was time to retire the identity of the girl who fought against her family so that I could become the woman who stepped into her power. Externally, I had left the battleground. Now I had to put down the sword *inside my mind*. No one told me this would be way harder.

My ego continued to replay reels upon reels of relentless holiday explosions. But as the dark night wore on, these moments hooked me less and less. Their appeal began to diminish. Soon, these memories felt like cheap, empty thrills. I was evolving before my very own eyes.

Now that I was Chava, there was no way to run from the truth. The role of the Wounded Warrior was suddenly incongruent with my soul. Chava was proud of her sharp tongue. She didn't cower or apologize for it. Sure, she was still an outsider, but she wasn't bothered by that. Chava understood that it was possible to be strong without being immersed in an incessant fight. She even began to understand why her parents hadn't been able to stand up for her. That was new. Something was changing. I could feel it in my bones.

* * *

My dark night of the soul had one final reveal: I began to realize that I had become a writer. I had always loved to write, but now that desire was even more powerful. Writing had become Chava's microphone. It was the way my soul chose to communicate with the world. I survived my dark night of the soul by writing. I wrote poetry and I wrote prose. I wrote my way through my own grief. I put down my sword and picked up my pen. That was also new.

In late September of 2019, I began to emerge from my cocoon. I will never know exactly what facilitated this moment. But just as a butterfly knows when it is ready, so did I. As I began to take my first steps out into the world, I wrote this poem:

Life (before)

    Life is a giant labyrinth
    And we are all
    Winding
    Pining
    Stumbling
    Climbing
    Through it.

    We are doing our best
    (Or not).

    It's taken me a long time to accept
    That the maze of my life is mine
    It was so much easier
    (And also harder)
    Before.

TWO STEPS FORWARD, ONE STEP BACK

September 2019

As I pulled myself out of the dark night of the soul, I began to re-enter the world slowly, methodically. Everything around me remained unchanged, but I was unequivocally different. Some of these changes were the result of trauma, and some of them were signs of new growth. I avoided making eye contact on the bus because I didn't want to be possessed again. I cried most nights, realizing that I had no idea how to live inside my new life and my new skin. But every time I looked in the mirror, I saw a glimmer in my eyes that hadn't been there before. In these moments, I could feel Chava peeking through all the layers of social conditioning as she beckoned me forward.

The dark night changed me forever. I retired the Wounded Warrior and vowed to step more fully into becoming Chava. However, as I placed the first few bricks in the foundation of my new life, I continued to climb over jagged pieces of debris left over from the tower. I wondered how long I would feel this way. Two steps forward, one step back.

* * *

One night at the end of September, I attended a new moon circle at Inner Sense Healing Arts, a local wellness studio I had come to frequent. The studio held yoga classes, but it also offered tarot, energy healing, and astrology seminars. I had steadily deepened my relationship to the Archangel Michael ever since he appeared as the security guard in my building the year before. As I continued down this road, though, I didn't know anyone who could truly relate to my newfound spirituality. I began searching for communities of people who understood this realm. I became more acquainted with my tarot deck. I began to work with crystals. And slowly, deliberately, I began to tell my story. That's when I found Inner Sense Healing Arts. Between the trauma-informed yoga classes and the spiritual seminars, I was beginning to meet my people. Chava's people. I felt like I belonged somewhere for the first time in my life. I had no idea how badly I had been craving that kind of space until I found it.

I had become a regular participant at the Inner Sense moon circles, especially during my dark night of the soul. Inner Sense held moon circles around the new moon of every month, and I always looked forward to them. Through attending these gatherings, I learned that new moons are a perfect time for setting intentions and for calling in more abundance: two things I desperately needed as I rebuilt my life. I made sure to attend these circles as often as possible. As I continued to seesaw my way through grief and liberation, these moon circles grounded me. They provided me with community, and a ritual around planting the seeds of my new life. It was a welcome change from all the destruction of 2018.

One evening in mid-September, I attended another Inner Sense moon circle. We pulled oracle cards and participated in a guided meditation. We took turns sharing, just as we always did. I didn't speak about anything particularly triggering that night. But my story was beginning to reveal itself in spurts during these events. One night, I shared that I had estranged myself from my parents. Another night, I shared that I was in the process of rebuilding my material possessions after *losing them quite abruptly.* And on this night, I don't even remember what happened in that group. All I remember is that when the moon circle ended, I found myself in the throes of a giant identity crisis.

After the moon circle, I texted Heather to see if she was around. She invited me to come over for a late dinner after she put Willa to bed. I usually lingered after these moon circles; eager to connect further with my newfound spiritual community. But on that night, I left the studio in an instant. I slid into my car, managing to shut the door right as I burst into tears. I had no idea why I was crying. As I drove to Heather's house, I said aloud: "I don't know who I am anymore."

I walked into Heather's house thirty minutes later as I tried to dry my eyes. She asked me if something had happened in the moon circle. I told her it hadn't. We sat in her kitchen as she made me a late-night grilled cheese sandwich.

I burst into tears again. "Heather, I don't know who I am. I have spent so much time crying over this. All those weekends when I said I was busy … I wasn't. I was going through a massive identity crisis. Marilyn called it 'the dark night of the soul.'"

Heather's eyes grew wide with concern.

I continued, "I avoided talking about it because I don't think you can ever really understand what this feels like. Sometimes I still feel like I don't know who I am without my family, Heather. And it's even worse than that. It's so much worse. Ever since the depossession, I don't know who I am without her. I can't say her name. You know … *her*."

Heather sighed as she walked over to the kitchen table and sat down across from me. She looked into my eyes lovingly as she passed me a tissue. I could tell that she had no words.

"Maybe there's something else I need to do," I said. "I mean, I spent so long ripping out all the things that don't really belong to me. But I haven't put very much back in there. The Mikvah was amazing, but maybe that was just the beginning. I think I need a lot more reconstruction. I want to learn more about who I really am."

Heather nodded.

"Honestly, I don't even know where to start, Heather. Becoming Chava has been amazing, but sometimes, it's hard to hold onto her. Most of the time, I feel like I'm a shell of a person. I can't go on like this. Something has got to change. This isn't where my story ends. It can't be. There must be something that comes next. I just have no idea what that might be."

Heather grabbed my hand and held it in hers. "Lauren, why don't you reach out to Linda? She has always been there for you. I bet she has an idea of where to go from here."

My eyes lit up. "Of course! Linda! That's such a good

idea, Heather. I haven't seen Linda since that hypnotherapy session when she told me I had been possessed. I sent her the transcript from my session with Diane, so she knows what happened since then. But you're right. It would be such a good idea to see her. I think I need her help again."

I looked at the time and realized it was incredibly late. I scarfed down my sandwich, acutely aware of the fact that I had burst into Heather's home and cried for the past twenty minutes straight. And now, it was time for me to go. It might have made more sense for me to call Heather on my way home from Inner Sense instead of barging into her place for a grilled cheese sandwich and a quick cry. But, somehow, I knew I needed to soak in Heather's calming presence that night. I also knew that Heather didn't mind.

But I did. I yearned for our friendship to go back to the way it was *before*. I yearned for the weekends when we took long walks with Willa and laughed about something insignificant that happened at work or in our dating lives. I was growing weary of how many Saturday nights I had spent crying at Heather's kitchen table while we attempted to make sense of my epic hero's journey. I was ready for that to change.

It was time to call Linda.

NO ONE WAS EVER GOING TO SAVE YOU

September 2019

Linda and I met for an energy session the following week. I hadn't seen her since I picked up a tennis racket in our hypnotherapy session almost exactly one year prior. Luckily, I had filled her in by text. She didn't seem very surprised to learn about Mary Frances. Even though I was still reeling from that reveal, it made sense to me that Linda had anticipated it. She was always a few steps ahead. That was exactly the kind of person I needed in my life right now.

As Linda and I made our way up to the attic for our energy session, I felt relieved to be returning to the room where we typically met. The last time I was in her house, we had ventured into the basement for over three hours, and I left with a gift bag full of spiritual cleansing materials. Now we were back in Linda's energy healing space, and everything felt right. I sat down across from Linda in a broad armchair and allowed my back to press firmly against the large cushion.

I wasted no time. "Thank you so much for sending me to Diane. She found Mary Frances and got rid of her. Everything got so much better after that. The plagues are over. Everything is over. I don't know what to say, Linda. I don't think I would be alive without you."

Linda smiled warmly as I continued:

"I need to be honest. I am not in a great place, emotionally. I have been immersed in a dark night of the soul for months. It's been so intense. I think I'm finally ready to rebuild my life. But I don't know how to do that. Honestly, I don't know who I am anymore. Without my family, and without Mary Frances."

Linda's expression changed as she quickly rearranged herself in her chair. "Lauren, I would caution you against saying that you don't know who you are. That kind of energy may open you up to another possession. There are spirits everywhere and some of them are on the lookout for an opportunity. You don't want the wrong one to hear that."

My eyes grew wide as a chill ran down my spine. "Linda, are you serious? Oh my God. I can't go through this ever again. What do I need to do? I'll do anything!"

Linda leaned closer as she said, "I don't want you to walk around freaked out, Lauren. Let me say a little more. Diane removed a spirit who was taking up a lot of room inside of you. And now there is a hole, a hole you will want to fill with your own soul. That's how you make sure this kind of thing doesn't happen again. Once a surgeon removes a tumor, the body regenerates its own cells to fill in that space. That's what we need to do for you right now."

I sat forward in my chair. "Ok … how do I do that?

Linda took a sip of water. "You will need to do a soul retrieval session, Lauren. That's when a healer helps you find parts of your soul from this lifetime or past lifetimes that split off from your body during difficult moments. For Mary Frances to have taken up that much space, you must have lost a lot of your own soul by the age of eleven. We need to go in search of your soul parts and ask them to come home to you. That will fill in the space that Mary Frances left."

I began to nod. "Diane said something about this before we did the depossession. She said that for me to lose this much of my soul, I might have past-life trauma in addition to all the childhood trauma that I already know about. Honestly, I don't know if I believe in past lives. What do you think, Linda?"

Linda crossed one leg over the other. Then she said, "I can't tell you what to believe in, Lauren. But in my opinion, a soul retrieval session is the next step in your journey. When a healer calls out to the lost soul parts, we never really know who will come back. Some parts may not want to return, and other parts may be grateful. They may have been waiting for you to find them for a long time. It's possible that you will retrieve parts from another lifetime. Do you think you can remain open to that?"

I rolled my neck from side to side and paused. "All I know is this, Linda. I never want to be possessed again. So I am willing to do just about anything to make sure that doesn't happen. When all this started, I didn't believe in angels, and I didn't know anything about spiritual possession. Look at me now. I am communicating with the Archangel Michael and attending new moon circles. So if I need to stretch my beliefs again, I think I can do it. Especially if there is a soul part from another lifetime who wants to come back."

Linda smiled. "Good, Lauren. That is perfect."

I changed the subject. "There's something else, Linda. During my dark night, I really grieved my parents. And not only that, but it also seems like there is a never-ending well of pain over what they did (or didn't do) when I came forward about being sexually abused. I don't know how to live with that betrayal. It cuts so deep."

Linda took another sip of water. "I know, Lauren. I know that pain is incredibly deep. On the surface, they did betray you. But I am wondering if you can see that there is a deeper layer to everything you experienced in your family."

I folded my arms over my chest. "I am not sure I understand what you mean, Linda."

Linda took a deep breath. Then she said, "Can you see what this was all for? I know you wanted your whole life to be different. I know you wanted to have parents who protected you from all that abuse. I know that it will always be painful that they didn't stand up for you. But I hope you can see it now. No one was ever going to save you. Not your father; not your mother. This was your journey. Everyone signed up for this, including you. Can't you see? You had to claim your place as the cycle breaker. Everyone did their job well."

My eyes bulged as my cheeks began to flush. I dropped my arms to the side. "Linda, I need you to understand that my parents fucked up. They should have saved me. They should have protected me from the Black Square. But they did nothing, and they lost me forever because of that. I would have given anything to have it all go differently!"

I stared at the floor, enraged.

Linda began to speak: "I received intuitive guidance to say this to you now, Lauren. All I ask is that you consider the deeper meaning of my point. Your pain is real, and it is justified. There is no silver lining here. What I am saying exists on a different plane. Mull it over when you are ready. That doesn't have to be today."

We sat together in silence as I watched the clock. Our time was winding down, and we hadn't even made it onto the healing table. I hugged my legs close to my chest and buried my head in my knees.

I couldn't deny that Linda had been right about so many things. She had been right about the possession, and it had saved my life. I began to wonder if she might be right about this too. Perhaps there was more to my own story; more to my own family than I could even see. Perhaps she was a few steps ahead of me again.

I began to search for clues. "Wait a minute, Linda. Do you remember that letter my mother wrote to me last January? Well, that letter ended up being the catalyst for my entire estrangement. It was the last straw. I've been so angry at her for writing it, but now I am beginning to wonder if it was also a gift."

Linda smiled. "Yes, Lauren. I knew my inner guidance was right. I think you can see it now."

I glanced at the clock again as I realized that our time together had come to an end. I placed my hands into a prayer position and thanked Linda for her guidance. She smiled back at me as she brushed her salt and pepper bangs to the side. Linda often spoke with so much wisdom and presence that she reminded me of Glinda, the good witch from *The Wizard of Oz*. That was especially true today. Our session felt like a riddle. A riddle that she wanted me to solve on my own.

LET IT GROUND YOU

January 2018

It had been a year since the iPad Thanksgiving, and I could barely contain my anger. I couldn't believe my father had betrayed me at that dinner table, and in front of everyone. He blew through my boundary with so much force that it left me breathless. I had mimed *NO* with so much exaggeration that it was impossible for me to pretend that he didn't fully understand what he had done. Still, I desperately didn't want to lose my father. So I wrote him an emotionally charged poem that ended with the line, *There's no room for your old shit in my new life.* He never responded. That was my last-ditch effort.

I had barely spoken to my parents since I ran out of their condo on Thanksgiving carrying large shopping bags filled with my contraband dinner. While my father had been the one to draw the iPad toward me, my mother had called in the order. There was no way I could stand to see or talk to either of them. But I still wasn't ready to leave. I hoped that with time and space, the pain I felt would subside into a numbness I could tolerate.

In the meantime, it felt like I was suspended in thin air. Was I a member of this family, or not? Would I be able to spend time with my parents, or not? I never wanted to completely estrange myself. I was content to stay in a low-contact situation indefinitely. The goal of going low contact with my parents was ultimately to *save* our relationship. I was afraid that if I saw them more often, they would betray me beyond the point of no return. And I knew I could never endure another iPad Thanksgiving. But then something happened. There was a catalyst. Something pushed me out of low-contact purgatory for good.

At the beginning of January, I received a handwritten letter from my mother. The truth is, when I first saw it, I was filled with hope. She had never written me a letter before. I wondered if this was the moment when things were finally going to turn around.

I stood at the kitchen island in my treehouse apartment and tore open the letter. The suspense was killing me. I immediately noticed that the letter was long, multiple pages. This was very uncharacteristic of my mother. I read a few lines and gasped.

My mother's unique blend of cursive and print handwriting suddenly morphed into a blur of blue ink. The letter was all about how I needed to *drop this grudge* I was holding against her and my father and *just get over it.* She talked about how she didn't understand what my problem was at this point. She told me that everything with the Black Square was *over,* so it was time for me to move on. She reminded me that she had *cut him out of our lives,* making no mention of the fact that it took her six years (and a giant fight with me) to ultimately do it. She told me that she didn't need to apologize to me for anything, instead she was simply owed my forgiveness. I couldn't even finish reading the letter. I threw my arms up and stormed around my apartment in a fit of rage.

I paced back and forth, as I role-played my rebuttal:

"What the fuck? You don't get to demand my forgiveness, that's not how any of this works! I will forgive you when you take accountability, which you still haven't done! You are still blaming me for the demise of this family! The Black Square tore us apart. And then you tore us apart even further. How is it possible that you still can't see that?"

I continued to shout into the void, shaking the letter in my hands:

"And you expect me to move on when you are *still* betraying my boundaries? I just walked out of another Thanksgiving! I will forgive you when you change! But you haven't changed at all!"

I went back into the kitchen and tried to read more. But before I could turn the page, I felt a wave of nausea rush over me. I threw down the letter, scattering its pages everywhere. I ran into the bathroom, cowering over the toilet, and dry heaved until I burst into tears. I slid down the wall of my bathroom until I came face to face with the toilet. I stayed there for a while, just in case. I felt paralyzed. I couldn't bear to find out what else she had said.

All of a sudden, my curiosity got the best of me. I grabbed onto the towel rack behind my head and pulled myself up from the floor. My body was heavy and listless. I felt dizzy and disoriented. I placed one foot in front of the other until I had finally re-entered the kitchen. I felt like I was creeping up on a spider. I didn't want to go near it, but I also couldn't allow it to remain in the center of the floor.

I slowly gathered the contents of my mother's letter. As I picked up each page, I glanced at parts of it, unable to look away. I read that letter completely out of order, as I filed its pages back into their original envelope. It almost made more sense that way. Once I had successfully digested the whole thing, I took the letter and walked back down the three flights of stairs to my mailbox. I placed the letter back into my mailbox and locked it away, hoping to forget that any of this had ever happened.

The next week, as I was rushing out the door to go therapy, I instinctively grabbed my mother's letter from my mailbox. I walked into Marilyn's office and threw the letter into her lap without any explanation. This was a test. I wanted to see what would happen if she was ambushed, just as I had been.

Marilyn opened the letter, read a few lines, and then looked at me. Her mouth was agape, and her eyes grew wide with disbelief. I even saw a tear begin to emerge from behind her ruby-rimmed glasses. She told me that she needed to walk down the hall before she finished reading it. All I could think was, *Oh my God. It really is that bad.*

* * *

I began working with Marilyn in the spring of 2015. Until then, I had a history of choosing therapists who didn't really confront me. But now I was in the field. I knew that a good therapist must often choose between being liked and helping someone heal. I was very proud of the therapist I had become. I was willing to journey to hard places with my clients. I wasn't afraid to relay my honest feedback. I had finally met my match in Marilyn. I wanted a therapist who was just as bold as me. I had also gotten to the point where I was sick of my own bullshit.

Marilyn wasted no time inspiring me to face myself. A few months into our relationship, she confronted me about my mother. She was the first therapist who was willing to truly dissect that relationship. Until that point, I had a habit of telling therapists that I was *so confused* about my mother's cold and stern treatment of me. I told therapists that *I guess I just had to accept it as love.* Every therapist I had ever seen agreed that my mother was cruel to me. But that's always as far as we got. No one ever offered me any alternatives.

A few months into my work with Marilyn, she said something completely new. Marilyn said, "Look Lauren, you need to stop saying that you're confused about your mother. I don't believe you. I know that you are a great therapist, and I know you see exactly what is going on here. And there is something you can do about it. You need to set better boundaries with your mother. Otherwise she will treat you like this forever."

I got angry at Marilyn that day. I had asked the universe for a therapist who was willing to confront me, and I received it. Careful what you wish for. My first instinct was to defend my confusion because that's what the brain does when someone is in the middle of destroying a defense mechanism that has been solidly in place for decades. But I knew she was right. Marilyn had effectively torn through my smoke screen.

I looked at Marilyn and I broke down. I admitted that I knew I needed to set boundaries with my mother. I knew there was no hope and that my mother would never treat me any differently. Despite my yearning for everything to change, the evidence to the contrary was bountiful. Marilyn was right. I was the one who needed to change. It was just too painful to say it out loud. But in the dim light of her office that day, we let the cat out of the bag. Over the next few years, I began to let myself grieve the mother I was never going to have.

* * *

A few moments later, Marilyn came back into her office and sat down across from me. She picked up the letter my mother had just written and continued to examine it. She shook her head as she sighed aloud. And then she looked at me calmly. "Well, this is pretty awful, Lauren. Although none of it is a surprise."

Tears began to stream down my face. "I know, Marilyn. A part of me still wants to act confused, but I know better now."

Marilyn nodded as she handed me a tissue. "That's right, Lauren. I know that doesn't make it any easier. But there is nothing clearer than this letter to show you that it's been a decade since your sexual abuse disclosure, and not much has changed. You are still running out of Thanksgiving, and she is still demanding that you move on."

I began to sob uncontrollably. "I don't think I can do this anymore, Marilyn. I think it's over."

Marilyn leaned closer to me. "I hope one day you can see that your mother is making it easier for you to walk away, Lauren. There's no coming back from this now. It's very clear. And perhaps that clarity can be a gift to you someday. If you ever find yourself second-guessing this decision, just think about this letter. Let it ground you."

I nodded as I wiped away my tears. I glanced at the time and noticed that our session was almost over. Marilyn carefully filed the pages of my mother's letter back into its original envelope and tried to hand it back to me. I immediately exclaimed, "Oh no, Marilyn. I can't take that thing home. You need to keep it here."

Marilyn threw the letter onto her desk reluctantly. "Well, I don't want it here either!

I laughed. That was something Coco would have said. We

continued to play hot potato with the letter until Marilyn finally acquiesced. She agreed to keep the letter in my case file at her office until we could figure out a final resting place. I watched as Marilyn walked over to her large tan filing cabinet and placed my mother's letter into my file, locking the door shut behind her.

I HAVE NOTHING LEFT

January 2018

Right after Marilyn locked my mother's letter in her file cabinet, I went on a long walk through the Chicago Loop. *Did I really just say that it's over? Am I actually done this time?* My head began to throb.

Luckily I didn't have to be at work for another hour. I walked down Michigan Avenue as a gust of frigid wind almost blew me over. I paused as I debated hailing a cab the rest of the way to my office but decided against it. I needed to breathe in the fresh, winter air. It helped me think.

Ten years had gone by since my sexual abuse disclosure. And yet my mother's letter was proof that no one was going to take accountability for how badly I had been hurt. I thought about the only fight I ever had with Coco all those years ago. I thought about all the holidays I spent at home with a can of soup. That letter my mother sent felt like the last straw. Marilyn and I had broken through the smoke screen for good. I forced myself to release the recurring daydream where my parents were sorry, and we moved forward together. It was time to get real. They had been consistent. I was the one who kept shifting.

* * *

The week after I showed Marilyn my mother's letter, I went boxing. I had grown up with Billy Blanks' Tae Bo videos, and I had taken the occasional kickboxing class. But I had never been to a real boxing gym before. After I received my mother's letter, I was overcome with the urge to hit something. I downloaded a free pass to try out the new, trendy boxing gym in my neighborhood, and I signed up for a Sunday night class.

Sweat poured down my face as I attempted to keep up with the pace of the beginner boxing class. I was in shape, but in that class, I felt like I was going to die. Nonetheless, I put my body through ninety minutes of hell. I hadn't sweat that much since I had taken an African dance class while living in Cape Town during college. As I grabbed my water bottle and vigorously poured water down my throat, our instructor told us that for the last ten minutes of class, we were about to go harder than we ever had before. I thought to myself, *Are you kidding me? I have nothing left!*

The instructor told us to face our punching bags and smash them until the music ended. We were allowed to forget about all the techniques we had sloppily picked up for the past hour. This was our moment to let it all out. I heard the loud beat of the latest hip hop track playing in the background, and a wave of energy came over me. The instructor said, "If you need some motivation, just think about someone you are really mad at right now."

That was it. My eyes grew wide. I looked at the punching bag, and all I saw was the letter from my mother. I punched the shit out of that bag. I punched the bag so hard that it began to shake uncontrollably. I started to let out tiny noises as my red rental gloves smashed into the bag. At first I felt silly. I looked around to see if I had disturbed anyone, but all the other students seemed very preoccupied with not dying. It felt good to let it out, so I kept going. Soon, my screams became increasingly more audible. I visualized myself back at my apartment, pacing up and down the corridor while I yelled at my mother's letter as if it was its own entity. The instructor walked over and egged me on. I slammed my bodyweight into that bag, wailing so loudly that everyone else stopped what they were doing. I felt like a rabid dog. The rage completely consumed me. Suddenly, I started screaming: "I CAN'T DO THIS ANYMORE. I AM DONE. DO YOU HEAR ME? IT'S OVER."

I burst into tears and collapsed on the floor. My sobs were uncontrollable and deep. I looked up and saw that the two women next to me were also crying as they watched me completely fall apart. They must have thought that I was going through a bad breakup. I was.

Class ended and I peeled myself off the floor. I avoided

making eye contact with anyone as I grabbed my gym bag and winter coat. I ran out the door of the gym and into my car. I checked my phone. My friend Jess had called and left a message. She wanted to catch up since it had been a while. Without thinking, I called Jess back and told her what had just happened. I told her I was done. Jess encouraged me to think twice about what I was saying, and that's when I heard myself for the first real time. I screamed into the phone as if it were an extension of the punching bag: "Did you not hear me? I said I can't take this anymore! It's been a decade of this shit and it's never going to change! I don't *want* to be done; I *have* to be done! It's all over!"

I hung up on Jess and continued to cry. I kept repeating those words, "I'm done. I'm done." I was so angry that Jess had just tried to talk me out of it. I felt like she hadn't heard me at all. And then I wondered if I had really heard myself.

My brain continued to fight with me in the car. *No, Lauren. You have been saying this for years. But you aren't really going to leave. That's not what you want.* It was the familiar rebuttal. I had almost left over the iPad Thanksgiving, but I had somehow managed to remain low-contact, even after my father ignored my poem. But that letter my mother wrote to me pushed me over the edge.

My heart had come forward at the boxing gym. That class was so insanely difficult that I had managed to shut off my brain long enough to hear the voice of my heart. My heart was wailing and screaming to be done. My heart fell apart on the gym floor.

As I sat in my car, I began to listen to my heart. She told me a completely different story. All this time, I thought I was staying in my family to please my heart. But she told me that it was breaking her to stay. My heart told me that she first broke during my disclosure in the spring of 2008, and with each betrayal that followed, she broke with more force and less room for repair. I was shocked. I couldn't let this happen anymore. I had to be done. I turned up the heat in my car as

I wiped away a mixture of tears and sweat. I slowed down my breath. I placed both my hands over my heart and closed my eyes.

And I promised to set her free.

GO, CHILD

As I walked out the side door of Linda's house, I thought about her warning that I could be possessed again if I weren't careful. Of course I didn't make it onto the healing table that morning. We had way too much to discuss. Clearly, this process wasn't over. I needed to figure out how to retrieve some of the soul parts that I had lost during my lifetime. *Or else.* A chill ran down my spine.

I passed by a string of daffodils and bright orange tulips on my way to the car. I was deep in thought as I pondered the riddle that seemed to emerge from my session with Linda. What did my mother's letter really have to do with all of this? I sighed aloud as I made my way across the street. Linda's words rang through my ears: *No one was ever going to save you.* Part of me already knew she was right. Before that part could take over, my chest began to fill with rage. There was no way my parents *did their jobs well* by allowing the Black Square to remain in my life for so long. Fuck that.

I unlocked my car and slid into the driver's seat. I remained in a state of confusion and disbelief as I drove away from Linda's house and toward Heaven on Sheridan. It was too much for me to consider that my soul had consciously signed up for this life. I wondered why the hell I would volunteer myself to be the scapegoat of our family. There was just no way. Then again, it also felt like something my soul would do.

Twenty minutes later, I parked my car in the garage of my apartment building and made my way up to my unit. I walked through the front door, as my eyes caught sight of the incredible lake view. I dropped my purse on the kitchen island and walked over to the living room window so I could stare straight ahead at the pier. It was a perfect afternoon in late summer. A few clouds drifted by slowly as rays of sunlight began to dance off the water.

I was standing in that exact spot when I first contacted the

Archangel Michael, when he appeared in the form of a security guard. That event had certainly bent my mind farther than I could have ever imagined it would go. I began to wonder if there was more to this life than I was willing to admit. I certainly didn't claim to have all the answers. I thought about Linda's riddle again.

I slowly began to analyze everything. Of course, I had yearned for our family to be completely different. I knew enough about trauma to understand that my desire came from parts of me that had been extraordinarily hurt. As I stared at the pier, another part of me took over. I began to realize that if I had grown up in a different family, there would be no need for anyone to break these patterns. But that's not the life any of us had. Somehow I knew these destructive patterns went back generations. Generations of children not receiving enough love from their parents. Generations of abuse going unchallenged and untamed. Generations of self-betrayal in the name of belonging. Generations of possessing each other and calling it love. Even though I was the one who experienced an *actual* possession, I had seen it all around me for my entire life. Everyone in my family was stuck together. They believed this made us a family. But attachment is not a bond. Attachment is a chain. I wanted to be in relationships that were free of chains. So I got out. Perhaps that was always meant to be.

My head throbbed. All I could think about was my mother's letter. *But why? What was the connection?* I had no idea why I felt compelled to ask Linda if the letter was somehow part of her point that my parents did their job well. That question came from a deeper place. A place my brain couldn't seem to access, even now. And then I realized that it came from the same place that had googled *psychic attacks* in the middle of the night while I laid awake in Heather's basement, driven to my brink by the final plague.

When I first received my mother's letter, I could barely get through it without screaming into the void. I read it aloud to my friends. I handed it to Marilyn. Everyone had the same reaction: shock and dismay followed by a harsh reality check. That's because my mother did what she had always done extraordinarily well. She forced me to give up on her.

My mother had always spoken to me in a way that cut through my bones. When we weren't together, it was hard for me to hold onto the severity of her words. I frequently relapsed into believing that she could change, and that perhaps if I confronted her one more time, she would take accountability for everything she had done. But each time I tried, she starkly held her ground. The day she wrote me that letter, I could no longer pretend. She told me that she wasn't going to apologize. Unfortunately, I needed that apology to remain in my family.

I stood in the middle of my living room window with my eyes focused on the glistening water below. I began to see everything differently. If my mother hadn't pushed me to the edge of the cliff, I might never have spread my wings. Before the letter, I had been wavering for years as I tried to figure out how to prevent an estrangement. Not even the iPad Thanksgiving was enough to get me out. But my mother had done something to move the pendulum. And I'm not sure I would have been able to move it myself.

It was almost as if my mother had whispered in my ear, *Go, child. Go and be free.* Of course the only way I was going to receive that message was for it to come in the form of language that almost made me throw up. That letter cemented the fact that my family had become an uninhabitable place. There was only one thing left to do. I had to step into my fate as a cycle breaker.

I began to see Linda's riddle more clearly. My mother's letter was the final straw in a long line of moments where each member of my family held on tightly to a system that I was designed to break. But that was just the tip of the iceberg. If my parents had defended me when I came forward about the Black Square, then I would never have left them. And if I hadn't left my family, then Mary Frances wouldn't have gotten so angry. And if Mary Frances hadn't gotten so angry, then she would still be with me. And if she was still with me, then my soul and my body would never be mine. Ever.

It was eerie to know that I could have lived an alternate life. A life where I remained in my family and Mary Frances remained inside of me. Alternate Timeline Lauren. I stood at the window as I pictured Alternate Timeline Lauren. I knew exactly who she was. She was lonely but trying not to admit it. She was telling her Wounded Warrior sob story to anyone who would listen. She was starved for love. She was accepting crumbs of attention and affection from anyone who would feed her and call it a meal. She was desperately yearning for a different life, but she couldn't see a way out.

She was still Leah.

THE CLYDESDALE HORSE

October 2019

In the weeks that followed my session with Linda, I found myself continuing to ponder the idea that I was destined to become a cycle breaker. My story began to feel more like a hero's journey and less like a victimhood narrative. Nonetheless, it was difficult to maintain this paradigm shift because it was such a departure from the way I had always viewed my life. I still had moments where the Wounded Warrior showed up, immersed in the despair of losing her entire family. It was hard to make room in my heart for the pain and the power that seemed to exist simultaneously in my story. But I did my best to try.

I also followed Linda's suggestion that I undergo a soul retrieval. I continued to shudder at the thought that without a soul retrieval, I might become vulnerable to another spiritual possession. There was absolutely no way I was willing to take that chance. I spent all my spare time researching local practitioners who performed soul retrieval sessions, and I allowed my intuition to guide me to the right person. That's how I found Joan Forest Mage.

Joan was an older woman with sparkling silver hair that she wore in a loose bob. She had the energy of a true crone. I began to realize that Linda, Diane, and Joan were all around the same age. I had inadvertently mobilized a force of crones to walk me through this journey. But it was more than that. These women filled a void in my life that I didn't even know I had. In the two years that followed the loss of my grandmother, Coco, I often felt comforted by the presence of older women. Especially those women who were clearly sent to help me heal.

* * *

Before we booked the session, Joan and I scheduled a phone call. During this call, Joan explained the purpose of a soul retrieval session in detail. I could tell that Joan was a different kind of crone. She practiced more traditional shamanic work and spoke about the fact that she would perform the soul retrieval by invoking her *power animal* through a combination of song and dance as she called in her guides. She also told me that during the soul retrieval, she would find out if I also had a power animal. I was intrigued. I liked the idea of a more experiential session. I also liked the fact that all of this was new to me.

Joan said that the goal of a soul retrieval is to call back the parts of someone's soul that have split off from the body. Joan reiterated what both Diane and Linda had told me, without even knowing it. She said that parts of our soul leave us during times of acute stress and trauma, but we may also begin this life with a hole in our soul if there is past-life trauma. I told Joan that I had experienced a lot of childhood trauma, and that I was also curious if I had experienced past-life trauma. I mentioned that I had undergone a depossession that left me with more questions than answers. Joan seemed to inherently understand. She shared that during the soul retrieval, I would lie down on a massage table as she invoked her guides to help retrieve any parts of myself that had gone missing. I was hopeful. I was ready. I wanted my own soul back.

Joan and I arranged a soul retrieval session for October 13, 2019. On the day of my session, I arrived at Joan's office right on time. She ran a center for shamanic healing called the Life Force Arts Ensemble. We conducted our session in the main room of the center that doubled as a small performance space. The room was bare, with beige carpet that looked to be about twenty years old. There was a slight draft that snuck in through the front door every time the wind blew. In the center of the room, I saw a large massage table. Nearby, there were two black folding chairs that were arranged to face each other. Apparently, this was where we would sit to process everything.

Joan smiled as I removed my light grey peacoat. She offered me a drink of water. I wasn't thirsty, but I walked over to the small kitchen and filled a red plastic glass anyway. Then Joan told me to climb onto the massage table when I was ready, and to lie down. We wasted no time. As I spread my body onto the table, another gust of wind blew through the crevices in the front door. The wind chilled my skin as goosebumps crept up my forearms. I took a deep breath, attempting to relax. Joan asked me to set an intention privately. And on that table, I asked any parts of my soul who had left my body to please return to me. I told them it was safe to come back home.

* * *

I awoke from the session as Joan finished her final chant. I had no concept of how much time had passed. My head was heavy and listless. I sat up and swung my legs over the side of the table. I looked at Joan, as if she was about to tell me whether the life-saving surgery had worked. And that's when she told me that it had. Joan had called out to the parts of my soul who had left me. Four of them came back.

I cried as Joan began to tell me about the parts of my soul that returned. The first part who came back was thirty-four years old. She was in deep grief over the loss of my grandmother, Coco. She left my body immediately after the funeral when she realized that she didn't want to exist in a family that was devoid of the only person who truly understood her. She floated directly out of my body and went searching for Coco. And she found her. Joan told me that this part seemed to be suspended somewhere in between the life and afterlife, where Coco had positioned herself ever since she died. I nodded. I knew exactly what she meant by that.

The second soul part who came back was five years old. Joan found her hiding under the deck of the house I was raised in. My soul part told Joan that she had been stuck down there for a long time. She told Joan that she ran away because she was afraid of her mother. She was so grateful that someone had come looking for her. She had come to believe that no one cared that she had been gone for so long. My heart began to ache.

Joan told me that the third soul part who returned was between seven and ten years old and she was from a past life. She told me that I had known my mother before, and we had been very poor. We were living in the 1700s, somewhere in Europe. Joan revealed that my past-life mother had been widowed, and she had recently remarried a wealthier man. This man began sexually abusing me. My past-life part had disclosed the abuse to my mother, but my mother told me that nothing could be done about it. That her hands were tied.

My jaw hit the floor. *Oh my God. That's what happened in this life too.* Joan went on to tell me that she had a very hard time extracting this soul part. Joan said that when she found her, this soul part was sitting in a chair bound by strong cords that were deeply connected to my past-life mother. My past-life part looked like she had been held hostage. When Joan tried to slice those cords, my past-life mother screamed: "YOU CAN'T TAKE HER!" Joan told me that she had to call in all her guides to face my past-life mother. She told me that an epic battle ensued. I couldn't believe it. And at the same time, *I could.* Nothing had ever felt more accurate in my entire life. Ultimately, Joan and her guides successfully sliced through the cords and removed me from the grip of my past-life mother. Joan described the way my mother continued to cry out with her arms outstretched as she tried to pull me back down with her. Joan talked about the fact that my past-life mother felt trapped as well, and she kept screaming, "If I can't leave, neither can she!"

As Joan shared these words, I felt them ricochet through my entire body. I knew that dynamic in my bones. My past-life mother was gripping onto me, believing that family is akin to possession. This story reminded me of the lobster races that my family held for years. Suddenly, I had a vision of my father insinuating that it was humane for one lobster to pull down the lobster who tries to escape from the pot of boiling water because none of them are getting out alive. I felt a chill run down my spine as I thought about my past-life mother binding me to a chair and screaming that I couldn't leave if she remained in confinement. I had been in the throes of this lobster pot for my entire life. But apparently, it was even deeper than that. My mother and I had been lobsters in the same pot more than once.

I barely had a chance to process that enormous reveal when Joan told me about the final soul part who had returned. The fourth soul part had a broken wrist. I nodded when Joan disclosed this to me. I didn't even need her to share the details. I knew exactly what had happened. This soul part was ten years old, and she was wearing a Brownie uniform. She had broken her wrist ice skating. This soul part had been walking around with a broken wrist for a week without telling anyone how badly she was hurt. She didn't want her mother to find out that it was broken because she knew she would get in trouble for *needing something.* This part was also very grateful to come home.

I sat across from Joan as I attempted to digest all this information. It felt so foreign and so familiar at the same time. I intimately knew the stories behind each of the soul parts that had returned from this lifetime. My heart ached for each of them; knowing they had each remained trapped in the worst moment they had ever encountered. However, I had absolutely no idea what to do with the past-life part. I didn't know who she was, and I didn't know very much about her. I didn't even know her name.

I asked Joan how she had re-integrated each part back into my body. Joan told me that she made a funnel with her hands and quite literally blew each soul part back into my chest. I told her that I felt the third gust of wind the strongest. And that's when she told me that the past-life part blew into my body with a force that far surpassed all the others. She told me that this soul part was most likely the missing piece that had opened me up to the possession. Joan said that I was born into this lifetime with a giant hole in my soul, and an incredibly thick, toxic chord that was already bound to my mother. I shivered. My relationship with my mother had been the most difficult and challenging relationship in my entire life, but it had also been the most powerful one. This was a fact I could no longer ignore.

Joan told me that I also received a power animal during the session. My ears perked up. I still didn't understand the concept of a power animal, but I was anxious to hear what she had discovered. Joan told me that my power animal was the Clydesdale horse. I looked at her with utter confusion. *The ... what?*

Joan talked about the fact that my power animal had come through as a very specific breed. It was not just any horse; it was the Clydesdale horse. I didn't know much about horses, so I asked Joan to tell me about this particular one. Joan told me that the Clydesdale horse is one of the largest breeds, with massive bodies and chunky legs so thick that they have fur lining their hooves. I sat across from Joan, acutely aware of my small frame. I remained perplexed.

Then Joan described the horse: "The Clydesdale horse is a work horse. They can carry tons of weight on their backs, it's actually incredible how much they can hold. They are gentle and compassionate, but incredibly strong. They are among the most powerful horses, so you don't want to mess with them. And they are intuitive. Incredibly intuitive. Like most horses, they are an incredible judge of character and can be very therapeutic."

I chimed in, "So when you say that horse can carry tons of weight on their backs, are we talking like ... an entire ancestral line?"

Joan nodded. "Now do you see it? This is your essence. You carried the weight of generations of unhealed trauma on your back. You were born into that role. Not everyone can take that on. But you can, and I think you know it. You have always been that strong."

I smiled. Yes. This was right. I was a strong, powerful horse.

I was an Aries sun and an Aries moon. I had been born into it. I had also been forced to be that strong, which was undoubtedly a trauma-response to the way I was raised. But I had always known that I had the soul of a warrior. The fire inside of me always burned brighter than the fire around me, and that is how I survived. It was the one thing I was sure about, even as I faced so much destruction and ego death in the dark night of the soul. This is the one part that always remained. I was brave. I was courageous. And that courage pulsed through my veins. I was strong enough to carry the weight of generations of unhealed trauma and then break that curse for all of us. I was the Clydesdale horse.

Joan smiled as she told me about the final piece of information that came through during my soul retrieval session. Joan asked if there were any deceased loved ones who wanted to come forward to offer me a gift. Joan made it clear that she asked for an energetic gift, rather than a physical one. Then she told me that Coco had immediately come forward to offer me a gift that seemed to bypass all the guidelines Joan had described. I laughed. That was right on brand for my grandmother, who always marched to the beat of her own drum. Even in the afterlife.

Joan laughed as she said: "Your grandmother was very specific, and she wanted me to pass along her request very clearly. She would like you to have a long-stemmed, sterling silver rose pendant. She knows you don't currently own that piece of jewelry right now, but she would like you to get in touch with her so that she can help you find it."

THEY CAME BACK

As soon as the soul retrieval session ended, I thanked Joan profusely. She stood up and gave me a hug. I stepped out the door and into the cool autumn air. It was a cloudy Sunday afternoon, but everything felt clearer. The sound of each car that drove by was exceedingly more pronounced. The fall colors on all the surrounding trees were even brighter. I was experiencing my life at full blast. Perhaps that was because the lost parts of myself had finally returned. There was more of me now, and I could feel it.

I walked across the street to go to Whole Foods. I figured that I would do my grocery shopping for the week since I was right there. As I stepped onto the escalator, I began to hear the voices of small children everywhere. I looked around, but I only saw adults.

I grabbed a green basket and began to walk around the produce section. The voices became louder and louder:

I want mac and cheese!

I want pizza! Yeah, pizza!

I would like some raspberry bars. Those are my favorite. Mother sometimes lets me get one when we go to the market.

Um … What the fuck.

I barely ate pizza, and mac and cheese wasn't exactly on my shopping list. Not even close. I was a plant-based, vegetarian-leaning, yoga-practicing adult. I didn't even know where the frozen food section was in that store. I wondered: *What the hell is a raspberry bar? Who says things like "go to the market"?* I paused. *Oh my God, I think my new soul parts are here.*

I felt like I had inadvertently taken a bus full of children to the grocery store that day. As I walked around the store, the three younger parts were all vying for my attention. It was almost as if I could feel them tugging at my sleeve as they tried to pull me toward all their favorite foods. At some point, I just gave in. Anyway, Joan told me to make sure to create a welcoming environment in the days that followed so that none of my soul parts felt the urge to leave again. I certainly didn't want that to happen.

I reluctantly walked over to the frozen food aisle of Whole Foods and grabbed a pizza. This made one of my soul parts happy. Then I filled a small cup with mac and cheese at the deli. The voices got a little quieter. Apparently, I had satisfied two of the three children who had come back to me. I still didn't know what a raspberry bar was, or who was asking for one. I turned my head to the floor, so I could speak to myself aloud without arousing any suspicion inside the store: "What is a raspberry bar, and who is asking for that?"

Then, I heard her.

Mother and I both like raspberry bars. I hope they have some here. I would really like one of those. It's such a special treat when mother lets me have one, but only after I have eaten my ration of potatoes.

My eyes grew wide. *This must be my past-life part.* It was so strange to hear her voice. In some ways, she felt like me. After all, we had both experienced such similar traumas in our families. But at the same time, I didn't know her at all. She spoke differently. More formal. It was clear that she was from a different time. She was very serious, especially for her age. I figured that had to be because of everything she endured.

I walked over to the baked goods aisle, hoping to find something that would resemble this so-called raspberry bar. I told the past-life part that it may not be possible for us to find it. This was a different kind of market than the one she was used to. As we approached the pastries, I heard her become increasingly elated. Then I looked down. I saw a package of four pastries that said: Whole Foods Raspberry Oat Bars. My soul part politely asked if I would buy those for her. I had never eaten anything like this in my life. But I placed a package of dessert bars into my basket along with all the other junk food that had been requested that day.

Once I was back at Heaven on Sheridan, I prepared one of the unhealthiest meals of my life. I stared down at my plate and laughed. Two slices of pizza, a scoop of mac and cheese, and a dessert bar. It looked like I was eating dinner at a little kid's birthday party. I suppose that wasn't far from the truth. I was having a party for all three of the children who had gone missing during such terrible moments. It was their very own homecoming party. It became very important for me to celebrate them.

After the children had been fed, I was still thinking about the raspberry bars. My past-life soul part seemed to recognize them immediately, and that made me curious. So, I googled raspberry oat bars and gasped when I saw the top result. It said: old world raspberry oat bar recipe. I clicked on the recipe and learned that this dessert bar originated in Europe. And that's when I knew that something synchronistic was happening here.

* * *

Joan had provided me with a handout entitled: soul retrieval aftercare. It contained directions for integrating the new soul parts back into my life. Joan mentioned that the first few days after a soul retrieval are essential because it is common for some folks to lose their soul parts again if they don't work hard to make their parts feel at home. Joan suggested that I create a ritual around integrating my new soul parts right away. She told me to consider drawing a bath that evening and asking each part to come forward so they could tell me their story. She directed me to pay close attention to why each part left, what they want me to know, and how I can begin to help them feel at home.

Of all the spiritual practices that I had encountered during the past year, this one felt the most natural to me. Joan was describing a practice that closely resembled one of my favorite therapeutic techniques: parts work. I often used this approach with clients who had experienced complex trauma, and I had already done it in my own therapy. At least I was about to venture into somewhat familiar territory.

I drew myself a bath and filled the tub with a stream of

essential oils. I bent down as I inhaled the vibrant combination of lavender, frankincense, grapefruit, and ylang ylang. I undressed and slowly stepped into the bathtub. My body sank into the warm water as I sighed with intense relief. I examined every inch of my body and felt into its newfound density. Something had changed. I felt full. And it wasn't just the pizza and mac and cheese sitting in my stomach.

I pulled out my phone and opened the Notes application. I decided it would be a good idea to record what came forward during this parts work session. I immediately chose a practice I often used in therapy. First, I would meditate to connect to the new soul parts. Then I would listen to what they had to say. And finally, I would respond to each of them.

This is what happened.

Soul Part One: Grieving Lauren (Thirty-four Years Old)

Well, I guess I'm back now. Honestly, I'm not sure how I feel about that. You remember how hard it was when I lost her. That's why I left. I couldn't bear to live the rest of my life without Coco. And especially in that family. So I floated out of my body, and I went to be with her. Frankly, I almost didn't come back today. But Coco said it would be alright. She said it was time for me to go back. Actually, she never wanted me to split off from my own body to be with her. She kept saying that I had my whole life ahead of me. But I was just so sad. It was so awful when she died. Anyway, if I am going to stick around this time, you need to hear the whole story. You need to witness me.

The night before Coco died, I went to temple, and I told her that it was alright for her to pass on. I bet you remember that. I told her that I knew she was holding on because of me. Actually, I had known that for years. You know how awful everything got after I came forward about the sexual abuse. I still can't believe that she ended up being right about Dad. I really thought he was going to support me. But Coco was right. She knew her son. So yeah, things were so awful for me in that family. I needed her. And when she started dying, I freaked out. So, I kept asking her not to go. She held on for years because of me.

But something changed at temple that night. I realized it was selfish of me to keep Coco here. So I sat in temple, and when we were all in silent prayer, I sent these words to her:

"Coco, I know you can hear me. I know you can feel me. I'm sorry that I've been holding onto you so tightly. I'm just really scared to do this without you. I'm not sure I can. But I know it's time for you to go. I know you are ready. And I want you to know that I will find a way to live my life without you."

Dad called me at eight the next morning. I'm sure you remember that too. My heart sunk into my stomach because I already knew what he was going to say. He told me that Coco had passed away overnight. I bet she died right after I told her she could go.

I walked into my bedroom after I got off the phone with Dad, and I burst into tears. I tried to pack for the funeral in New York, but I collapsed on the floor instead. I started wailing in my bedroom.

All of a sudden, my bedroom was filled with the strongest scent of mothballs. I stopped crying and started laughing. Mothballs, seriously? Why couldn't she make my room smell like her perfume, Chanel Nº 5? Well, the mothballs certainly got my attention. It smelled just like her closet. I knew that she was there. That was the first time I realized that maybe there is something beyond death. I could feel Coco trying to tell me that I would be alright without her. I just didn't know what to do with that. Anyway, that was really hard. That was when I started to feel my chest ache from a place I didn't even know existed.

I want to back up for a second to talk about the card I wrote Coco on Mother's Day that year. Somehow I knew that Mother's Day 2016 would be our last one together. So I wrote her a card, and I really went there. I was a little nervous because I didn't want Mom and Dad to read it. But I needed to say everything to Coco before it was too late.

I really told the truth in that card. I told Coco how much I loved her. I told her that she was the only person in the family that ever understood me. I told her that I felt like I belonged with her. I told her that she was really my mother. I told her that I wouldn't have been able to survive my life without her.

Now I want to talk about the last time I saw Coco alive. I think it will help you understand why I left, and how much pain I was in. I know it's difficult for you to relieve this memory, but I need you to do it for me.

When I walked into Coco's bedroom the week before she died, I noticed that the card I had given her for Mother's Day was right next to her bed. She couldn't talk much anymore, but her eyes filled with love as soon as she saw me. I pulled up a chair and sat at her bedside; my hands were clasped in her hands. I closed my eyes and tried to hold on as tightly as I could. I looked at her, and I told her that I loved her. I also told her that I wasn't sure I was going to be able to stay in this family without her. I said I was sorry for that. She pulled me toward her, and I felt her gulping down air. I knew she was preparing to speak. And then she pushed out these words: "Lauren, do what you need to do."

We both cried. Then Dad knocked on the door and told me it was time to go. I didn't want to. I wanted to climb into that bed and stay with her. But instead, I started to unclasp my hands. She gripped them tighter and pulled me back in. Then she said: "I love you."

Tears rolled down my face. I kissed her cold cheek and said: "I love you so much, Coco. I will love you forever."

I pulled my hands away and she let go. I backed out of the room slowly, but still facing her. That's how I said goodbye. It was perfect. I am bringing this up because I want you to remember that moment forever.

Losing Coco hurt like hell. I tried to pack for New York, since we had to go there for the funeral and burial even though she lived in Chicago with all of us. She wanted to be buried in that Jewish cemetery on Long Island next to Grandpa. In a lot of ways, I get why Coco wanted to be buried there. I know she loved New York more than any other place. But damn, I was so glad she had moved *to Chicago before I was born.*

I got my period the day before we left for New York. Naturally. I packed my suitcase, and I went to the drugstore on the way to meet Mom and Dad at the airport. I went to that CVS around the corner from my apartment, you know, the one I went to all the time. For some reason, I got super lost looking for the tampons that day. I walked up and down all the aisles, getting increasingly more frustrated. Finally, I turned to one of the clerks and screamed: "Can you just tell me where the fucking tampons are in this store!? Jesus Christ. Nothing is where it's supposed to be! Everything is so fucked right now!"

The clerk looked at me in horror. I burst into tears. Then I said it. "My grandmother is dead, ok?"

I didn't even wait for the clerk to tell me where the tampons were before I bolted out of that store. Anyway, it might seem random that I'm telling you this story. You need to remember how much pain I was in. I yelled at a clerk over some tampons. You know that I don't do that kind of stuff. I was mortified.

New York was hard. Really hard. For some reason, I was hoping this moment would bring us all together, but I have never felt more alone in my life. Sure, at times I felt close to Dad during the funeral. Mostly because he knew how much Coco meant to me. But it was impossible for me to be around Mom. Impossible. I couldn't even look at her.

I'm glad that I had my own hotel room while we were in New York. Coco totally came to visit me in there. At first I tried to tell myself that the mothball incident was a fluke, but then something else happened. On the day of the funeral, I saw this black shadow jetting back and forth by my closet, super early in the morning. I looked around, trying to make sense of what I had just seen, and I couldn't. The lights were off, the blinds were drawn, and the room was filled with natural daylight. Nothing in the room could have naturally created that shadow. Anyway, I knew it was her. Then I realized that she was over by my closet because I think she wanted to know what I was going to wear to her funeral. Can you believe it? That's Coco for you. Still picking out my clothes in the afterlife.

Even though I was exhausted, I got up and started talking to her. I opened the closet and took out my pre-planned funeral outfit. I had chosen a purple shirt with a tan knee-length skirt that had a black lace overlay. She loved that skirt. It was her favorite thing that I owned. I showed her the outfit in the early light. I could feel her excitement. I had also brought heels, and I did my hair in an updo, just the way she liked it. She always said I looked so elegant with my hair up. Getting ready for the funeral was a little humorous because I was talking to Coco the entire time. I really felt like she was standing next to me in the bathroom as I placed bobby pins in my hair.

Later that morning, I was dressed to perfection and ready to go. I took the elevator down to the lobby, but when the doors opened, my heart sank. I saw the rest of our family waiting in the lobby, and no one else was dressed like me. Not even close. Then again, I doubted that Coco had bothered to help anyone else get dressed for her funeral. All the other women were wearing plain black clothes with flat shoes and no makeup. Meanwhile, I looked like I was going to a ball. Dad looked at me and he smiled. He got it.

The first part of the funeral was indoors at a parlor, followed by some prayers that we had to recite at the gravesite as we buried Coco. I hope you remember how great the rabbi was. I was really worried about that, especially because Coco didn't go to temple. Somehow, that rabbi really captured the essence of who Coco was. That was helpful, at least.

When we arrived at the parlor, we were all taken into a private room. That's when I saw the casket. It was closed because you know: Jews. But I could feel her in there. I looked around, wondering if anyone else could feel her. I think it was just me.

The rabbi asked if anyone wanted to say a few words. I immediately spoke up and said that I wanted some time alone with Coco. So I went last. When it was my turn, everyone left the room. But I could feel them hovering right outside the doors that were still open. I walked across the room in my three-inch heels, and I proceeded to shut the wooden double doors. I felt everyone back up. I had written something that I wanted to read to Coco, and I didn't want anyone else to hear it.

I put my hand on the casket, and I took out my speech. I started to read it to her. I told Coco that if I ever got the chance to name someone after her, I would. When I said that, I felt the casket vibrate. My whole hand went numb. She heard me. She heard me say that I wanted to name someone after her. I sealed it in fate. Then I got a little nervous, like I had overpromised something. You know, I was never sure whether I wanted kids. But it felt right to tell her I would name someone after her for some reason.

The gravesite was hard. I kept crying. Dad put his hand on my shoulder and that helped. I knew that everyone understood how close I was to Coco. I just wonder if anyone really thought about what it would do to me to lose her.

After we buried Coco, I got back into the car with Mom, Dad, and Peter. I honestly don't even remember what happened next, I really don't. All I know is that Mom said something, and it completely pissed me off. I snapped at her and she snapped back at me. And then Dad did what he always does. He yelled only at me.

That's when I left. I looked out the window, and I left my own body. I remember thinking that I couldn't bear to be stuck here on Earth with these people who thought I was a nuisance when I had just lost the most important person in my life. That moment in the car seemed to summarize everything. Mom said something mean, I tried to defend myself, and Dad yelled at me. Why couldn't anyone see the whole picture? I couldn't take it anymore. I think you probably understand.

I tried to float around, looking for Coco. I left so I could go be with her. And now I am back, and I need to be honest. I would still rather be with her. So if you want me to stick around this time, you need to reassure me that it's better now. I also need you to find that sterling silver rose pendant that Joan talked about. And I need you to promise me that you will never, ever take it off.

Dear Grieving Lauren,

I know it must be so hard for you to come back to me. I

completely understand why you left. I remember that moment in the car, and I remember looking out the window and wishing with all my might to be taken elsewhere. It's kind of eerie to know that actually happened.

Knowing what I know now, I'm not surprised that Coco died right after you gave her permission to go. She was absolutely holding on for you. And I know that things were especially difficult for you around that time.

You were right about it all. You knew that it would be almost impossible to stay in the family after Coco died. I see that her death really wasn't the death of one person, it was the death of the whole family. I'm so sorry that it would be a few more years before I got us out. But I want you to know that it is better now. I did get out, just like you hoped for. And we are never going back.

Thank you for reminding me about the card you wrote to Coco on Mother's Day of 2016. That was only a month before she died. It's incredible that you had that kind of insight. I am indebted to you for writing that card, and for making sure that Coco knew just how much she meant to you. The last time you saw her was so powerful to relive. I know it was hard. So hard. But the fact that you made sure to get that closure made all the difference.

You had the right idea about what you wore to the funeral, but I don't even think you need me to say that. You looked perfect. And Coco loved it. She absolutely loved it. I wish I still had that skirt, but I ended up losing all my belongings last year. Never mind, you don't need to worry about that.

Of course I remember the mothballs. And the shadow dancing by that hotel closet. Those were the first moments I saw real evidence of the afterlife. Thank you for reminding me about how powerful those moments were for you. Don't you think it's amazing that Coco showed up right away to be with you? That's how much she loves you.

I know that you are still new to the whole idea that Coco can visit from the afterlife. But she can, and she often comes to see me. I bet you left because you thought that was the only way you could be with her. I'm here to tell you that she is HERE. She is here with me so often. She is here right now! She wants you to know that she's glad you came back to me. And she wants you to know that she will help us find that sterling silver rose necklace she told Joan about.

Honestly, if you hadn't been open to the mothballs and the dancing shadow, I'm not sure I would be alive right now. That's occurring to me as I write this letter to you. I went through so many supernatural experiences in the last year, and I doubt that I would have believed in any of it without the experiences you had right after Coco died. I might not have undergone a soul retrieval. But I am so glad I did. Because now you're here.

Just so you know, I talk to Coco all the time. I do this ritual where I get out a pint of chocolate ice cream and two spoons (I bet you already know where this is going). I leave one of the spoons out for her. Then, I dish it, just like she and I used to do. I tell her everything. That's right, I still have dish-it sessions with Coco. The only problem is, now I have to eat all the ice cream. It's totally unfair. We laugh about that too. The next time I do a dish-it session, I'll invite you to join us.

There's something else I want to make sure that I tell you. I did name someone after Coco, just like you promised her. You sealed it in fate, and I never forgot that. I know, at the time, you wondered about whether you would name a child after Coco. But bringing a child into this world didn't end up feeling right for me. I did one better. I named myself after Coco. And I did that for you too.

Love,
Lauren

Soul Part Two: Little Lauren (Five Years Old)

Hi! Psst. It's me. I know it's dark under here. That's the whole point, haha. Hey, wanna see the book I'm reading? It's called The Berenstain Bears. I don't even like it that much, but it was the only one I had time to grab. Shhhh! You need to be quiet if you are going to talk to me. I'm hiding from Mom. It's ok if we whisper. Katie says I have a loud whisper voice, so I'm sure you will still be able to hear me.

Hey, do you think the Berenstain Bears are Jewish? It seems like they might be. I mean, that's a pretty Jewish last name. I wonder if other kids know what a Jewish last name is. Oh, guess what? I just found out that Katie is half Jewish! How cool is that? I love Katie. She's my best friend.

I bet you're wondering what I'm doing under this deck. Especially since you know how much I HATE spiders. Don't worry, I'm still looking for a better hiding place. I try to wiggle around whenever I see a spider, or anything else that I don't like. Dad says that most spiders won't hurt me, but I'm afraid of them anyway. Especially when they start moving around. I'm fine if they stay put. But eeeeeeew I don't like their legs. Why do they have so many legs? I mean, I only have two legs and that seems pretty good. I don't get why they need so many.

I'm down here because Mom was being scary again. I was in the living room playing with Lincoln Logs and they fell over. I don't even like Lincoln Logs, but Peter was playing with them, so they were already out. You know how Mom doesn't like it when we make a mess. So I was trying to be good. But then all the logs fell over. I think I put the roof on wrong. The roof is really hard. Anyway, she ran into the living room, and she started screaming. She said a lot of mean things. She said that she wished I would stop bothering her. I don't really know what that means. But then I just started thinking that maybe she wanted me to go away. I mean, I know how to turn the front doorknob the right way so that it opens. It gets stuck a lot, but I know how to do it. So I just left. Don't worry, I didn't lock the door so I can get in later. Maybe she'll be happier now that I'm gone.

It's so hard to make Mom happy. I don't really know how to do it. I guess she seems happy when she listens to the Beach Boys. She loves the Beach Boys. Also, I do not. I think they sound really weird. Why do their voices go up so high? I like Elton John. He's my favorite. I love "Your Song." Yesterday I was almost late for school because I kept listening to that song on the record player. But then Mom said that Jack from down the street was here. We have to walk to school together even though he's really weird. So I had to go. But I kept singing that song so it would get stuck in my head.

I run away a lot, but don't tell anyone I told you that. I can tell you about the first time I walked out the front door all by myself if you want. I was SURE that Mom was going to try to stop me. I don't think I'm supposed to walk around alone. My teacher is always saying not to cross the street without holding someone's hand, but I don't think she knows about Mom. When Mom gets mad it's the worst thing ever. She doesn't really yell at Peter. It's just me. I don't think Mom really likes me that much. Also I don't think she likes being a mom. But Dad says none of that is true. Also in case you're wondering, I know not all moms are mean. I actually just learned about that. I just started being able to have sleepovers with Katie, and her mom is super nice to me. It's so weird.

Oh, and there was this one time when I ran away, and I got really lost. I think I was over by Sabrina's house, but I'm not really sure. It was so scary. I didn't mean to go that far. I just walked all over the place until I saw the Treasure Island grocery store. Then I knew how to get back.

I get lost a lot, but I know how to make that funny. Katie and I made up a game where she spins me around a lot until I get super dizzy, and then I fall down. But wait, that's not the best part. Then I pretend that I don't know where I am, and I pretend that I don't know my name, and I make these googly eyes like I'm really confused. Haha. It's so funny. I bet you would think it's funny. I am just playing though. I always remember my name. Don't tell her I told you that! I don't want her to know I'm just playing.

I don't really want to be under this deck, but it's the best hiding place I could find. I used to walk around the block looking for better places to hide. But the lady who lives next door saw me once and asked if my mom knew where I was. I didn't want to get found out. So now I stay here. That's how I got under the deck. Yeah, it's a little dark down here, but there are so many games you can play. I mean, I'm kind of playing hide and seek. Except it's not as fun if no one *comes looking for you.*

Sometimes I get sad down here. I mean, at first it always feels really good. When I first come down here it's like, phewwww! I did it. I can breathe! She can't find me. Ahh that feels sooooo good. But after a while, I get sad. I wonder why Mom hasn't come looking for me. I want to know what she is doing inside. I start to picture Mom having conversations about me. Like, "Where's Lauren? Has anyone seen Lauren? She's been gone a really long time!" Then I figure that if I just wait a little longer, she will DEFINITELY come looking for me. But that doesn't really happen.

Aw man, now my heart hurts. Does your heart ever hurt? I think it's funny that I can feel my heart. Yesterday I didn't want to be called on in school, and my heart started beating really fast. But then my teacher didn't call on me after all, and my heart went back to normal. I knew the answer, I just don't like to talk in class. It's funny because I can be really shy sometimes.

I bet you're wondering how long I stay down here. I try to go inside right when Dad gets home. That's when everything gets a little better. But I don't really know what time he gets home. I just know that it's right before dinner. Don't worry, it's easy to figure out when Mom starts cooking 'cause she makes a lot of noise with the pots and pans. So that's when I decide to go back inside. Plus I don't really want to miss dinner. It's usually something good.

Sometimes I go meet Dad at the train. But I have to sneak back into the house first. I have to be really quiet, so Mom doesn't know. I open the door really slowly, and I go into the front hall closet and put on Dad's coat, and I walk to the train station and wait for him. He's always really happy to see me. I get so many cute points for showing up in his clothes, so that's why I do it. You are probably wondering what cute points are. Well, I made that up, haha. When I do something cute and someone notices, I get a point. It feels so good. Sometimes I try to do things just so I can get cute points. They are so easy to get from Dad.

Anyway, when Dad gets off the train and sees me in his coat, he runs down the street and scoops me right up. That feels so good. Then he carries me all the way home. It's funny, he never asks if

Mom knew where I was. Oh wait, he did ask one time, and I lied. That felt bad. It kind of ruined all the cute points I got that day. If Dad knew I lied, it would be like getting negative cute points. Sometimes I feel like he takes cute points away when he's mad at me. That makes my heart hurt.

I don't really want to talk about this anymore. Can you take me to get some ice cream? Mint chocolate chip is my favorite. There's a place right down the street. Don't worry, I promise we won't get lost. I bet you don't believe me. That game I play with Katie is just pretend. I really do know how to get there. I think we have a little time before Dad gets home. But it's ok if you don't want to. It's just that I'm ready to come out now, but I don't want to go back inside.

Dear Little Lauren,

Thank you so much for talking to me today. I am so glad that you decided to come back. I really missed you. I want to make sure that things are different around here. I understand why you left when you did. I know that it was too much for you to stay under the deck, hiding from Mom. You did such a good job of keeping yourself safe. It's really quite incredible. But you don't have to worry about hiding from her anymore. I want you to know that I ran away for good. I don't think I could have done that without you.

I am so sorry that you didn't feel safe in your own house. I am so sorry that you had to stash toys all over the place so that you would have something to do while you were hiding from Mom. I am so sorry that this was your life, and that you don't even know how much better it can be. I am so sorry that you taught yourself how to be safe. I want you to know that it was never your job to do that.

It makes me really sad that no one ever came looking for you. It also makes me really angry. I know that you don't understand why I would be angry. That makes sense because it's a very adult thing. It's completely unacceptable that you went missing for hours, and you had to keep coming back on your own. Someone should have come looking for you. You don't have to be angry about it, but I am. I am angry for you. I totally understand why your heart hurt so much when you were hiding under that deck. It makes my heart hurt too. It also makes my stomach burn with rage. But don't worry, I'll hold onto that for you.

One more thing. You reminded me about the cute points! I totally forgot that you did that. While that is an adorable game you played, I also feel really sad that you had to work so hard to receive love. I know that doesn't make much sense, so let me try to explain it. You don't need to go out of your way to get cute points from me. I just love you. All the time. Yes, it's very cute that you dressed up to go meet Dad at the train. But I know you did that so that he would show you more love. And that makes my heart hurt. I want to do things differently now that you are back with me. I want you to feel loved all the time. No more cute points. We don't need them. I can tell that you're a little scared about what will happen without the cute points. Don't worry, I will show you how it's done.

Oh, and to answer your question from earlier, I don't know if the Berenstain Bears are Jewish, but you have given me something to think about!

Would you like to get some ice cream now? I know exactly what kind you want, and I know the place. Don't worry, I also remember how to get there. If you forget the way, you can rely on me. We won't get lost. You won't get lost. I never want you to lose you again.

Love,
Lauren

Soul Part Three: Alice (Seven to Ten Years Old)

Hello, my name is Alice. It's a pleasure to meet you. So you want to know a little bit about me? Well, Mother and I live in the big house down the way. You need a horse to get there, and there is a special road that only we can take. The house has a big gate in front of it with servants. I look at the servants, and I remember when Mother and I were dressed like them. Mother seems to have forgotten all about that, but I haven't. I remember everything.

Don't tell Mother about this, but sometimes I miss our old life. The new house is nice, but I get lonely here. I liked it much better when we lived in town near the market. I know we just had a small house back then, but I liked it. I didn't need much. But Mother wasn't happy. She's never really been that happy. Not since my father died. That happened a long time ago. I don't even remember him. I think he died around the time I was born. Mother used to say she wished that God had taken me instead of him. Sometimes, I use my nightly prayers on that. I ask God to switch me with my father. To bring him back to Mother, so she could be happy. But I don't think God has heard me because I am still around, and my father is still gone. Don't tell anyone I told you that. Mother says that prayers are private.

When we lived in town, I used to take care of everything around the house because Mother was sad all the time. We barely had enough for one ration of potatoes and milk. But when I would walk to the market, everyone would take pity on me because they knew about my mother. Henry, from down the way, used to give me a nice, hot piece of bread every time I would go see him. He would wink at me and put his finger to his lips like I wasn't supposed to say anything. It was our secret. The bread tasted so good. Have you ever tasted Henry's bread? You really should.

I would come back from the market with just enough potatoes for Mother and me to eat for a few days, if we made sure to ration properly. Sometimes, I would give Mother extra rations to see if that would make her happy. I know what you're thinking. Then I went hungry. That's true, but it really wasn't so bad. Did you know that if you take some stale bread and you soak it in water for long enough, it's almost like a meal? I did that a lot.

Anyway, we don't really have to do that stuff anymore, now that Mother married the new man. He is rich, and Mother says I should thank her because she did this so that he would take care of us. But I don't feel very thankful. Please don't tell her I said that. I don't want to seem ungrateful. I am very grateful to have a big house and more food than I could ever eat in a day. But the new man is not a good man, he's a bad man. I call him the Bad Man because he makes me do bad things.

The Bad Man hasn't been around for that long. Mother met him during the last harvest season, and now it's winter. When he started coming around, he was always nice to me in front of Mother. He brought me gold coins to play with as a toy, and I thought that was funny because we barely had enough for a week's worth of food before. Sometimes I would take the coins he gave me and go buy some of Henry's bread, the proper way. That made me feel good.

The Bad Man made me do bad things. He touched me down there. The first time it happened, I cringed. Then he told me that it was ok, that he was allowed do to this because he's family. That didn't feel right. I thought no one was supposed to lift my petticoat except for Mother and the maid. So I was confused. But he told me it was ok, so I guess I let him do it.

But then he put my hand down his trousers. I didn't like that. I took my hand away, and it smelled funny. It was all so strange. I ran out of the room, and I went to wash my hands. The cook was in the kitchen, and she saw me washing my hands so much. She asked me what was wrong, and I just ran away. I didn't want to say anything. I didn't want to get anyone in trouble.

But the Bad Man kept being bad. And I ended up telling Mother what he did to me. I know what you're thinking. I shouldn't have done that. I only told her because the Bad Man kept sneaking into my room at night after everyone had gone to bed. That's how I knew it was wrong. Mother said that no one except the maid is allowed in my room, but he came in there. So I told Mother about all of it. That didn't go so well. Mother slapped me across the cheek and told me never to say something so vile again. Then she told me that I needed to keep quiet because our life is better now that we have money. She said that she didn't want to go back to being poor, and that she was staying with the Bad Man to give us a better life.

Then she told me that I should be grateful to her. She said I should be thanking her for marrying the Bad Man. And then she washed my mouth out with soap.

Dear Alice,

It is so nice to meet you. I am glad that you came back to me from a past life. I have to admit, I had no idea that you were a part of my soul, but it makes more sense than you can even imagine. I know that you are from a very different time and a very different place than we are currently living in. I just want you to know that I am so grateful to have you here, and I want to do as much as possible to help you feel like you belong with me.

I want you to know that what you went through with the Bad Man is truly awful. I am so sorry that you had to endure all those terrible things. You are right, he is a bad man. And I am so sorry that no one else could see it. We have that in common too. There's a bad man who did bad things to me, and my mother reacted just like your mother. It's kind of chilling.

Joan told me that I was connected to my mother in a past life, and when she went looking for the root of that connection, that's when she found you. Isn't that wild? I bet that's why I feel like we had the same mother. In many ways, we did.

I know that it feels weird to be here without Mother, but it doesn't sound like you were safe in your old life. And besides, Mother wanted you to stay and burn in the lobster pot with her. I promise I will explain what I mean by that when you are ready. But just because Mother was unhappy, doesn't mean that you had to keep living an unhappy life with her. You had every right to leave and come back to me. Mother didn't protect you from the Bad Man, and she asked you to continue to endure more abuse when you told her about it. You don't have to live that way anymore.

I made the choice to free you, and in doing that, I hope we also set Mother free in her own way. Even though she may not know it, those cords weren't good for her either. I know how hard it was for you to leave her. I did the same thing in my life. I walked away from my mother and the rest of my family. I did that because parents are not supposed to ask their children to continue getting abused.

I hope that you can begin to build a life here with me. It's 2019, and I live in the United States. I know all of this must be a big shock to you, and it's such a different time and place than where you came from. But I promise I'll explain everything, over time. The Bad Man can't find you here. Mother can't find you here. It's just the two of us and those delicious raspberry bars I bought for you from the market.

Love,
Lauren

Soul Part Four: Brownie Lauren (Ten Years Old)

Hi! It's me! Look at this cool cast on my wrist. It makes my whole arm look so much bigger than it is. I think that's funny. I know, you probably don't think it's really that funny because I got hurt. I guess you'll want to know what happened.

Well, I knew my wrist was broken pretty fast. I was in the small rink and ice skating class was almost over. That's the thing. I just wish class would have ended and I would have just gotten off the ice. Why did I have to get hurt right at the end? Ugh!

I was trying to do a t-stop, and I slipped and fell. I shouldn't have tried that. I'm a lot better at the snowplow stop. As soon as I fell, I put my left hand behind me so that my butt wouldn't get hurt. I should've used my right hand. You know, since I'm left-handed, just like Coco. I didn't want to mess up the hand that I write with. I just started learning cursive. Coco says I write really pretty.

Anyway, my wrist hurt a lot that night. Mom was looking at me real funny. She kept asking if something was wrong. But she wasn't really asking. She was doing that thing where she stares at me like I'm already in trouble. I didn't really want to tell her the truth. I know that's bad 'cause I'm supposed to tell the truth.

Then it was dinner time. Taco night, my favorite. The only problem was, it hurt when I tried to pick up the taco. I think I made a face. Then Mom looked at me again, like she didn't believe that I was ok. I said I was fine, and then I did this thing to prove it. I bent my wrist all the way backwards, and my wrist didn't hurt at all! I thought it was going to hurt so bad, but it didn't!

Don't you think it's kind of weird that I could bend my wrist all the way back without it hurting? I think that's weird. Most of the time, my wrist really did hurt a lot. Like when I had to get dressed in the morning. It hurt SO much to pull my pants up. I couldn't do it. I had to sit on the bed and use my right hand to get my pants on. That was kind of funny. I bet you would have laughed if you had seen me. I don't like using my right hand to do things. I'm way better with my left.

Anyway, I bet you already know why I didn't want to tell Mom. She gets mad all the time, even at regular stuff. She gets mad when she has to drive me places, or when I get sick. I know she really hates it when I get sick. It seems like me getting sick is the worst thing that could happen to her. Well, maybe not the worst. She had to talk to this policeman one time. He made us stop on the way to school, and he told Mom she was driving too fast. She said a lot of bad words after he left.

One time, I threw up in the morning, and Mom had to miss work and stay home with me all day. She hated that. I heard her on the phone telling one of her friends about it. She said it was "so annoying." Mom told me to stay in my room, so I stayed up there and I didn't come down—not even once. At least she rented Anne of Green Gables from the library so I could watch it. Have you ever seen that movie? Well, it's my favorite. I love Anne. I wish I had red hair like her. Sometimes I braid my hair just to be like Anne.

So now you get why I try not to tell Mom when something is wrong. She didn't like it when I threw up that one time, so I knew she would get really mad about a broken wrist. She'll probably tell all her friends that I'm so annoying for breaking my wrist.

Anyway, I bet you can see that now I'm in this cast. I've never had a cast before … it's my first one. And guess what? I got to choose the color. I really wanted my friends to sign it, but the markers don't really work. This one boy in my class has a sling, and he gets a lot of attention. Teachers are always asking if he needs anything. So that seems pretty cool. Maybe people will think that my cast is cool too.

Oh, I don't like that boy. I don't want you to think I like him just because I talked about him. It was only 'cause he has a sling.

Ok, I bet you are wondering how I got this cast. Well, everything was going fine with me pretending not to be hurt. But, then one day, I had Brownies after school. Did you know that I am in Brownies? Yeah, it comes before Girl Scouts. You have to be in Brownies if you want to be in Girl Scouts. And I want to do Girl Scouts because of the cookies. But I like the Brownie outfit better.

Anyway, I had to wear my Brownie outfit to school the day I got my cast on. I like wearing it because I get to show everyone that I am in this club and it's cool. Like sometimes, I wear my skating sweatshirts to school so that people will ask me what it's for, and I can tell them that I am an ice skater. I like telling people that I am an ice skater. Especially the other kids who don't skate. They think that's cool.

You can tell that I'm still wearing my Brownie outfit right now. I didn't want to take it off. It's this brown jumper with white tights. But guess what, so many people forget about the tights. Maybe that's because we have to get those on our own. Coco says that the tights are part of the outfit. She says that you have to wear the whole outfit for it to work. So, I end up reminding a lot of people to wear their tights, but most of the girls still don't do it. Anyway, you can bet that I had my tights on. I always wear the whole outfit.

When I was at school, it really hurt to pull my tights up when I had to go to the bathroom. So I kept trying to hold it. I really do need both hands to pull up these tights.

After school, we had a Brownie meeting in the cafeteria. Crissy's mom is the Brownie leader. I like her, even though I'm not really friends with Crissy. My wrist hurt a lot that day, probably because of the tights I just told you about. So I was walking around holding onto my wrist. Crissy's mom came up to me asked me if I was hurt, and then I was like, oh no! I am going to get found out. So, I told her that I was ok. She kept asking though. It was kind of annoying, but it also was nice. Then she asked if my mom knew. I begged Crissy's mom not to tell my mom, and she looked confused. But then Crissy's mom said that we should tell my mom when she came to pick me up. I asked if she could do it for me.

When Mom came, I watched Crissy's mom go and talk to her. I was peeking out from behind the corner, but don't tell anyone I saw. At first, Mom acted surprised when Crissy's mom told her that something might be wrong with my wrist. That made me feel confused 'cause Mom already knew about it.

But I watched Mom talk to Crissy's mom, and she was being so nice. They were both laughing, so I thought it would be ok. So we said goodbye to Crissy's mom and walked out of school. Mom put her hand around my shoulders, which was weird, but kinda nice. I thought, wow, maybe it's going to be ok. But then I got into the car with her. Mom turned around and started screaming at me. I started crying. I asked her not to take me to the hospital because I was scared. She told me that we had to go to the hospital. I cried the whole way there, and she just kept yelling at me.

Anyway, I don't really want to talk about this anymore. Mom promised me a stuffed animal if I did a good job at the hospital. Can I go pick it out? Then I would like to go home and watch Duck Tails.

Dear Brownie Lauren,

I'm so glad that you came back to talk to me. And I am so sorry that you had to go through all of this. I know it was hard when you got sick, and you needed Mom to take care of you. I know that you tried not to need her as much. But the truth is, that's all backwards. When you get sick, your parents are supposed to take care of you and not make you feel bad about something you can't do anything about. I want you to know that everything is going to be really different from now on.

You didn't do anything wrong by pretending that your wrist wasn't broken. I know that's confusing because it seems like a lie. But if you had felt safe, none of this would have happened. Nothing about that is ok. None of this is your fault.

And I am so sorry that you had to watch Mom act so differently with Crissy's mom. I am also upset that Crissy's mom didn't try to figure out more about this situation. She put you in a bad position. I have a lot of feelings about the way that you grew up. I think that because it was such a nice area, and Mom was so nice in public, no one really thought to ask you what was going on at home. And that's not fair at all.

I want you to know that our life is so different now. One of the biggest changes is that when you aren't feeling well, you get to come to me instead of Mom. So I want you to try to tell me when you aren't feeling well. I want to know when you need something. I am here to help you. And it wouldn't even occur to me to say that helping you is annoying. It makes me so angry that you dealt with that for so many years. Getting sick and getting hurt are natural parts of life. There is nothing wrong with that. The last thing you need, on top of a broken wrist, is to feel guilty about it.

I want to be there for you in all the ways you needed and didn't get. I know it will take some time. I don't expect you to trust me right away. Maybe the next time you aren't feeling well, we can sit down and watch Anne of Green Gables together. I would like to do that with you, so you don't have to be alone. Also, I still love that movie. I still love Anne.

I do remember the Brownie uniform. It was totally cool. And thanks for reminding me that you felt special when you belonged to a group. I want to think of ways to show you that you belong here with me.

You're probably wondering where Mom and Dad are. Well, we never have to see them again. I know that seems crazy, and I can feel you looking at me like you don't understand. But trust me, it's so much better this way. Now, when we get sick, there is no one there to make us feel bad about it.

Would you like to pick out your stuffed animal now? I think

I remember the one that you wanted from the hospital gift shop. We can do that anytime you want.

    Love,
    Lauren

A LONG-STEMMED STERLING SILVER ROSE

I stepped out of the bath and wrapped myself in a lime-green towel. I tried to process everything I had just learned during the parts work ritual, but my mind was abuzz with all this new information. *Alice? My past-life part is named Alice.* I couldn't get over the fact that Alice had been abused by the Bad Man, and I had been abused by the Black Square. These two men felt as though they had been cut from the same cloth. And the same could be said about our mothers.

When I came forward about the Black Square a decade ago, my mother had acted as though her hands were tied. She kept insisting that she couldn't rock the boat or attempt to shake up the dynamics in our family. I pointed out repeatedly that the Black Square was the one who had shaken up our family, but my mother seemed to be wholly incapable of hearing that point. I couldn't believe that Alice went through something strikingly similar. Her mother had chosen to stay with the Bad Man, and in doing so, she sacrificed the well-being of her own daughter. Both mothers seemed to believe that the sexual abuse their daughters endured were just the residue that went along with belonging to a family. Both mothers essentially told us to *deal with it.* I knew every ounce of this story.

Despite all this mounting evidence, my mind still couldn't fathom the fact that Alice was real. All of a sudden, I was overcome with the urge to pull out my phone and play the recording from my soul retrieval session with Joan. As I listened to my own voice on the recording, I realized that I told Joan that I had been sexually abused, but I didn't tell her much more than that. What were the odds that Joan managed to find a soul part who could present a story I already knew in the depths of my bones? It didn't seem like those odds were very good.

I stopped the recording and put my phone down. My brain was playing devil's advocate again, even though my soul quite literally recognized Alice's mother as my own mother. I began to think even more deeply about all the ways I had felt especially connected to my mother. From the time I was very young, I related to her from a place of total exhaustion that made absolutely no sense. Until now.

And there was another striking similarity between us. My mother and I were both incredibly frugal. That made no sense given the fact that both my parents were solidly upper middle class, and I was raised in a very affluent suburb of Chicago. I watched my father tease my mother for all the coupon-cutting and bargain shopping she did. I watched my mother scold my father for ordering too much Chinese takeout, almost every time. And during these moments, I always came to my mother's defense. I argued that saving money was always the smart move and that bargain shopping was important. Peter and my father always looked at us perplexed during these moments. But my mother and I seemed to be perpetually afraid that we would end up losing everything. This was the only way we could truly relate to each other. And now, I began to wonder if that was because we had been poor together in another life.

* * *

As I put on my pajamas, I began to think about the other soul parts who came back. My heart ached for Little Lauren as she hid under the deck. Once she started talking, I could feel all her emotions pulsing through my veins. The fear. The pain. The nervous excitement of a lonely child who suddenly had a visitor. It was all deeply familiar. I didn't have a ton of intact memories from that era of my life. But I knew I ran away from home a lot. Somehow this made the story of my estrangement fit even more securely within the fabric of my larger experience in my family. All those emergency bags that I packed. All those cans of soup on Thanksgiving. Little Lauren had taught me how to escape.

And then I thought about Brownie Lauren. I definitely remembered breaking my wrist while figure skating. I also remembered being so afraid to tell my mother about it that I pretended not to be hurt for a week. I had forgotten about the way my mother acted when she came to pick me up at school that afternoon. The way she had been so kind to Crissy's mom, and so mean to me in private. This dichotomy was such a common experience in my life. I felt that my mother was often one way in public and another way at home. But hearing Brownie Lauren move through such big feelings while she had a broken wrist was heart-wrenching. I could certainly understand why she left.

I sighed as I attempted to digest all these stories. These soul parts had shared so much valuable information with me, and frankly, I was surprised. Sometimes during parts work, it can take a while before the parts are willing to share their exile stories. But this was different. Joan had called into the abyss, looking for parts of my soul who were at least somewhat willing to return. And these four parts had answered the call. However, I had a feeling that I had lost more than four soul parts over the course of my traumatic lifetime. I began to wonder about all the other exiles who refused to return to me. I felt my chest tighten.

A few minutes later, I walked into my kitchen in Heaven on Sheridan. I decided to make myself some tea. There was no way I was ready for bed. I turned on the television and plopped down on my dark grey couch. I whipped out my phone. It was time to search for that sterling silver rose pendant that Coco told Joan about during the soul retrieval. I had taken good care of the three younger soul parts. They had been coddled and fed. I needed to spend the rest of the evening with the adult soul part who left my body during Coco's funeral. Honestly, I was the most afraid of losing Grieving Lauren again. The three children were glad to be rescued away from the hellscape Joan found them in, but this soul part felt differently. It was clear that she had reluctantly come back. If I didn't find this rose necklace, and quick, I feared that she may decide to drift out of my body once again. I didn't want her to join all the other *lost girls*.

I was cautiously optimistic that I could convince Grieving

Lauren to stay. On the day of Coco's funeral, I had no idea that Coco would be so accessible from beyond the grave. So Grieving Lauren must not have known that either. These parts seemed to be frozen at the time of each traumatic event when they left my body. They were each little time capsules, suspended at the age and developmental stage that they were in when they departed. It was up to me to teach them what I had learned since then.

I got excited as I realized that I had an opportunity to show Grieving Lauren that Coco was still very much here. Since Coco's passing, I had been able to communicate with her quite regularly. Sometimes I would feel a chill drift through the air. Then, I would hear, "Yoo-hoo, Mrs. Bloom!" That's always how she got my attention. And it worked, every time.

It worked because Coco used that phrase incessantly when she was still alive. And it certainly wasn't a part of my regular vernacular. Apparently, it was a catchphrase from a show called *The Goldbergs*, which Coco proudly declared to be one of the first sitcoms about an overtly Jewish family in the Bronx. It ran during the fifties, and she loved it. Coco had been blunt and obvious when she was alive, and she was no different in the afterlife. I was so grateful for that.

I poured myself a cup of ginger tea and returned to my couch. I spoke into the center of the room, which is how I began every session where I wanted to speak to my grandmother. I said, "I call Coco to join me. Thank you for coming to my soul retrieval session today. I know you want to help me find that rose pendant, so can you guide me toward it now?"

I waited a few minutes. Then I heard her:

"That was fun today, Lauren, but that lady almost got my gift wrong! At first, she said that I couldn't give you a real gift, it had to be fake or something. But I thought, why would I do that? I want Lauren to have a good piece of jewelry from me. She thought I was trying to give you a pineapple necklace. No! I kept shouting at her: IT'S NOT A PINEAPPLE, IT'S A ROSE!

She got confused because there are little dots on it, and that's true, but the dots are on the leaves of the rose. You'll see. The necklace is on that site you like so much. I don't know the name—"

"Etsy?" I responded.

"Yes, that's the one. Go on Etsy and type this in, exactly like I am saying it to you: A LONG-STEMMED STERLING SILVER 925K ROSE PENDANT."

Coco had been a jeweler, so none of this felt surprising to me. I didn't even know what "925k sterling silver" meant. But anytime Coco told me to do something related to fashion or jewelry, I complied. She was always right. There was clearly a specific necklace that she was guiding me to, and I was determined to find it.

I opened the Etsy app on my phone and typed in the exact phrase Coco had given me. An array of options popped up. As I began scrolling, I heard her voice, loud and clear:

"No, no, keep going … no, no … not that one, that's not real silver!"

Even though I liked a few of the options on the page, I continued to scroll until I heard her yell:

"STOP. THAT'S IT. THAT'S THE ONE!"

I opened the listing. It was a long-stemmed, sterling silver rose pendant with a delicate chain. It loosely resembled the rose from *Beauty and the Beast.* I liked the way the rose hung down from the chain stem first, so that the petals would be closest to my chest. The listing was from a jeweler in the United Kingdom. I could hear Coco talking about the fact that she liked that attribute. Coco told me that she could tell this jeweler took great care and precision in her work, and Coco also liked the fact that there were also cleaning instructions. She was very particular about that part:

"This is high-quality sterling silver, Lauren. That means you need to take care of it. You will need to polish it regularly because the necklace will tarnish over time. There's nothing wrong with that. All good silver requires a little maintenance. I will show you how to do it. You don't need any fancy polishes. Those are a rip-off. You just need to soak it in some white vinegar."

I asked her why she was giving me a rose.

She said, "Listen, Lauren. I want you to wear this necklace every day. I want you to wear it and remember how much I love you. That's why I want you to have a rose. It's the greatest symbol of love, and it always has been. It's classic and timeless. Just like us. I worry about you now that you don't have the rest of the family. I want you to feel my love every day. You will always have me. I want you to know that I will love you forever. That's what this rose is for."

I burst into tears. I had always overlooked the rose. It never meant very much to me. I had felt more of a camaraderie with other flowers, like the lotus. The rose felt overused and generic. Until now. I stared at the listing for the necklace, and I noticed a small detail. The petals had small lines on them that almost resembled dots. It surely wasn't a pineapple. But it was the exact necklace that Coco had described to Joan. I had found it. I placed a hand on my heart and called in Grieving Lauren. She was overjoyed. I ordered the pendant immediately.

* * *

Since it was shipping from England, the necklace took a few weeks to arrive. And the wait was excruciating. I could feel Grieving Lauren yearning for that necklace with an urgency that I couldn't seem to temper. I checked the tracking information multiple times a day as I tried to imagine how it would feel to receive that necklace and place it around my neck for the first time.

I crossed each day off my calendar. And on the day that the necklace was set to arrive, I couldn't focus on anything else. The bus ride home from work seemed to take forever. When I finally arrived at my apartment, I bolted through the lobby and ran directly over to my mailbox. I opened it and peered through the small container. There was nothing inside.

I almost lost it. I had been waiting for this moment for so long. I couldn't wait any longer.

I checked the tracking information again, and this time it said: *delayed.* I emailed the jeweler immediately and asked her if she knew what was going on with my package. She did not. I began to cry. Not only was this necklace taking forever to get to me, but now it was *lost*. I sunk into my grief. Concave and complex. I felt like I lost Coco all over again. I became concerned that Grieving Lauren might really leave over this. I could tell that she was incredibly upset. I attempted to talk her down from that ledge as I frantically paced around my apartment.

* * *

The next day, I took an earlier bus home from work. I checked the tracking information again. The rose necklace was still suspended somewhere in the abyss. I departed the bus and sprinted through the lobby of my building. I opened my mailbox anyway. Nothing. I went up to my apartment and called my local post office. No one had any idea what was going on or where my package was. I began to cry again. I could feel Grieving Lauren beginning to revolt. She was about to leave me again. There was nothing I could do to stop her. I couldn't lie to her anymore. It wasn't better down here. It wasn't better without Coco. She knew it. And I knew it too.

Suddenly, I felt a chill at the base of my neck. The room felt different.

"Yoo-hoo, Mrs. Bloom!"

I burst into tears. "Coco? Are you here?"

"Yes, it's me, Lauren. Hold your horses. There's nothing wrong with your package. I have it."

I had been pacing nervously around the room, but now my feet were frozen in place. "What do you mean, you have it?" The breath left my body as I waited for a response.

"I have been holding onto the necklace so you can tell me when you want to receive it. Don't you see? It will be just like

I am really giving it to you, Lauren. So tell me when you want it, and I will make sure that it's there. That way, the rose will really feel like a gift from me. Just like old times."

I dried my tears and began to laugh uncontrollably. My brain screamed, *what?* But my soul was at peace. This made complete sense. Coco was the kind of person who took great satisfaction in physically handing a gift to someone she cared about. She loved to watch people open her gifts, so she could witness their joy and amazement. Of course she held up this package. She wanted to watch me open it. She wanted to watch me put on that rose necklace. Just like old times.

I stared into the center of the room and threw my hands into the air. "Well, I want it right now!"

And then I heard her: "Ok, Lauren. Go downstairs and check your mailbox again. It will be there."

I bolted out of my apartment and into the hallway. I frantically pushed the button on the elevator multiple times. My legs shook in place while I waited to be transported back down to the lobby of my building. As I got into the elevator, a wave of fear and hesitation came over me. *I just checked my mailbox. What the hell am I going to do if it's not there?*

As the elevator reached the lobby, my heart began to pound. I walked over to my mailbox and closed my eyes. I was instantly terrified. I knew that if this necklace was not there, I would have a very hard time believing that Coco was really talking to me. Everything would change. I would cease to believe in so much of the magic that had transpired over the past few months. I would lose faith in the angels and the spirit world. I would lose faith in my own knowing. I would probably lose Grieving Lauren all over again. I paused. *Everything was riding on this moment.* But I had to look. I had to know. The only way out is through.

I placed the key into my mailbox and turned the lock slowly. I closed my eyes. Slowly, I pulled open the small door and glanced inside. At the base of the box sat a small package. I pulled out the package as tears began to stream down my face.

It was from England.

I held the package close to my chest and burst into tears.

THE HEART WORD

I want to tell you a secret.

I didn't want to write another word after the chapter about the rose necklace. It was so tempting to end this book right there. In fact, I fought with my editor over it.

In a perfect world, I hoped you might place this book down (while ugly crying) as you imagined Coco giving me the rose necklace in the most magical way possible. I thought about how you might phone a friend (still ugly crying) and tell them all about this memoir you just read about angels, possessions, and fairy grandmothers who say, "Yoo-hoo Mrs. Bloom." I wanted you to read the story about the necklace and believe in it all. In the rainbow that appeared without a drop of rain. In the Archangel Michael, who introduced himself to me by posing as a security guard. In the orbs of light that danced around my apartment in Heaven on Sheridan. And in the spirit of Coco, who continued to find ways to show me that I could never truly lose her.

Perhaps I wanted that for you because that's what receiving the rose necklace did for me. It made me believe in everything. And I mean, *everything.* Even as I write these words, the necklace still hangs down from my neck. And Coco still shows up, every so often, to remind me to clean it with white vinegar.

Unfortunately, this is not a book about proving that spirits exist. There is more to my story than magic, although that is certainly a part of it. This is a book about something else, something much deeper.

This is a story about what happened when I began to follow my heart.

This book opens on Mother's Day of 2018 for a reason. That was the first time in my entire life that I made a heart-based decision. Until that point, I had been listening to my mind. And there is no way that my mind wanted to leave my family.

Instead, my mind told me to pack emergency bags on Passover. My mind told me that perhaps I had asked for *too much* when I said I never wanted to see the Black Square again. All the while, my heart was breaking. Slowly, methodically. Without me even knowing how bad it was. But something happened when I woke up crying in my bed on Mother's Day. My heart was done.

Had I not listened to my heart, I would still be Leah. I would be stuck in a family that didn't really love me. I would be pining for their attention and their basic respect. I would be fighting with my parents over the Black Square. I would be eating cans of soup on Thanksgiving. And Mary Frances would still be living inside of me.

Instead, I followed my heart. And that was the source of my liberation.

As I write these words, they feel a little trite. Perhaps that's because the adage *follow your heart* feels overused to the point where we have all become numb to it. I wonder why that is. Why we don't understand the sheer power of our hearts. Truthfully, I used to be someone who felt that *following your heart* was about as generic as the rose. That concept seemed to be reserved for Hallmark movies and memes on my social media feed. I wasn't into it. Somehow, I didn't think that *following your heart* had anything to do with me.

Now I see that following my heart was an essential part of my story. My heart led me out of the life I had inherited. My brain wouldn't let me leave. My ego certainly wouldn't let me leave. But my heart was a free agent. She wasn't bound by reason or convenience. She was only bound by the truth. And the truth was that running away was not the same thing as freedom. I couldn't continue to put duct tape on that vault. I had to come forward about the Black Square. It *was* a psychic attack. My name was really Chava.

I had to lose it all to find myself.

And yet, following my heart was much more grueling than Hallmark wanted me to believe. My heart took me down a path filled with the most terrifying, gut-wrenching decisions I have ever made in my life. When my heart woke me up on Mother's Day and told me to estrange myself, it was wholly inconvenient. I learned that my heart didn't care about the life I had built, or how hard I had worked to maintain it. In fact, this book is filled with an array of the most inconvenient string of events that I could have ever imagined. From the estrangement and the plagues, to the depossession and the soul retrieval, there is nothing about this story that follows a typical path.

Now I see why it was almost impossible for me to operate as Regular Lauren during this timeframe. Regular Lauren was an ego invention. A façade. An outward-facing version of myself that I had grown accustomed to portraying. But as I ventured deeper into the journey of my heart, Regular Lauren struggled to exist. My heart took me away from my wounded warrior past and into my new life as Chava. Once I began to live more fully from my heart, there was no turning back.

* * *

Even though I regret nothing, I want to be clear about the fact that following my heart was brutal. Perhaps some folks follow their hearts and live out the plotline of a Hallmark movie. But in my case, my heart asked me to demolish almost every inch of the life I had known. And that was an incredibly painful road. Truthfully, it still is.

It's not necessarily better on the other side. I can't give you that. I mean, I had to survive a depossession to get to where I am today. But every time I think about whether my life was better before, I arrive at the same conclusion: no matter what *Regular Lauren* wanted you to believe, my life was highly problematic, and I knew it.

A year before my estrangement, I made a pro and con list. And on the side of the pros, I wrote "identity congruence." I know exactly what I meant by that phrase. I was referring to the fact that Regular Lauren was a lie. It may have taken a plague of moths for me to ultimately part with her, but Regular Lauren hadn't been working for a long time. Whenever someone would ask me how my Thanksgiving had been, I would smile and say that it had been lovely. But there was nothing lovely about deploying emergency bags and eating cans of soup. That's for sure. I had been pretending to belong in my family for so many years, possibly my whole life. And I just couldn't do it anymore. Ultimately, I wanted identity congruence so badly that I risked everything to get it.

Now, I've chosen to go a step further into my newfound identity congruence by telling this story. As terrifying as that is, I also know it's the only way I can live my life from this point forward. With integrity. With truth. From my heart.

* * *

In the five years that have passed since my depossession, I have learned a lot about myself. Clearly, I have claimed my place as a writer. But I have also been afforded the chance to explore other aspects of my identity in more detail than I could when I was younger. I spent so much of my life trying to escape abuse. And all that trauma robbed me of the privilege of being able to learn about who I really am, until now. While a part of me will always grieve this truth, I know there was no alternative. My early life was riddled with incest, my teens and twenties were overshadowed by multiple rapes, and my thirties were spent divesting from my family. In my forties, I can finally grow into the full expression of my personality. Diane warned me that after someone survives a depossession, they often change in ways that might appear drastically different to the outside world. That has certainly been true for me.

While I was writing this book, I struggled with the fact that readers would most likely assume that I am heterosexual. Ultimately, I decided to leave it that way because this story exists as a time capsule, and I wanted to stay true to my thoughts and feelings at the time it took place. And for many years, I believed that I was straight. However, in the spirit of identity congruence, I now identify as bisexual.

After Mary Frances departed and parts of my own soul came back to me, I developed a deeper understanding of who I am and how I see the world. And I see the world through the eyes of a queer woman. My life and my relationships make more sense this way. I've colored in more of the picture. I've come home to myself.

Of course this book was written by someone queer. Trust me, I see that now. From my refusal to adhere to an unhealthy family system, to my desire to change my name and live more authentically in the world, to my yearning for relationships that don't fit into a box: this is a queer story. And I am honored to join such a powerful, vibrant community of survivors and innovators. This is where I belong.

* * *

When I think about what I have learned about my journey by writing this book, one word keeps rattling around in my mind: courage. Every time I lost my way, my bravery always sustained me. It was the one attribute I knew I could rely on. It was the true staple of my identity congruence. It was my throughline. My courage got me through the ants and the moths. It got me through the moment when I almost took my own life. My courage always kept me going. For a while, it was all I had.

A month after I received the rose necklace, I tattooed *the heart word* on the inside of my wrist in my own handwriting. I wanted to find a way to consolidate the path that began with my estrangement and ended when I received the necklace from Coco. And even though my journey will never be over, the first phase of it seemed to come to an end with that rose.

After taking French for so many years, I knew the word courage stemmed from *coeur,* which meant heart. Instinctively, courage felt like the voice of my heart. The way my heart chose to show up in all my relationships. The way my heart blew up my life for all the right reasons. The way my heart changed my name so that I could live more authentically in the world.

The way my heart was right about everything.

Just to be sure; I googled the word courage. And I came across a quote from Brené Brown: "The root of the word courage is cor – the Latin word for heart. In one of its earliest forms, the word courage had a very different definition than it does today. Courage originally meant, *to speak one's mind by telling all one's heart.*"[9]

Brene Brown went on to share that courage is a heart word. I couldn't believe that she used the exact phrase that my heart had already identified. Maybe it was a synchronicity or maybe it was just Google, but the day I found this quote, I began to trust my heart even more.

My tattoo made all the sense in the world the day I chose it, but it makes even more sense to me now. When I decided to write this book, I knew exactly what to call it. The title came from a place deep inside of me. A place of sheer knowing. A place that logic and reason couldn't touch. An inconvenient place. A place filled with magic and truth. A place only my heart could truly understand. That's why my heart wrote this book to you.

After all, it's her story to tell.

THE ROGUE LOBSTER

August 2023

Dear Claire,

Congratulations on making it all the way to the end of this book. I am sure it has been quite the wild ride. As you can imagine, I had hoped to take this story to my grave. I mean, why would I ever want folks to know that I survived a real-life depossession? There's only one reason I decided to come forward about all of this. And you are that reason, Claire.

Perhaps you are wondering why I have chosen this name for you. To me, Claire is a placeholder. She's an archetype. She's the part inside of us that hasn't succumbed to the pot of boiling water. She can still feel her wild nature. She knows what she wants, and at times, she still believes she can have it. She is tossing and turning. Pacing and yearning for a different life.

There's another reason I chose the name Claire to represent this part of us. Claire is the middle name that my mother was given at birth. The name she was given when she entered this world with a clean slate, before the terrors of the world got to her. My mother dropped the name Claire when she married my father. As a result, I never got a chance to see Claire, or the joyful innocence that I imagine she once embodied. I was raised by someone else. Someone who had already been burning in that pot for so long. By the time I came into the world, Claire, along with her desires, had been steadily washed away.

Sometimes, I wonder if Claire still lives deep within the soul of my mother. For years, I tried to excavate her; to hold onto the hope that my mother could rekindle her hopes and dreams. But that wasn't meant to happen in this life. The good news is that a book is immortal. And that's why I felt inspired to hold a torch for Claire. Perhaps when my mother leaves this Earth and returns as someone else, Claire will make that journey along with her. And maybe, just maybe, the next version of Claire will see herself in my story and know it will always be for her.

What happened to my mother is incredibly commonplace. That's because the world does a fantastic job of trying to chip away at our spirit. This seems especially pertinent as I close my book during an era where our civil rights are being stripped away, one by one. So, I feel even more compelled to deliver this message. The most effective form of resistance is to keep Claire alive in a world that wants her dead. Liberation will always be an inside job. No one is coming to airlift the rogue lobster out of that pot. The rogue must always claw her way to the top if she wants to escape.

* * *

I wrote this book because I had a feeling there were a lot of other Claires in the world. So I gathered my strength and poured all my time and energy into bringing my story to life. Not because I wanted you to tell your friends all about Mary Frances, although, you are welcome to do that. I wrote this book because I hope that my story travels through your bones until you see that my liberation is your liberation.

Let me tell you what I mean by that. I dedicated this book to the part of you that knows you were meant for more than the life you are currently living. The voice deep inside of you that is beckoning your soul toward something greater. I heard that voice calling out to me for many years, but I was stuck in a pot of boiling water, burning alongside the other lobsters in my family. My environment drowned out the voice of my own heart for most of my life. Until Mother's Day, when I became the rogue lobster and escaped from that pot for good.

Just like there are multitudes of Claires in the world, I know I'm not the only rogue lobster. It may seem like stepping onto the path of a rogue lobster is out of reach for many of us. I'm not going to pretend that we can all get there. It takes more than sheer will to escape from a pot of boiling water. I got out in large part because I had built up enough economic and social capital to survive without my family and their resources. I am not sure I would be here today without my steady career, my grandmother's savings account, and the incredible hospitality of my friends.

Even though our stories may vary, I will say that all the rogue lobsters I know have one thing in common: we finally listened to Claire. That may seem rather simple, but it is an incredibly painful road. You watched me travel down it.

The road will always be difficult because Claire wants us to change every aspect of our lives that isn't in alignment with our true purpose. That could mean leaving behind everything from our jobs, relationships, and families to the names we were given at birth. And those are only a few examples. Stepping onto the path of a rogue lobster isn't for the faint of heart. But I have a feeling that you already know the alternative. If you allow Claire to wither away, that is not a life.

At this point, I wonder if there are any lobsters out there who are beginning to wake up to the possibility that they are stuck in a pot of boiling water. So many of us are born into situations where we are burning along with our families, our communities, and our countries. And we are often surrounded by people who have been burning for generations. It's very hard to connect to that deeper part, the part that wants more, when all we can hear is the rumbling of boiling water and the voices of other burnt lobsters telling us that there's nothing wrong with staying inside the pot.

I want to talk about how this happens. How we end up believing the pot of boiling water is a lovely hot tub instead of something that is killing us slowly. I spent so many years participating in lobster races without ever realizing they were inhumane. Now, that might seem completely nuts, from the outside. But I wonder if you have your own example of a family lobster race. I wonder if there is a generational pattern that you learned how to tolerate. A pattern that seems impossible to change and exists deep within the shadow of your own ancestral line. A pattern no one wants to talk about.

I bet there is.

And that's because it's quite easy for families to end up like lobsters in a pot of boiling water. There are so many reasons this can occur. For starters, the pot always represents some force from the outside that is placing pressure onto the family unit. It will never be the fault of the lobsters. It will always be the fault of the system that put us there.

I'll use myself as an example. I come from a long line of Ashkenazi Jews descending from Eastern Europe. There is a generation of lobsters in my family that had to survive the Holocaust. And a generation of lobsters who immigrated to the United States. And a generation of lobsters who bore the brunt of all that excess steam and heat. That's when I entered the pot.

I can see exactly how this happened to us. Our family was ripped apart by the Nazis and then spread out all over the Jewish diaspora. In fact, we didn't learn that we had an entire branch of our family living in Israel until I was in college. And one of those relatives successfully escaped from a concentration camp the day before it was liberated. Talk about a rogue lobster.

When I zoom the lens out, I can understand why my parents acted the way they did when I came forward about the Black Square. To them, nothing that happened inside the confines of our own family would ever be as bad as the atrocities that were done to us. This was an unspoken rule in my Jewish American family.

Now, I am going to do something I never thought I would do. I am going to defend every single lobster who came before me. I firmly believe that everyone did their best, with the tools they had available. By the time I came into this world, that pot had been taking us down for at least four generations. I can't even imagine how hard that must have been for my ancestors.

But we are each born into a role. And my role was clear: I was destined to become the cycle breaker. I began to see the pot, as well as our behavior inside of it, as equally toxic. And I was the first lobster to make that claim. I tried to pull the other lobsters out of the pot, but no one was ever going to join me on the other side. That's because the rogue must act alone.

No one tells you that liberation is a cold, lonely mess. I hope I've illustrated that process in this book. Granted, each rogue who escapes will have their own story to tell. And the world needs every single one of our stories. And now, I've told you mine.

Before I go, I want to leave you with one final request. The worst thing you can do is close this book and resume your life, exactly as it stands. That's the quickest way to lose access to Claire.

If you made it to the end of this book without throwing it across the room, I know for a fact that Claire still lives within your heart. And I suspect that she has a few things she may want to say to you.

Luckily, getting in touch with her is quite simple:

Just close your eyes,
Place one hand on your heart,
Slow down your breath,
And listen.

A LOVE LETTER TO MY EDITOR

This book would not be possible without the incredible work of my editors Maggie McReynolds and Sky Kier, and the fierce network of writers at Un-Settling Books. *The Heart Word* is the result of an effortless collaboration between Maggie, Sky, and me. Both Maggie and Sky brought their unique and invaluable perspectives to the table. They provided me with honest feedback throughout this process, which allowed me to trust them even more. I knew that both Maggie and Sky felt a genuine connection to my story and to the way I chose to tell it. That really kept me going during all the tough moments when I doubted myself and my capacity to finish this book. They were always in my corner cheering me on, and that truly made all the difference. I am grateful for their time and effort, but most of all, I am grateful for their friendship.

* * *

I want to take a moment to center the work of my main editor, Maggie McReynolds. I fear that she might be slightly uncomfortable with that, but she'll just have to get over it (as she edits her own appreciation letter). After all, I can't imagine bringing this book to print without first declaring my respect for Maggie's time, her talent, and all the Zoom calls that made this book a reality.

From the moment I was first introduced to Maggie, I knew that she was the only person on the face of the Earth who would be able to help me bring this story to life. I remember the day when we had our first phone call. It was August of 2021, and I was driving across the country from Illinois to Colorado. I had packed up my entire life and decided to move thousands of miles away from where I was born and where this story took place. I was finally ready to part with my karmic relationship with Chicago, and it felt like the universe was allowing me to leave. I was also in the process of legally changing my name to Lauren Chava Rose. With the time and distance that I was about to carve out for myself, I was beginning to feel an urge to tell this story.

Somewhere between the border of Nebraska and Colorado, Maggie called me. She asked me to explain the basic plot of my memoir. I took a deep breath. Then, I did my best to regurgitate an abridged version of this book: First, I left my family. Then, weird things began to happen in my apartment. And yada, yada, yada, it turns out that I had been possessed by a spirit when I was a child. *Any questions?*

I paused as I waited for Maggie to respond. I was clearly testing her. But I needed to put all my cards on the table to see if she would be able to handle it. I knew exactly what I wanted out of a main editor for this book. First, it was essential for my editor to believe the details of this story. There was no way I was about to work with someone who placated me. And then, I needed to know that my editor was capable of diving deep into the horror of the four plagues and the spirit who possessed me. Those were the things that I screened for that day.

Maggie passed both tests with flying colors. She wasted no time as she launched headfirst into the plot of this book. She talked about common pitfalls in writing about the metaphysical world and how we could avoid them. She talked about the right tone for this book and ways I could best achieve it. She told me that it had all the makings of a great story. A powerful story. One that could stay with readers for a very long time.

Maggie clearly understood me, and she also understood the bones of this book right from the start. I was a little shocked that she didn't trip over any of the supernatural details that I had shared. Her calm demeanor reminded me of the way that both Linda and Diane had responded to this exact situation as it was happening. It was clear that I had mobilized another crone. Everything about this felt right.

Working with Maggie was a breeze. It was truly an effortless partnership. We both seemed to know exactly what we wanted out of this book, and we put our heads together on a regular basis for the next two years until we got there. Maggie helped me design a storyboard that made sense for the rough draft. Then, she watched as I demolished it and wrote an entirely new storyboard right before we were slated to begin the second draft. I made it abundantly clear from the moment we met that I didn't care how hard I had to work on this memoir, or how many drafts it took, I needed it to be great. Maggie was on the exact same page. Neither one of us ever wavered.

During this entire process, Maggie exhibited the patience of a saint. Patience is a virtue that doesn't seem to exist in my DNA, so I truly admire that quality when I see it manifest in someone else. Maggie sat with me as I experienced multiple breakdowns where I became petrified to tell this story. One of those breakdowns rendered me useless for a few months. I couldn't write a single word without thinking about the way this book might be received. I became consumed by the fact that I would be forever known as *the girl who got possessed*. I understand that is still a likely scenario, but at some point, it became more important for me to share my story with the world than to give into my egoic obsessions around how I would be viewed. That's when I knew that I was ready to finish this book. And Maggie was waiting patiently in the wings, ready to help me bring it to fruition.

Step by step, Maggie sat with me until I found the strength to keep going. She never tried to rush me past my own process. Instead, she held back until I rediscovered the courage that was necessary for me to choose this book all over again.

I know, from being a therapist, that it's not possible to *get someone* to a different place. They must elicit that change work on their own. Maggie has an intuitive gift of sensing these stages of change in her clients. And I needed exactly what she provided at every stage. I needed a few months where all I did was roll around on my floor in the fetal position and cry. Then, I needed to persevere through all those sleepless nights where I feared that telling this story would be a mistake. And finally, I needed to get my shit together and finish this book. Maggie accepted me through it all.

If Maggie hadn't been along for this ride, I am not sure *The Heart Word* would exist. So, if you enjoyed this memoir, please know that I did not accomplish it alone. Healing doesn't take place in a vacuum. We need community care. We need each other. The same is true for writers.

Thank you, Maggie.
Thank you from the bottom of my heart.

ABOUT THE AUTHOR

Lauren Chava Rose is a writer, poet, and psychotherapist with over a decade of experience in the field of trauma-informed care. Her writing has been featured in *Elephant Journal, Body Politic,* and *Medium. The Heart Word: How I Lost It All and Found Myself* is her debut memoir. Lauren is dedicated to helping people bring their stories into the world. When she isn't living life as a rogue, you can find her in the mountains. Follow Lauren's work on Instagram (@laurenchavarose) and via her website (www.laurenchavarose.com).

THE HEART WORD: A READER'S GUIDE

1. Lauren follows her heart for the first time on Mother's Day, 2018, when she mails estrangement letters to both her parents. When was the first time you followed your heart?

2. *The Heart Word* explores the idea that intergenerational trauma can also be inter-dimensional. What do you think about this concept?

3. Lauren talks about the heart and the mind often being at war when faced with a difficult, life-altering decision. She says that the mind will almost always fight to remain in the status quo, while the heart is the only part of us that can make a different choice. How do you relate to this inner struggle?

4. Lauren uses the story about her family's lobster-racing tradition to illustrate familial entrenchment in cycles of intergenerational trauma. No one else in her family can see the horror of racing lobsters and then plunging them into a pot of boiling water. Does your family have their own version of a lobster race? What patterns can you see in your family or community that other people fail to see?

5. Lauren's journey contains both darkness and light. What stands out to you about the light workers (both alive and otherworldly) who help Lauren along the

way?

6. Mary Frances turns out to be a wounded little girl, just like Lauren. Both girls feel like orphans who desperately want to be seen and understood. How did this relationship land for you?

7. Lauren's grandmother is the most stable, reliable figure in her life. In trauma-informed care, we refer to Coco as a protective factor. What protective factors do you have in your life?

8. Lauren dedicates this book to Claire, or "the part of you that knows you were meant for more than the life you are currently living." What did you feel in your heart when you read that passage?

9. Lauren receives the rose necklace from Coco and suddenly believes in all the metaphysical elements of her story. Have you ever experienced a meaningful synchronicity or a gift from another realm?

10. Lauren feels like most of her family members are possessing each other and calling it love. How does this dynamic manifest in the book?

11. Lauren says that "liberation is a cold, lonely mess." How can you relate to this concept?

12. Lauren undergoes a Mikvah ceremony where she chooses to leave Leah behind and be reborn as Chava. Have you ever been through something so transformational that you feel like a different person on the other side?

13. Lauren closes this book by writing a letter to Claire. Take a few minutes to write your own letter to Claire. What do you want her to know? What wisdom do you want her to share?

[1] The anniversary of a loved one's passing as observed in Judaism.

[2] Alex Myles, "Psychic Attacks and How to Respond to Them," *Elephant Journal*. June 29, 2018. https://www.elephantjournal.com/2018/06/psychic-attacks-how-to-respond-to-them/

[3] A coming-of-age ritual in Judaism that takes place around the age of thirteen. Jews who identify as female are given a Bat Mitzvah, which serves as their entryway into adulthood within the Jewish faith.

[4] The Jewish prayer for repentance that is recited on Yom Kippur, which is one of the most holy days of the year and the time when Jews come together to repent for the sins of the previous year.

[5] A brimless cap traditionally worn by Jewish people who identify as male.

[6] Aaron L. Raskin, Kabbalah of Jewish Names: Chava. October 25, 2017. https://brooklynheightsjewishacademy.org/kabbalah-of-jewish-names-chava-חוה-eve/

[7] A talk or essay given in English that is an interpretation of the lessons from the weekly Torah portion.

[8] No relation to The Wounded Warrior Project, which is an organization that provides support to veterans of war.

[9] Brene Brown, *The Gifts of Imperfection*. (Minnesota: Hazelden Publishing, 2010). Page 12.

Made in the USA
Monee, IL
29 November 2023

47717830R00215